# In Common

The architects of our lives are divided. There are those who insist that there is still no alternative to neoliberalism. Despite the many crises it has provoked, they continue to push for competition in every sphere of life, to widen the wealth gap, to ignore climate change and to pursue the steady dispossession of our rights and commonwealth.

Then there are those advocating change, those who seek to persuade us that capitalism can be saved from itself. They conceal capitalism behind a human face. They tell us that environmental disaster can be averted through technological solutions. They say that deeply rooted social injustices can be cured with a little more economic growth. That we'll be safer with more police on our streets.

And yet, we know that capitalism is dying, that its lies have been unmasked, that its grip on our world and our lives is maintained only through expropriations, dependency and commodified desires. In Common is a collection of works that see an end to capitalism without apocalypse. It provides us with techniques for building another world, and it narrates practices of alternatives and theories of hope. It is a glimpse into our shared present, for a future in common.

In Common is published by Zed Books, under the creative commons license. You are free to share this material, transform and build upon it for non-commercial purposes.

**Series editor:** Massimo De Angelis

## About the author

Stavros Stavrides is an architect, activist and associate professor at the School of Architecture, National Technical University of Athens, where he teaches courses on social housing design, as well as a postgraduate course on the social meaning and signifi-cations of metropolitan experience. His publications on spatial theory include *The Symbolic Relation to Space* (1990); *Advertising and the Meaning of Space* (1996); *The Texture of Things* (with E. Cotsou, 1996); *From the City-Screen to the City-Stage* (2002, National Book Award), *Suspended Spaces of Alterity* (2010) and *Towards the City of Thresholds* (2010).

# Common Space

## The City as Commons

Stavros Stavrides

**Zed Books**
London

*Common Space: The City as Commons* was first published in 2016 by Zed Books Ltd, The Foundry, 17 Oval Way, London SE11 5RR, UK.

www.zedbooks.co.uk

Typeset in Minion by Sandra Friesen
Index by Rohan Bolton
Cover designed by Dougal Burgess
Printed and bound by CPI Group (UK) Ltd, Croydon, CR0 4YY

A catalogue record for this book is available from the British Library .

ISBN  978-1-78360-328-2 hb
ISBN  978-1-78360-327-5 pb
ISBN  978-1-78360-329-9 pdf
ISBN  978-1-78360-330-5 epub
ISBN  978-1-78360-331-2 mobi

*For Eugenia and Zoe*

# Contents

# Acknowledgements

Chapter 2, 'Expanding commoning: in, against and beyond capitalism?', includes parts of the article 'Common Space as Threshold Space: Urban Commoning in Struggles to Re-appropriate Public Space', in *Footprint*, 16 (2015), 9–20, as well as parts of the article 'Re-inventing Spaces of Commoning: Occupied Squares in Movement', in *Quaderns-e* (Institut Català d'Antropologia), 18(2) (2013): 40–52.

Chapter 3, 'Shared heterotopias: learning from the history of a social housing complex in Athens', is a developed version of the chapter 'Heterotopias and the Experience of Porous Urban Space', in K. Franck and Q. Stevens (eds.), *Loose Space: Possibility and Diversity in Urban Life*, London: Routledge (2007).

Chapter 4, 'Housing and urban commoning', includes a version of the article 'Housing and the City: Re-inventing the Urban Commons', in Binna Choi and Maiko Tana (eds.), *Grand Domestic Revolution Handbook*, Utrecht : CasCo Projects (2014).

Chapter 5, 'Metropolitan streets as contested spaces', is a reworked and extended version of the chapter published under the same title in Greek in K. Giannacopoulos and G. Giannitsiotis (eds.), *Contested City-Spaces*, Athens: Alexandreia (2010).

Chapter 6, 'Occupied squares, societies in movement', is an extended and revised version of the article 'Squares in Movement', in *South Atlantic Quarterly*, 111/3 (Summer): 585–96. Some of the thoughts in this chapter were first formulated in a working paper titled 'Communities of Crisis, Squares in Movement' (2011), available at www.professionaldreamers.net/prowp/wp-content/uploads/Stavrides-Communities-of-crisis-fld.pdf.

Chapter 7, 'Practices of defacement: thresholds to rediscovered commons', is an extensively reworked version of the paper 'Defacement and the alternative politics of urban memory' presented at the ISA Forum of Sociology, Barcelona, in September 2008 (RC21: Rethinking Cities and Regions in a Troubled World, Session 3, New Urban Cultures: Public Space, Public Art, Performance and Popular Cultures).

Chapter 9, 'Representations of space and representations of emancipation', includes parts of the chapter 'Espacialidades de emancipacion y la "ciudad de umbrales"' (in Spanish), in J. Holloway, F. Matamoros and S. Tischler (eds.), *Pensar a contrapelo. Movimientos sociales y reflexion critica*, Buenos Aires: Herramienta Ediciones (2009).

# Foreword

by Massimo De Angelis

The debate on commons and commoning has grown exponentially in the twenty-first century. In the 1990s it was virtually non-existent, apart from the neo-institutional contribution of Elinor Ostrom and her affiliates, which was nevertheless mostly unknown to radical scholars and activists. The contemporary radical literatures were just beginning to tackle new interpretations of the notion of original accumulation, enclosures and, later, accumulation by dispossession (to name different interpretative varieties), that is, the strategies used by capital and the state to destroy commons. At the same time, social movements in the global north were starting to wake up after the big defeats that accompanied the establishment of neoliberalism, and a new generation began to realize that the period of neoliberal TINA ('there is no alternative') was instead a period of TAMA ('there are many alternatives'), practised in full self-awareness by peasant and indigenous movements in the global south and by many other individuals and groupings in the global north.

Alter globalization movements coupled with the World Social Forums have further opened the cracks of hope first made unexpectedly for many of us by the unknown indigenous groups of the Zapatista Liberation Army, entering the world stage with their taking of San Cristobal de las Casas, in Chiapas, southeast Mexico, on 1 January 1995, the day the North America Free Trade

Agreement came into force, which, incidentally, proposed the privatization of the *ejidos*, the land held in common by Mexico's indigenous people.

Twenty years and several wars after those eye-opening events, we find ourself with a burgeoning critical literature on commons and commoning, commonwealth and the common. Even the mere mention of these nowadays gives us a momentary break from the grip of fear and insecurity brought by our times of war and austerity. On Friday 13 November 2015, I was writing this foreword when news broke of the Paris attacks. These were perpetrated by youths from a forgotten banlieue, turned fanatics for lack of alternative practices of hope and 450 euros a month – by youths who killed mainly young people doing some very innocent socializing at restaurants, a football game and a gig. Daily life stuff for global middle-class citizens. The response from the socialist president of France was not a measured reflection on the previous reactions of the global north on similar occasions. No, it was the same as that of the neoconservative US president in Afghanistan and Iraq following the 11 September 2001 attacks, a response that escalated deaths by terrorist attacks in the global north and around the world by 4,500 per cent and caused hundreds of thousands of civilian deaths in US-led interventions. The French fries are thus back in US restaurants, and there is further bombing of Syria, murdering yet more civilians, while in Paris the state of emergency is intensified and the authorities are ready to close roads to demonstrators in view of the approaching climate change talks. Daily life space becomes a space of war and security.

The neoliberal state finds money to buy bombs and missiles, but it cuts money from everywhere that money is useful for social reproduction, in the attempt to intensify the conditions of competitiveness and of the rat race. Neoliberal capital always seems to reach a point of crisis, but then it re-emerges with new emergency laws. In 2008, neoliberal states used public funds to save the major banks which had speculated with mortgages and been hit by the bursting of the financial bubble. Nowadays, the banks are playing instead with repackaged student loans or healthcare debt. Will the state save them again when the next financial bubble bursts, giving us another round of austerity? Greece perhaps epitomizes the case for the scenario of doom. After years of austerity imposed by the Troika (the European Union, the European Central Bank and the International Monetary Fund), at the beginning of 2015 there seemed to be some hope with the election of the new Syriza government. That hope lasted about six months, until the Greek government was forced to accept continued draconian cuts and privatization. Daily life space here is a space of austerity and hopelessness.

However you look at it, whatever channel you choose, our current condition seems to be reproducing hopelessness and powerlessness, and it seems impossible to approach an egalitarian and socially just society, or even think about one. It is in this context that this first book of our new In Common series, by Stavros Stavrides, is so important, in that it opens a space of hope where there seems to be none, a space in which the vicious circle of war and austerity is replaced by the relational dance of diverse subjectivities in heterotopic spaces. Stavrides challenges our daily perception of space, and thereby makes us see opportunities for acting in common, for locating or producing threshold places that allow us to create the conditions of entry or exit into heterotopias of commoning practically everywhere: in roads and public spaces, in housing, occupied spaces, parks and other places.

This is the first theoretical book of its kind, the first book to problematize space as commons and not only as commodity or state-managed space or pure ruin brought about by war. It is a book on the best of the Lefebvrian tradition, but also engaging with contemporary social and political thought – Foucault, Turner, Bourdieu, Hardt and Negri, Zibechi, Holloway and others – all interlaced with rigorous observations on contemporary and older social movements, and on the intersection of 1930s architectural movements with contemporary square commons. What types of subjectivities could develop when we cross the thresholds separating alienated life with other spaces? What type of experience of emancipations will we live by leaving behind a practice measured by capital and the state and encountering others in heterotopias, other spaces where differences meet and establish a practice of doing in common or commoning? These are open questions that invite each of us to get involved and experiment. The threshold between hopelessness and hope, powerlessness and power is, after all, in our own hands and spirits.

# Introduction

The contemporary urbanized world is a world predominantly ruled by interests organized around the economic extraction of profit. Urban environments, contemporary cities and especially metropolises are important shaping factors of ruling organized interests, whether they take the form of banks, corporations, state enterprises, industry complexes or trading companies. At the same time, a diverse geometry of hierarchical relations between such organized interests casts its shadow on metropolitan everydayness, dominating the city's spatiotemporal transformations.

Is it that contemporary cities have become merely the channels and the tools of such a dominating arrangement of power relations that focuses on extracting profit from each and every activity that unfolds in urban worlds? Is it that predatory capitalism in its contemporary neoliberal or even post-neoliberal phase exploits the cities and that city life merely reflects the process?

An attempt will be made in this book to explore the emerging potentialities of resistance and creative alternatives beyond contemporary forms of domination in today's cities. Whether commoning, this relatively new term, has a role to play in such a prospect is something that has to be explored: do contemporary city-dwellers discover in and often against current forms of urban order opportunities to appropriate their own city, to create or even reinvent shared spaces and inhabiting practices based on cooperation? Are the meanings, the stakes and the values of a possible urban civilization being questioned today in and through practices of commoning? Do people in many parts of the world fight against corrupt governments, unjust policies and everyday exploitation not only by demanding what they need but also by organizing their common life themselves?

This book attempts to study the meaning and production of spaces of commoning in the context of today's urbanized world. Understood as distinct from public as well as from private spaces, 'common spaces' emerge in the contemporary metropolis as sites open to public use in which, however, rules and forms of use do not depend upon and are not controlled by a prevailing authority. It is through practices of commoning, practices which define and produce goods and services to be shared, that certain city spaces are created as common spaces.

Commoning practices importantly produce new relations between people. They encourage creative encounters and negotiations through which forms of sharing are organized and common life takes shape. Commoning practices, thus, do not simply produce or distribute goods but essentially create new forms of social life, forms of life-in-common. That is why those practices may be projective (hinting towards possible forms of life-in-common), expressive (attempting to draw attention to the values shared by those who participate in the commoning processes) and exemplary (partially establishing social relations that exceed the limits imposed by dominant models of sociality).

Common space is a set of spatial relations produced by commoning practices. There are, however, two distinct ways through which those relations are organized. They may either be organized as a closed system which explicitly defines shared space within a definite perimeter and which corresponds to a specific community of commoners, or they may take the form of an open network of passages through which emerging and always-open communities of commoners communicate and exchange goods and ideas.

Throughout this book an effort will be made to explicitly connect commoning with processes of opening: opening the community of those who share common worlds, opening the circles of sharing to include newcomers, opening the sharing relations to new possibilities through a rethinking of sharing rules and opening the boundaries that define the spaces of sharing. Opposed to such levels, practices and rules (or, more precisely, institutions) of sharing are the rules and practices of capitalist social organization which promotes and establishes a 'desocialization of the common' (Hardt and Negri 2009: 258). This is based not only on the appropriation of the products of commoning by capital (considered as a social relation and not simply as money) but also on an all-encompassing strategy that may be termed a strategy of enclosure (De Angelis 2004, Midnight Notes Collective 1990). This term evokes an image connected to the fencing of an area – a spatial image, no doubt. But the capitalist enclosure of the commons is not only a process of fencing in areas of production or the uses of certain goods and resources but also a process of obstructing those commoning practices that tend towards an openness of sharing: self-managed cooperation which is open to newcomers, knowledge 'production' which is not limited to those who understand it, create it or 'finance' it and festive and joyous events which do not separate consumers from artists, and so on.

What possibly justifies the theoretical adventure of this book in focusing on common space is that enclosure in this case retains both its literal as well as its metaphoric value. This is because, as we will see, space is not only a product and therefore a stake for commoning but a means of establishing and expanding commoning practices. In and through space, dominant strategies of capturing, limiting, commanding and appropriating commoning have to face the dispersed tactics of resistance which defy, destroy or challenge the limits of literal and metaphoric enclosures.

Commoning is a process that is shaped by social antagonism that often leads to historically contingent and ambiguous results: commoning may be fenced in within the limits of a specific community that explicitly tries to keep the commoning products and advantages for its members only. In this case we can say that commoning is enclosed, although the very clear distinction between enclosure and commoning as a clear-cut distinction between two opposed poles remains theoretically valid and important. This is why, as we shall see, enclosure through literal or symbolic barriers of a community's common space may signal the death of space-commoning (and commoning through space).

Common space, defined through acts of spatial enclosure, may end up either as 'collectively private' space (as, for example, the outdoor space of a gated community) or as 'public space' managed by authorities which act in the name of a community (as, for example, the space of a municipal park or a town square). Both these forms of closed common space tend to 'corrupt the common' and to block the liberating potentialities of commoning practices.

Expanding or open common space explicitly expresses the power commoning has to create new forms of life-in-common and a culture of sharing. Threshold spatiality, a spatiality of passages which connect while separating and separate while connecting, will be shown to characterize such spaces produced in common and through commoning. Thresholds may appear as boundaries which separate an inside from an outside, as, for example, in the case of a door threshold, but this act of separation is always and simultaneously an act of connection. Thresholds create the conditions of entrance and exit, prolong, manipulate and give meaning to an act of passage. This is why thresholds have been marked in many societies by rituals which attempt to control the inherent potentialities of crossing. Guardian gods or spirits dwell in thresholds because the act of passage is already an act that brings into potential connection an inside and an outside. Entering can be taken as an intrusion, and exiting can convey the stigma of ostracizing.

Considering common spaces as threshold spaces opens the possibility of studying practices of space-commoning that transcend enclosure and open towards new commoners. Exploring the idea of expanding commoning, this book is in search of examples of practices and experiences which may reveal the emancipating potentialities of commoning for, in and through space.

Collective inventiveness flourishes in the production and use of threshold spaces. Comparisons between emerging identities are made possible as people use those spaces through constant negotiations. Communities which inhabit them are thus always communities-in-the-making. Entering an important discussion on contemporary forms of political subjectivation, this book will attempt to show that commoning and the creation of common spaces involve subjectivation processes which do not produce closed collective identities. J. Holloway, M. Hardt and A. Negri, and J. Rancière all share in their theorizations on political subjectivation a common horizon: subjects of political action emerge today by threatening, upsetting or even dismantling dominant social taxonomies and the corresponding established identities. In this process, contemporary urban space, which necessarily expresses and reproduces these dominant taxonomies, can possibly be transformed through collective action. Threshold spatiality can insinuate itself into the dominant spatial order in the same way that emergent 'non-identities' (Holloway 2002), 'newcomers' (Rancière 2010) or inherently multiple 'singularities' (Hardt and Negri 2009) can insinuate themselves into the dominant social order.

The book explores the interconnections between processes of spatial transformation and processes of political subjectivation, focusing especially on socio spatial experiences which reveal the potentialities inherent in contemporary metropolitan life. Drawing from research focused on inhabited spaces (including social housing, everyday uses of metropolitan streets, and occupied squares), this book attempts to show that common space is produced through collective inventiveness, which is either triggered by everyday urgent needs or is unleashed in the effervescence of collective experiments: in the self-managed settlements of the homeless movements in Latin America and in the encampments of the occupied squares of the Arab Spring, in initiatives which reclaim and transform public space, in building squats and in the creation of open neighbourhood centres or in self-organized 'reclaim-the-city' events (often connected to anti-gentrification struggles).

Envisaged common spaces, spaces imagined or sought for through expressive gestures, play an important role in shaping

practices of space-commoning. Possible spatialities of commoning emerge in the form of images which trigger thought.
People develop ways through which they attempt to think about,
imagine and express the characteristics of common space and
by doing so they invent possible forms of space sharing and
sharing-through-space. Can dissident politics escape the trap
of the 'liberated enclave' imaginary and discover the power that
the representations of common spaces-as-thresholds have for
the pursuit of collective emancipation? Perhaps yes, if people
attempt to think about the common through thought-images
that do not trap the future in projected city-like utopias of social
harmony or liberty.

Space-commoning is not, therefore, simply the sharing of
space, considered as a resource or an asset, but a set of practices
and inventive imaginaries which explore the emancipating potentialities of sharing. Common space is both a concrete product
of collectively developed institutions of sharing and one of the
crucial means through which these institutions take shape and
shape those who shape them.

Experiences of space-commoning emerge latently or explosively in many places in the world. I wouldn't attempt to create
a theoretical perspective on common space if I had not had the
opportunity to share some of these experiences. I strongly believe that we must learn from these experiences and try carefully
to develop out of them generalizations and theoretical proposals. Like every piece of research which is immersed in its subject
and like every theory which is influenced by collective aspirations and enthusiasms, this book runs the risk of being more
oriented towards the defence of people struggling than towards
offering a distantiated look at their struggles. I really don't know

if I have managed to develop a strong enough critique of space-commoning in order to be able to show the important stakes involved. I do know, however, that the discussions and literature on commons and commoning definitely shape a contested area. One should take sides in these discussions, and one should realize that value choices and views about the future of societies are directly involved in them.

Learning from struggles and collective experiences means, I think, being able to dwell sometimes on a threshold: the threshold that separates and connects at the same time acts and criticism, praxis and theory, experience and representation, and participation and distantiation. I am very thankful to those who gave me the opportunity to linger sometimes on such thresholds by realizing that this was my way of supporting our common aspirations and dreams. Active members of the Alexandras Prosfygika Inhabitants Coalition in Athens taught me how to remain an academic while being part of an urban struggle. People from Brazilian homeless movements and young activists in Buenos Aires *favelas* taught me how a feeling of solidarity and the sharing of common values may produce common ground for fruitful debates. In the Syntagma Square occupation in Athens I learned how important it is to participate in egalitarian cooperation, an experience that produces its own shared space. Maybe during the long night of *pasalo* in Barcelona I realized how people may almost instantly convert the city centre to common space. Maybe matatu drivers in Nairobi and immigrants and street traders in Athens showed me how important it is to observe space-commoning at the very molecular level of everydayness.

I don't know if my education as an architect and my affiliation to a School of Architecture has been the main reason for my interest in the spatial aspect of commoning. I believe, however, that space matters a lot for commoning and that studying cities through theories and research on commoning is as important as studying commoning through theories and research on cities. Perhaps I was able to understand and experience more deeply the Red Vienna pioneer architecture which concretizes a view on a collectively organized public culture through my research on common space. Maybe this research made it possible for me to draw comparisons between this kind of architecture and the architecture of social housing in Latin America as well as in Greece, architectures that I was able to observe and study.

My 'threshold' research would not have been possible, however, if my theoretical and political trajectory had not crossed the Zapatistas' road to autonomy and social emancipation. Their social and political experiences are perhaps the most important contribution to the search for connections between today's struggles and tomorrow's just society. Without the Zapatistas, discussions on the emancipating potentialities of commoning would be less equipped with examples, less developed in concepts, less connected to the history and cultures of different communities, and probably less inspiring.

After I have said all that, maybe it is clear that thanking people and acknowledging their role in shaping this book cannot take the form of a catalogue of names. Most of those people already know that I owe a lot to them, my students at the National Technical University of Athens included. Mentioning a few by name, then, does not mean that I have forgotten all the others.

A great number of research exchanges and political discussions have influenced my explorations in space-commoning. To name some of those who offered me such opportunities:

Andrea Brighenti, Xenia Chrysochoou, Massimo de Angelis, Ana Džokić, Michael Hardt, John Holloway, Michael Janoschka, Giannis Margaris, Marc Neelen, Haris Tsavdaroglou, Carlos Vainer, Raul Zibechi and the members of the research group on Critical Research Methodology in Athens.

Zed Books is, I believe, one of the most appropriate publishing contexts for this book – being a workers' cooperative. Kika Sroka-Miller, my commissioning editor, has always been supportive and encouraging.

With Maria Kopanari I have been discussing matters connected to the ideas and observations presented in this text for many years now, sometimes fiercely debating but always probingly reflecting on the process of human emancipation. Evgenia Michalopoulou was always there: inspiring in her explosive temperament, active in establishing connections with movements and engaged thinkers, and always sharing dreams for a better world. I owe her a lot more, then, than many creative years of common life.

Zoe Michalopoulou Stavrides seems to be my most relentless critic but also one of the most inspiring people I know for younger generations to learn from. I only hope that she and Evgenia will once again forgive my dark moods in periods of disappointment or inefficient efforts at writing ...

Part one

# Commoning space

Chapter 1

# An urban archipelago of enclosures

## The contemporary metropolis and the normalization project

The contemporary metropolis appears as a chaotic agglomeration of urban environments and flows. If Simmel's big city was already a real ordeal for the senses and a difficult place to live in, today's metropolises seem to have evolved to a paroxysmal accentuation and disarticulation of conflicting and overlapping urban rhythms. And if in modernist art's imaginary the big city could have been envisaged as the possible locus of a city-symphony (Stavrides 2013: 35), in today's metropolis only cacophony seems possible.

What appears as an incoherent and fragmented locus of human activities is characterized, however, by forms of spatio-temporal ordering that are meant to be compatible with each other. The city must be controlled and shaped by dominant power relations if it is to remain a crucial means for society's reproduction. True, the city is not simply the result of spatio-temporal ordering, in the same way as the society is not simply the result of social ordering. Order, social or urban, is a project rather than an accomplished state. It is, however, important that we locate the mechanisms through which the project of urban ordering is being shaped and implemented if we want to find out against which forces that resist or overspill this ordering such mechanisms were crafted. Ordering mechanisms, thus, do not simply execute certain programmed functions but constitute complicated self-regulating systems that interact with urban reality and 'learn' from their mistakes. Urban ordering, the metropolis itself, is a process, is contested, much in the same way that dominant social relations need to be reproduced every day. Capitalism itself is a process rather than a form of social organization that repeats itself throughout its micro-history and its macro-history (Holloway 2002 and 2010).

If urban ordering is an ongoing process, what is, then, the role of urban ordering mechanisms? And what exactly is urban order when we talk about the contemporary metropolis? We could say that urban order is the impossible limit towards which practices of spatial classification and hierarchization tend in order to ensure that the city produces those spatial relations that are necessary for capitalism's reproduction. It appears as obvious that ordering mechanisms are mechanisms of control: the city can indeed be depicted as a turmoil of activities and spaces that need to be controlled. Ordering mechanisms, however, are not meant only to tame a complicated and highly differentiated form of human *habitat* (perhaps the most complicated one in human history so far). A rhetoric that attempts to legitimize them presents them in this way. However, those mechanisms are, to use Foucault's bold term, mechanisms of social normalization. Foucault insists that normalization is not simply the result of the legal system: 'techniques of normalization develop from and below a system of law, in its margins and maybe even against it' (Foucault 2009: 56).

In terms of urban ordering, normalization includes attempts to establish spatial relations that will encourage social relations and forms of behaviour which will be repeatable, predictable and compatible with the taxonomy of the necessary social roles. Normalization shapes human behaviour and may use space (as well as other means) to do so.

Normalization is a project which is always explicitly or latently contested. It is not simply imposed, it has to infiltrate every capillary vein of society in order to be effective. It has to be connected to words and acts that mould everydayness but also to acts of dominant power that frame those everyday molecular practices. Normalization is undoubtedly a project of domination, a project that seeks to mould society's subjects. It thus has to be the result of a certain arrangement of power relations.

Exactly because a complete and unalterable urban order is an impossible fantasy of those who rule, a complete and total normality cannot be imposed. Normalization will always have to deal with deviations and exceptions. What is more important, normalization can treat exception as a propelling force. What will follow in this book will be an attempt to observe the mechanisms of urban ordering as they shape the project of normalization in a constant and complex interaction with mechanisms of exception.

There is a certain image that may prove useful to a project that attempts to discover the kind of order towards which the city is forced: the image of the archipelago. Today's metropolis appears to be shaped in the form of an urban archipelago. Urban space appears as a vast sea which surrounds urban islands of various sizes and forms. As with every analogy that supports a certain interpretative idea, this image needs to be treated with caution. We need to select metaphors carefully when we talk about space if we want to examine how space is always understood through socially inculcated ideas and concepts.

The image of the archipelago may better be considered not as an analogical representation of the city but as a thought-image, an image through which thoughts about the city can be moulded rather than simply illustrated (Stavrides 2014b, Richter 2007). Thus, the urban archipelago image can be used to conceptualize spatial order (or non-order) as well as to interpret it. An emphasis on the chaotic aspect of urban space may be taken to correspond to images of unexplored or, even, untamed seas. Urban islands, in such a perspective, would be enclaves of order in the middle of urban chaos. Interestingly, an almost opposite view can also be developed. In Koolhaas's essay 'City of the Captive Globe' (Koolhaas 1994: 296), a model city is projected onto Manhattan's spatial structure, which is called an archipelago: the urban grid corresponds to the archipelago's sea and the urban plots are taken as islands. As Aureli has observed, in this conception of the archipelago 'the more different the values celebrated by each island, the more united and total the grid or sea that surrounds them' (Aureli 2011: 24). In this understanding of the urban archipelago the sea is the organizing and ordering medium in which distinct enclaves of difference, 'cities within cities', are located.

Aureli's own positive conception of the archipelago is also characteristic of the polyvalence of the image. For him, architecture ('absolute architecture') can become the force to defy and criticize the all-encompassing 'extensive space of urbanization' (ibid.: 44) which engulfs the city. To 'exceed this sea ... from within' (ibid.), architecture has to mould the islands as separated fragments, 'absolute' parts which reintroduce the necessary ingredient of confrontation and agonism, 'political separateness', against the homogenizing principle of the endless and always-expanding 'sea of urbanization' (ibid.: 45).

The image of the archipelago is obviously related to a contra-distinction of order versus disorder in all of these interpretations. What this chapter will try to show is that this image can support the idea that urban ordering is a project that unfolds in different but complementary levels of urban space and that this project reveals at least three distinct mechanisms of power at work. The urban sea is being ordered in different ways than the urban islands, and parts of the archipelago (including delimited areas of urban sea and certain connected islands) are mainly ordered through a third kind of mechanism.

Michel Foucault has distinguished three distinct model-forms of power mechanisms in Western societies. The first one is described as the model of sovereignty, the second as the disciplinary model and the third as the security model (Foucault 2009). Although he convincingly presents these models as corresponding to successive periods in the West's history, he nevertheless insists that models coexist in contemporary society by having a different role and importance in the overall structure of power relations (ibid.: 8 and 107).

It is interesting that in some of Foucault's examples and remarks on the distinctive characteristics of power mechanisms, space plays an important role. One can even suppose that those mechanisms correspond to different ways of space ordering or, rather, to different normalization techniques that use space by regulating it. Thus, sovereignty is 'exercised over a territory' (ibid.: 15), 'capitalizes a territory' (ibid.: 20) and corresponds to a 'feudal type of territoriality' (ibid.: 20), whereas discipline structures 'an empty and closed space within which artificial multiplicities are to be structured and organized' (ibid.: 19) and security 'tries to plan a milieu in terms of series of possible events' (ibid.: 47). Territory, empty space and milieu: different spatialities are being defined by the different mechanisms of normalization. Let us see how this differentiation may be projected to the thought-image of the urban archipelago.

### Sovereignty and discipline in urban *enclavism*

'We are witnessing … a *resurgence* of a global gated urbanism' (Jeffrey et al. 2012: 1, 252–3). Urban enclaves are spaces in contemporary cities which are defined by specific recognizable boundaries within the city and are explicitly connected with specific protocols of use. Urban enclaves are the islands of the urban archipelago. Their perimeter is marked, and various forms of control are employed to ensure access to those who are qualified as 'inhabitants'. The logic of the enclave is to separate a spatial arrangement from the rest of the city and to enclose specific urban functions in this clearly demarcated area. Enclaves are much like territories defined by the application and enforcement of certain rules of use and behaviour.

In Foucault's reasoning, sovereign power is based on juridical mechanisms which regulate the behaviour of the specific community's members by explicitly excluding certain forms of social life and those who embody them. Thus, sovereignty creates, marks and eventually stigmatizes 'outsiders'.

Urban enclaves tend to be self-contained worlds in which specific forms of spatial ordering prevail. Ordering is guaranteed by rules that apply only inside each enclave. Thus, a peculiar site-specific sovereign power is established in urban enclaves in the form of an administrative apparatus that imposes obligations and patterns of behaviour and thus defines the characteristics of the enclave's inhabitants (temporary or more permanent ones).

Specific rules are applied in the ordering of a large department store, upon entrance to a bank or a corporate tower and in the layout and use of a shopping mall or a huge sports stadium. Urban islands can be huge building complexes, like the ones just described, but also closed neighbourhoods – especially those defined as 'gated communities'. Spatial ordering is connected with behaviour normalization in all those cases. And this process of normalization is explicitly or implicitly performed through the enforcement of regulations, which often present themselves as pure and innocent management decisions. The contemporary metropolis is 'an archipelago of "normalized enclosures"' (Soja 2000: 299).

Some gated communities have taken the form of completely barricaded urban areas to which public access is restricted. 'Legal agreements … tie the residents to a common code of conduct and (usually) collective responsibility for management' (Atkinson and Blandy 2005: 178). One can talk of a kind of 'private governance' whether or not those legal agreements are 'free' contractual choices or rules imposed in exchange for 'lifestyle preferences' (ibid.: 183).

Enclave-bound 'authorities' (such as, for example, a shopping mall's management or a gated neighbourhood's administration either elected or appointed by the corresponding corporation which constructed it) may assume responsibilities and control jurisdictions which used to belong to the state. They thus contribute to the strengthening of a localized 'post-political consensus' (Swyngedouw 2011: 28). These forms of governance can be considered as arrangements of 'governance-beyond-the-state' (Swyngedouw 2009) and may even be shaped as 'privatized governance regimes' (Graham and Marvin 2001: 271).

By employing Agamben's theorizations on the state of exception we could further discover an essential aspect of enclave-bound power arrangements. Rules that apply inside the enclaves are often exceptional when compared to the general legal framework that is effective in the corresponding society. This kind of spatial ordering is based on a peculiar state of exception. Not only are inhabitants' obligations are exceptional but the rules that define the enclave's relations to the rest of the city are exceptional too (for example rules regulating tax obligations, street maintenance, conditions of public space use, etc.). Enclaves are spatial forms of a normalized state of exception (Agamben 1998: 169; 2005: 86). To understand the implications of this paradoxical situation we need to trace the connection of normality to exception.

Schmitt has explicitly connected sovereign power to the right to suspend the law. For him 'sovereign is he who decides on the [state of] exception' (Schmitt 2005: 5). If sovereign power, like every power, is, according to Foucault, focused on sustaining normality, then the right to suspend the law must be proved compatible with this permanent orientation of power. Indeed, suspending the law is not supposed to destroy normality (although it obviously does) but to protect normality from a threat. No matter what threat sovereign power diagnoses, predicts or invents to excuse law's suspension, this threat is meant to be confronted with means sovereign law normally does not permit in order to be eliminated. Inherent in the act of suspension is a kind of governing reason which is focused on efficiency rather than on rights.

Exception as a form of suspension of rights is acceptable to the enclave inhabitants, or even desirable, because it is presented as a 'naturalized', obviously effective, administrative procedure. 'Outsiders' are not allowed to pass a gated community's gate, people can be searched upon entry at an Olympic Games venue, shoppers at the mall have constantly to prove that they are not thieves as they pass through electronic scanning devices, and visitors (and those who work) in corporate towers as well as travellers in airports have to be subjected to various, often humiliating, controls in order to prove that they are not terrorists. And, of course, in periods in which a certain kind of pervasive threat is presented as imminent, relevant measures will escalate.

Administrative procedures which routinize these forms of everyday control tend to normalize their exceptional status. Normalized exception becomes the generator of habits and everyday act sequences which, by being repeated, produce a peculiar kind of normality. If a state of exception – no matter how convincingly legitimized – permits to those who experience it some kind of awareness that legal guarantees and rights are suspended, a state of normalized exception tends to become a new form of localized normality. Each enclave is 'normalized' through different sets of rules. Situated rights (and privileges) become concrete, whereas 'universal' or 'general' rights become vague and abstract. Enclave-bound citizens or enclave-frequenting users learn to adapt to concrete obligations and space-bound habits without recourse to rights that unite them with the other inhabitants of the city. Urban enclaves shape a contemporary 'differentiated citizenship' (Holston 2008: 5) through localized states of normalized exception.

Disciplinary power is also present in the production and reproduction of enclave microcosms. According to Foucault, whereas sovereign power prohibits, disciplinary power surveys, classifies and tries to separate the normal from the abnormal not in terms of banishing the negative but in terms of carefully circumscribing and isolating the threatening 'other'. Disciplinary power prescribes rather than prohibits (Foucault 2009: 47).

In maintaining the order of the enclave, disciplinary power has to constitute it as a totally describable, totally knowable and totally organizable space (ibid.: 19). Surveillance is the most important of the disciplinary technologies imposed on the defined closed space of the enclave. And this technology treats the inhabitants as *quasi*-citizens 'by constituting and structuring perceptual grids and physical routines' (Lemke 2011: 36). Discipline for Foucault is not simply suppressive but actively contributes to the productive aspects of the human relations it shapes. The human body is made 'more obedient as it becomes more useful and conversely' (Foucault 1995: 138).

We could say that while sovereign power encloses and defines the boundaries of the enclaves, disciplinary power works on defining the characteristics of the enclave users. Whereas sovereign power uses space to control those people whom power identifies as subjects of a situated set of rules, disciplinary power uses space to situate, classify and mould those subjects not simply as subjects of law (or 'subjected' to law) but as members of a specific social articulation that reproduces itself through everyday life activities.

The mechanism of exception plays an important role in shaping disciplinary power too. This role can be detected in the very example Foucault uses for explaining the logic of disciplinary power: the example of 'the plague stricken town' (Foucault 1995: 195–8). To control the plague the authorities had to separate the infected from those who were healthy, had constantly to control the status of the city's population and had to create mechanisms

of surveillance which could locate and contain deviations from
the normal city life. Disciplinary power, in other words, needs
to know and classify (ibid.: 145) and needs to map and survey
the city. The *Panopticon* is more than a spatial mechanism which
supports surveillance by attributing to the surveyor's presence
a status of 'undecidability'. It is a disciplining arrangement that
distributes people in space in order to impose on them forms
of behaviour. According to Deleuze's interpretation of Foucault's
abstract machine of disciplinary power, this is a specific 'dia-
gram … a map, a cartography that is coextensive with the whole
social field' (Deleuze 1988: 34). A form of totalizing cartography
is imposed on the plague-stricken city 'where power controls the
whole field' (ibid.)

In the exceptionality of the circumstances of plague an exceptional model of controlling and thus governing the city emerged.
In the plague-stricken city 'the utopia of the perfectly governed
city' (Foucault 1995: 198) took shape. This utopia persists in the
processes of establishing and governing the urban enclaves.

After Foucault, Agamben too visited the image of the
plague-infected city in a short article he wrote on the 'red zones'
which were defined in Genoa's centre during the G8 leaders'
meeting in 2001. For him, authorities chose to confront massive
demonstrations as if they were some kind of plague threatening
the city. Police controls and the act of circumscribing the city
centre with an impenetrable barrier created an urban state of
exception. The urban centre was transformed during these days
to a temporary urban enclave with very rigid borders: a contemporary 'forbidden city' (Agamben 2001).

The logic of 'red zones' has, as we know, spread all over the
world. Especially since the 11 September 2001 terrorist attacks,

emergency circumstances are being diagnosed by the authorities during mega-events (Olympic Games, World Cups, etc.), in cases of state leaders' meetings, World Trade Organization or International Monetary Fund summits and public ceremonies, et cetera. Red zones are exemplary enclaves which may be produced under sovereign decisions to suspend the law in certain parts of the city but which effectively create paradigmatic acts of disciplining. Red zones contribute to an imposed and totalizing cartography of the city which classifies potential threats and thus categorizes behaviours especially by limiting access and by erecting sophisticated systems of entrance control. The utopia of a totally classifiable and transparent space is the inspiring principle of the surveillance systems that make red zones effective.

Red zones are spaces of exception and they usually last as long as the event which caused a security alarm lasts. They are, however, the very matrix of a normalized state of exception that urban enclaves concretize (Stavrides 2010b: 37–9). Learning to accept red zones means learning to inhabit exception. With one important difference: whereas in red zones law is explicitly suspended and prevailing urban normality is broken (allegedly in order to be protected), in established urban enclaves general laws may be suspended but site-specific laws and rules may replace them. From the outside, the enclave is a space of exception. From inside, however, it looks like a complete law-abiding universe. Agamben is right in insisting that exception is neither inside nor outside the law. Exception is declared 'in the name of law', but order is broken in the name of order. Thus, although exception creates a zone of indistinction between law and anomie (Agamben 1998: 37 and 2005: 23), it cannot nevertheless be presented otherwise than as being an act of power. What makes enclave exceptionality different is that in this case power simply presents itself as administration and the suspension of rights presents itself as efficient management of risks, and so exception is effectively presented as normality.

### Discipline and security in the urban sea

Disciplinary power also tends to engulf parts of the urban sea which spreads between the enclave-islands. As in the case of red zones, disciplinary power fences areas that normally are part of the city's public space. In contemporary metropolises the very tissue that gives the city a somewhat deceptive unity, the space of circulation flows and outdoor public spaces, seems to pose a threat to the dream of total control. The urban archipelago's sea, although it appears to be ordered through traffic rules and circulation planning, is inherently unpredictable and a threat to the urban ordering process much like the sea itself is unpredictable (although both the sea and the urban sea phenomena follow some traceable patterns).

Disciplinary power tries to conquer parts of this immense sea-milieu and to integrate them into its enclave policies. Gentrification projects certainly have such aspects because they plan to programme life and the practices of production and social reproduction by carefully bringing to view every hidden corner of the corresponding neighbourhoods: gentrified areas are ideally areas of total planning and surveillance (apart from being, of course, areas of capital investment and aggressive speculation). Grand projects (either connected to mega-events or to large-scale redevelopment interventions) are also acts of exemplary urban ordering through which parts of the urban sea are annexed to newly formed island enclaves. Resorts or prototype suburban neighbourhoods (like those, for example, planned by the pioneers of the so-called New Urbanism) equally represent acts of taming and appropriating the urban sea.

If the image of the urban archipelago is to remain useful, it is important to locate the limits of this comparison between a physical arrangement of places and a man-made production of spatial arrangements. Importantly and as opposed to geographical islands, urban islands are being created and can be destroyed (or can even be left for the urban sea to take over). The urban sea itself can even be converted to urban 'land': to space, that is, which becomes part of planned gigantic enclaves.

Urban sea, however, cannot be totally controlled. Urban sea poses problems to urban governance which escape any form of flows management. Urban sea is not simply what remains between urban islands in the form of spaces of circulation and open spaces of public use. Dominant enclavism tends to absorb parts of these sea-spaces and to convert them to urban enclaves of controlled public use. Fenced parks are exemplary cases, as are gentrified areas which may also end up acquiring the characteristics of a public entertainment enclave.

The very process of delineating islands in the urban archipelago leaves the sea to contain various urban spaces that potentially escape total surveillance. If at one end of the spectrum we have the urban metro network as part of a tamed urban sea (which in many cities becomes a completely controlled world, though not in Mexico City, and not even perhaps in New York either), at the other end of the spectrum lie areas like those which surround *villas miserias* (slums) in Buenos Aires or *periferias* (slum areas around the city) in São Paulo: ambiguous zones of urban fabric in which acts are not easily predictable by authorities.

When dominant forms of urban governance fail to enclose and thus normalize patterns of urban life, they attempt to control space through recurrent but essentially temporary and metastatic interventions. Random identity control in the streets in search of 'illegal immigrants' (or those accused of illegal acts) may be considered as the emblematic act of authorities in this respect. It is a different form of power that concretizes in these acts. What Foucault terms the security mechanism is at the core of a politics of governing the city and especially the urban sea. It aims at studying, checking and interpreting a highly complicated (urban) reality in order to be able to predict and intercept unwanted acts and behaviours. Security tries 'to plan a milieu in terms of events or series of events or possible elements' (Foucault 2009: 21). Planning has always to readjust its ambitions, however, because reality often escapes models imposed on it. Urban governance focused on the most unpredictable and thus ungovernable parts of the urban sea has to be flexible, metastatic and always open to new knowledge concerning possible patterns of urban life in order to be able to intervene and regulate. Sampling is the form of research and action power takes when it deals with these problems. And it is through practices of sampling that security power attempts to control not individuals but populations, urban populations par excellence. Baudrillard's work on the importance of codes for the pre-normalizing of behaviour through normative simulation can be very useful in this context (1983: 115–22).

Foucault insists on the seriality of possible events that power tries to infer and thus control. Maybe it is better to talk about the imposition and the control of urban rhythms (Stavrides 2013). Normalization may be understood as the successful politics of rendering social life completely transparent: knowable and available to planning. Rhythmicality will be in such a context the essential characteristic of social life. Lefebvre's promising sketch of a possible 'rhythmanalysis' (Lefebvre 2004) shows us that rhythms can shape control mechanisms but can also give form to practices that exceed dominant rules. To borrow from De Certeau, power works through strategies that calculate space and time, whereas the 'weak' only use tactics: they are 'always on the watch for opportunities' (De Certeau 1984: XVII). However, both the strong and the weak actually attempt to navigate in and through urban rhythms. If dominant power was to become able to absolutely control rhythms then the very mechanisms of domination would become pointless. Domination is a project. And social life rhythms constitute a contested terrain.

Security power, thus, rather than prohibiting or prescribing, tries to calculate and include those very habits through which urban life manifests itself. That is why security mechanisms were supported by the advancing liberalist reasoning. A belief in the market's and, eventually, society's self-regulation through the coordination of the acts of free individuals is illustrated in the very practices of security power. What makes this kind of power effective is its very flexibility.

Take, for example, the problem of surveying the city as posed by nineteenth-century cartography. As Joyce shows us, the 'standardized map' reduced the city to a homogenizing 'clarity of the line' even though differences between different spaces were depicted, in terms of geometry, accurately (Joyce 2002: 105; see also Joyce 2003). This is indeed characteristic of the 'social imaginary of liberal democracy' (ibid.) in which the unity of society (and the city) is established through acts of power that present themselves as 'natural' (exactly in the way that the standardized map presents itself as objective). Security power is 'liberal' because it seems natural. However, security apparatuses activate the power models have in order not only to predict but also to mould behaviour. Security, thus, understands normalization as the 'plotting of the normal and the abnormal … in different curves of normality' or, in other words, understands 'the norm as an interplay of differential normalities' (Foucault 2009: 63).

The problem of normalizing the urban sea is thus a problem of urban governance that requires new mechanisms of power. A power that calculates and constructs models has to work with mechanisms of discipline and sovereignty, as we have seen. But this kind of power coordination has to deal in a different way with exception. Exception may become a propelling rather than a paralysing force in the enactment of security power. The security mechanism's flexibility above all is based on its ability to learn from exception, to incorporate exception and to use exception in order to readjust models and predictions. Let us remember that Foucault uses the project of smallpox epidemics' control as an example of this advancing form of normalizing power during the nineteenth century. Smallpox was to be studied through the statistics of the disease and the rate of deaths, et cetera. If the normal was taken to coincide with the healthy and the abnormal with the pathological (the sick), then sickness was to be studied as a recurrent exception. Anthropology is actually full of observations on how different societies treat a potential disaster by using rituals that try to avert it. Scientific knowledge has supposedly managed to go well beyond such 'prejudices' and has offered to societies the power to control the unpredictable by calculating possibilities and constructing models. For those in power, the will to normalize and thus to control the society is often projected on the reassuring certainties of models that come from science (although those certainties are contested in those very sciences too).

Thus, a complicated but also value-connected reasoning is developed in the policies of security power. Exception cannot be eliminated and urban rhythms are permeated by unavoidable 'cacophonies', but the urban sea itself must be tamed. Exception thus becomes a mechanism that establishes the ground of new potential rules. An example comes from the contemporary Brazilian metropolis São Paulo. A peculiar collective habit has been developed recently by the city's youth. They organize ad hoc feasts in front of large shopping centres which they call *rolezinho* (roughly translated as 'little excursions' or 'outings'). Do these young people, who mostly come from the peripheries, threaten the city's normality as they bring the *periferia* culture in front of the city's emblematic spaces of security and consumption? Or do they simply construct popular hymns to capitalism, as some analysts reassuringly have declared? Exceptional behaviour poses problems to authorities: metastatic control has to face metastatic resistance, or what may potentially evolve into resistance. Unpredictability is a condition that power has to process, limit, but which it cannot completely suspend.

Chapter 2

# Expanding commoning: in, against and beyond capitalism?

## Common worlds may overspill enclosures

Through the process of normalization, domination crafts social worlds in which the different groups of the society find their place. In those defined worlds, belonging becomes important in shaping social relations and in producing different forms of consent. In contemporary capitalist societies, distinct social worlds can be established on various levels of social organization. Urban enclavism, however, tends to become the prevailing mode of circumscribing a common world for people to recognize and, indeed, to 'inhabit'. Common worlds tend to be defined and reproduced as worlds with recognizable boundaries. In them, belonging crafts consent and consent crafts belonging.

Within the boundaries of a common world, people accept and perform shared identities, shared habits and, often, shared values. As subjects of belonging to this common world, people tend to experience it as explicitly separated from a hostile or simply alien outside. Participating in a common world is often connected to practices of securing the limits of this world and to practices that reproduce this separation. This is why, as we shall see, common worlds are not necessarily linked to practices which overspill the boundaries of a community, no matter how 'real' or 'imagined' this community may be. Common worlds may be crafted as homogeneous and homogenizing structures of beliefs and habits. But in the process of their creation and reproduction lies the possibility of transforming them to worlds of commoning. Worlds of commoning are not simply worlds of shared beliefs and habits but are strongly connected to ways of sharing that open the circle of belonging and develop forms of active participation in the shaping of the rules that sustain them. Worlds of commoning are worlds in movement.

Rancière attempts to retheorize 'community' starting from the notion of 'common world'. He emphasizes the importance of being able to recognize a socially crafted 'distribution of the sensible world'. This world, however, according to him, is always more than a shared ethos and a shared abode. This world 'is always a polemical distribution of modes of being and "occupations" in a space of possibilities' (Rancière 2006: 42). Reducing this 'space of possibilities' to a rigid social order means replacing politics with 'police'. For Rancière, what is at stake is a constant redefinition of what is considered as common. This is what creates a common world and this is what, consequently, is at the basis of understanding and symbolizing community. 'Police' is characterized by a way of conceiving community 'as the accomplishment of a common way of being', whereas 'politics' conceives community 'as a polemic over the common' (Rancière 2010: 100). Inherent in the community is a process which recognizes the common as an issue rather than as a fact or an unambiguous norm. When this dispute or polemic over the common is silenced, community ossifies. Community becomes an ordered social universe rather than a process. Interpreting Rancière's understanding of the bond between community and politics, we could say that he sees community as an open political process, through which the

meaning and the forms of living together are questioned and potentially transformed.

In this context, Rancière is against consensus, which he describes as a form through which 'politics is transformed into
police' (ibid.). Can we, however, introduce to this theorizing of
community a way of understanding consensus and dissensus
that may describe the multifarious processes of creating agreement between people?

Communities may keep on defining the common worlds
which their members inhabit through processes of negotiation
and dispute without necessarily being reduced to endless battle
over the common. The production of a common world does not
need to be the result of a homogenization process. It does not
need to be the explicit and unavoidable result of normalization
power strategies. If we understand a common world as the result
of social relations (which are necessarily open to the history of
minor or major transformations), then common worlds not only
may permit differences but are the means of establishing a common ground between them. It is this kind of common world that
is being expressed in public space, if public space is understood
not as the locus of domination but as an always-contested area
(Hénaff and Strong 2001, Loukaitou-Sideris and Ehrenfeucht
2009).

We can possibly compare different societies in terms of how
open to changes and negotiation practices are the common
worlds which express and sustain them. In the search for ways
towards social emancipation we can possibly learn from those
societies (and communities) that actually open or keep open the
processes through which common worlds are being developed.
But this is not as simple as it seems. We need to explore first what

kind of practices potentially prefigure social emancipation and what kind of values seem to be connected with them. This is where the political importance of the discussion on commoning becomes evident and challenging. As Linebaugh convincingly suggests, 'the commons is an activity' and this is why it 'expresses relationships in society that are inseparable from relations to nature' (Linebaugh 2008: 279).

According to this approach, it is politically meaningless to separate common goods (goods meant to be shared) that are 'natural' (resources such as the air, the forests, etc.) from those that are produced by human societies, that is 'artificial'. By the very process through which a society defines and describes a certain 'natural' good and the rules of its appropriation, such a society literally creates it as socially meaningful good. Commoning is not a process of production or appropriation of certain goods meant to be shared. Commoning is about complex and historically specific processes through which representations, practices and values intersect in circumscribing what is to be shared and how in a specific society. We generally think that what is to be shared has to do with goods and sharing is an economic process or a predominantly economic process. On a first reading, D. Harvey's definition of the common, no matter how broad and anti-essentialist, corroborates this view: for him, the common is not 'a particular kind of thing' but 'an unstable and malleable social relation between a particular self-defined social group and those aspects of its actually existing or yet-to-be-created social and/or physical environment deemed crucial to its life and livelihood' (Harvey 2012: 73).

However, the distinction between the two terms 'life' and 'livelihood' may possibly hint at a complementarity: social life comprises a multitude of practices that express and perform so-cial relations of power. Assigning meaning to those relations is a crucial aspect of social reproduction.

Livelihood is undoubtedly important for a society's persis-tence. But social life is by no means reduced to processes that sustain a society's livelihood, and the efforts to ensure social livelihood are not the sole explaining factor of social life. Com-moning unfolds in all levels of social life. To reduce commoning practices to practices focused on social livelihood is an econo-mistic fallacy. Relations of production and relations of power jointly (albeit not necessarily in harmony) shape the specific historical status of a specific society. Both sets of relations are ex-pressed in social struggles, and especially through struggles over the definition, the control, the representations and the forms of appropriation of the common.

If commoning is based on practices which give form to shar-ing processes, then those practices are characterized both by the means they employ and by the subjects who participate in them (Bollier and Helfrich 2012). Commoning practices shape both their subjects and their means; commoning practices literally produce what is to be named, valued, used and symbolized as common.

On the subject of what is considered as common in a specific society, discussions necessarily include specific historical anal-yses of the social context in which 'commons' are recognized as crucial social stakes. Enclosure acts have been analysed in many studies according to the different characteristics of the corre-sponding societies and communities, including the structure of power relations (Linebaugh 2008, Linebaugh and Rediker 2000, De Angelis 2007, Federici 2004).

What Hardt and Negri explicitly propose is that new forms of commons have emerged in contemporary capitalism: those especially connected to immaterial goods which can be shared as knowledge, information codes, but also affects and forms of social relationship (Hardt and Negri 2009: 132). From this catalogue it becomes clear that these new potentially shared commons directly involve human relationships not simply as the means of producing commons but, essentially, as products of commoning themselves.

It seems that this reasoning attempts to locate a specific historical period in capitalism in which commoning has to do predominantly with the production of subjectivities. This view is highly debatable, however, if we take into consideration the fact that subjectivities are indeed the most important products of a society that aims at ensuring its self-reproduction. Is it that commoning becomes the new condition of this production? This also is not easily provable. Different societies in the past contained differing sets of commoning practices (not necessarily immaterial but connected, for example, to land cultivation) through which social subjectivities were established and reproduced (Godelier 2011, Esteva 2014).

What seems to be at the core of the Hardt and Negri argument is that in today's capitalism commoning practices produce subjectivities which acquire characteristics that threaten this society's reproduction. Giving new form to the Marxian idea that capitalist society contains and produces relations that may undermine it (the idea of contradictions such as the immense potential of development of means of production which is thwarted by private ownership), Hardt and Negri discover the constitutive contradiction that may lead to contemporary capitalism's destruction. This is probably what they try to locate in the dynamics of the multitude (Hardt and Negri 2005, 2009). The multitude is considered as a vast agglomerate of potential subjectivities which emerge in the context of contemporary commoning. The multitude is a set of 'singularities' which are inherently multiple and are connected through multiple forms of coexistence. Exactly because the multitude is produced through commoning and produces various kinds of commons (especially those already referred to as 'immaterial'), the multitude may potentially constitute itself as a multiple political subjectivity that surpasses capitalism (Hardt and Negri 2009: 165–78).

Why do contemporary forms of commoning possibly give rise to political subjectivities which threaten capitalism's reproduction? Is it because inside capitalism commoning is always a source of anti-capitalist struggle? From the examples already referred to, it becomes apparent that commoning is not necessarily an anti- or post-capitalist process. Commoning may support the reproduction of existing communities and their struggle to defend their collective symbolic or legal ownership. This kind of ownership may have been the product of enclosure practices which limit access or define privileges of use, as in the case of common facilities and open space in a gated community, a 'private' club or a 'whites only' playground. Furthermore, commoning in general may create areas of conflict between different communities or societies. Can these conflicts be resolved by reference to principles connected to commoning, or is this a problem which lies outside commoning reasoning?

In the search for answers to this question let us return to the historical specificity of contemporary in-capitalism commoning. Practices of collaboration obviously pre-exist today's capitalism. Practices of capitalist command exercised on various collaboration forms obviously have their history in capitalism's transformations. It seems that at least two very important new qualities characterize contemporary collaboration practices that connect them to commoning: the tremendous rise of information and transmission technologies and the predominance, as a result, of the model of networking in social relations. Affects and knowledge(s) used to bind people in various epochs. Codes and languages too become crucial aspects in almost all forms of human collaboration. It is the networking model (Castells 2010, Castells and Cardoso 2005) that seems to create today unprecedented possibilities of human collaboration and interaction (De Peuter and Dyer-Witheford 2010) which may proliferate in ways that capitalist command fails to predict and control. Information technologies have widely diffused the networking model. This model, however, is at the same time a very powerful tool of social control. We already know that dominant control mechanisms can seriously affect information flows, can efficiently connect dispersed units of domination and can process data with speeds that may put them ahead of collaborative acts of resistance.

We probably need, then, to distinguish between those practices of collaboration, communication and cooperation that may escape command or appropriation and those that are part of domination and exploitation processes. This is possible if we develop certain criteria through which we can evaluate commoning practices or processes according not to their pro- or anti-capitalist 'essence' but according to their beyond-capitalism dynamics. Commoning retains such a dynamics, I maintain, only if it is always expanding beyond the limits of any community that gives it ground and develops it. In terms of collaboration, this necessarily presupposes an ever-expanding community of potential collaborators. To develop the means and the rules that may include ever-new participants in the collaboration-cooperation-communication practices of commoning is the most important prerequisite for commoning to exceed the limits capitalism imposes on it through enclosures and privatization of the products of commoning and through controls that subsume commoning under capitalist command.

The networking model surely creates new opportunities for expanding commoning. It is not enough, though, to insist on these opportunities if we don't accept that networking can be the very form of capitalist command (and of the capture of the common). The problem of retaining the anti-capitalist potentialities of commoning (Caffentzis and Federici 2014, Hardt 2010, Harvey, Hardt and Negri 2009) is indeed a political problem. That is why the means of expressing these potentialities have to do with the characteristics of collaboration that sustain commoning practices. If commoning creates potential political subjectivities, it is important to know what kind of social relations actually open or orient those subjectivities towards sustaining and expanding commoning. What kind of practices of social relationality keep commoning alive and equip it with the power to escape the traps of enclosure and control? Can we really talk about forms of repeatability of those practices that not only expand the circle of potential commoners but also open the field to new forms of commoning, to new forms of commons and thus, necessarily, to new forms of cooperation? Can we really speak, in this context, of practices that invent open institutions of expanding commoning?

## Institutions of expanding commoning

For commoning practices to become important prefigurations of an emancipated society, commoning has to remain a collective struggle to reappropriate and transform a society's common wealth (Hardt and Negri 2009: 251–3) by always expanding the network of sharing and collaboration.

Dominant institutions legitimize inequality, distinguishing between those who know and those who do not, between those who can take decisions and those who must execute them and between those who have specific rights and those who are deprived of them. Thus, dominant institutions focused on the production and uses of public space are essentially forms of authorization which stem from certain authorities and aim at directing the behaviours of public space users (Stavrides 2012: 589).

True, there also exist dominant institutions which appear to be grounded upon an abstract equality: real people with differentiated characteristics, needs and dreams are reduced to neutralized subjects of abstract rights. Thus, in public space general rules appear to be addressed to homogenized users, users who can have access to a specific place at specific hours of the day and under specific conditions (including discreet or straightforward surveillance).

In spite of their different role in social normalization, both types of dominant institutions classify and predict types of behaviour and deal with only those differences which are fixed and perpetuated through the classifications they establish. There are, obviously, differences in terms of content: an institution that aims at guaranteeing a certain form of equality (no matter how abstract) is different from an institution that openly imposes discriminations.

Institutions of commoning established in a stable and well-defined community may very well look like the dominant institutions in the ways they regulate people's rights and actions. Institutions of expanding commoning, however, explicitly differ from the dominant ones as well as from the institutions of what can be termed enclosed commoning. This makes them potentially different 'social artifices' which are oriented towards different social bonds.

Three necessary qualities characterize the institutions of expanding commoning. First of all, these institutions establish the ground of comparisons between different subjects of action and also between different practices. Subjects of action and practices themselves become comparable and relevant: what is at stake is to invent forms of collaboration based not on homogenization but on multiplicity (Hardt and Negri 2005: 348–9). Instead of keeping or creating distances between different subjects and practices (situated in a rigid taxonomy), institutions of this kind encourage differences to meet, to mutually expose themselves and to create grounds of mutual awareness. Mere coexistence does not capture the potentiality of comparison. Differences mean something because they can be compared. Differences are relative and relational.

Let us consider an example. In the case of the occupied Navarinou Park in Athens (a car park converted to a lively urban square and garden through a neighbourhood initiative), people could have created distinct working groups in which participation would be based on each one's knowledge and abilities. This, however, would have latently reproduced a role taxonomy based on the 'innocent obviousness' of existing differences. As a young architect who participated in the park's assembly recalls: 'People involved felt that they had to reposition themselves outside of their normal position and profession' (An Architektur 2010: 5). Even in areas of her expertise she was careful to express her opinion 'as one opinion among others, and not as the expert's opinion' (ibid.). What makes Navarinou Park an experiment of common space creation is that any form of work and cooperation is implicitly or explicitly an act of collective self-regulation and self-management. Collecting the rubbish can become a test in such a context, as can a discussion regarding direct democracy in the park's assembly. The rules established by the assembly formed institutions of commoning, as did the rules that established a rotation of duties (such as, for example, the collection of rubbish). Institutions of expanding commoning need to be flexible because 'newcomers' need to be included in them without being forced to enter a pre-existing taxonomy of roles. Comparability is the motor force of expanding commoning.

However, comparability is not enough. Institutions of commoning need to offer opportunities as well as tools for translating differences between views, between actions and between subjectivities, one to the other. If comparability is based on the necessary and constitutive recognition of differences, translatability creates the ground for negotiations between differences without reducing them to common denominators. 'An emancipated community is a community of narrators and translators' (Rancière 2009b: 22). Obviously, this is quite difficult, since dominant taxonomies tend to block those processes of establishing a socially recognizable common ground that are not based on the predominance of the ruling elites. Translation seeks correspondences but cannot and does not aspire to establish an absolute unobstructed mirroring of one language to the other. So does or should do an institution which keeps alive the expanding potentiality of commoning. Indeed 'the common is always organized in translation' (Roggero 2010: 368). Expanding commoning does not expand according to pre-existing patterns; it literally invents itself. Translation is this inherent inventiveness of commoning which always opens new fields and new opportunities for the creation of a common world always in-the-making.

The creation of common spaces involves practices of translation that build bridges between people with different political, cultural or religious backgrounds. In a collectively managed neighbourhood kitchen in today's Athens (or in Buenos Aires during the 2001 *Argentinazo*), people have to communicate in order to collaborate in facing urgent tasks connected to everyday survival. It is not only that pre-existing common languages and codes are employed in establishing these kinds of communication. It is always necessary to invent forms of translating 'experiences' or 'intellectual adventures' (Ranciere 2009b: 11), thus creating intersections between individual trajectories. Immigrants can join in the social kitchens as commoners only if such translations are being worked upon, but translation is not only necessary for establishing correspondences between different spoken languages. Immigrant cultures contain important seeds of commoning which can be planted effectively in a new collectively cultivated ground. Around a collective kitchen's pot, at the benches of an occupied square and during the long sleepless nights in front of the popular barricades of Oaxaca Commune (Esteva 2010), common space was weaved through acts of translation that created common stakes, new shared habits and views and new common dreams. The power of expanding commoning depends upon acts of translation that always invite newcomers without attempting to diminish or engulf their otherness.

A third characteristic of institutions of expanding commoning has very deep roots in the history of human societies. Social anthropologists have documented very well the existence of mechanisms in certain societies which prevented or discouraged the accumulation of power. Depending on the case, these mechanisms were focused on the equal distribution of collected food, on the ritual destruction of wealth, on the symbolic sacrifice of leaders and on carnivalistic role reversals, et cetera.

If institutions of commoning are meant to be able to support a constant opening of the circles of commoning, they need to sustain mechanisms of control of any potential accumulation of power, either by individuals or by specific groups. If sharing is to be the guiding principle of self-management practices, then sharing of power is simultaneously the precondition of egalitarian sharing and its ultimate target. Egalitarian sharing, which needs to be able to include newcomers, has to be encouraged by an always-expanding network of self-governance institutions. Such institutions can really be 'open' and 'perpetually in flux' (Hardt and Negri 2009: 358–9) but in very specific ways connected to the practices of expanding commoning. Power is first and foremost the power to decide. If, however, the power to decide is distributed equally through mechanisms of participation, then this power ceases to give certain people the opportunity (legitimized or not) to impose their will on others.

Raul Zibechi has carefully observed the way neighbourhood communities in the city of El Alto, Bolivia, have organized their struggle against the privatization of water (Zibechi 2007, 2010). He starts from the idea that 'Community does not merely exist, it is made. It is not an institution, not even an organization, but a way to make links between people' (Zibechi 2010: 14). By tracing the actual practices through which communities organized their struggle, Zibechi found out that those links did not only produce a stable form of centralized leadership out of a series of recognizable social bonds. In the Aymara city of El Alto, community was not simply transported as an enduring model of social organization from rural areas to urban areas. Community form was, according to Zibechi, 're-invented' and 're-created' (ibid.: 19). This kind of community was organized to cope with the everyday problems of a poor population which migrated en masse from rural areas and which based its survival on rich networks of solidarity. Community, thus, was really a network of smaller micro-communities (the smallest unit of which being the neighbourhood block), each one with its local council and distinct decision-taking assemblies. A form of dispersion of power was produced in practice which created various levels and forms of intra-neighbourhood cooperation (ibid.: 30).

During the days of struggle these communities fought against the usurpation of natural resources in many inventive ways. What characterized these methods was a dialectics, one could say, of dispersal and regrouping: 'First of all there is a massive sovereign assembly; Secondly a series of multiple actions in the community, deployed in parallel; And thirdly, a regrouping, or rather a confluence, but rather of a much larger scale than the original' (ibid.: 58).

Community thus, through the dispersed initiatives of the micro-communities which constitute its fabric, manages to fight both the external enemy, in this case the central privatization policy, and the internal enemy, the ever-present danger of concentration of power which inevitably creates hierarchies, exploitation and, of course, corruption.

It is important to note that consensus was pursued on the level of massive neighbourhood assemblies, but decisions were more like guidelines for dispersed and improvised initiatives of action, unified by the struggle's common cause as well as by a feeling of equal participation. In Rancière's reasoning, these communities should be considered as political communities, so long as acts and decision making were not contained in a pre-established centralized order ('police'). What Rancière perhaps misses is that consensus can be a practice; consensus can be a project which takes different shapes and does not have to reach a final and definitive stage.

In the recent Occupy movement, as well as in many other forms of direct democracy which were tried in neighbourhood initiatives, an open assembly explicitly tried to establish equality in terms of decision making. Everyone had the right to participate. In many cases decision making was based not on voting but on consensus reached through extended and sometimes exhaustive debate. Establishing equality of opinions is a difficult process. It depends on who is willing to participate, what is at stake in the decision, how decisions are linked to specific tasks and who chooses to take the burden. And of course an important issue is how a person forms his or her opinion and what kind of access to knowledge, education, experience and bodily abilities a person has. Often, advantages in all those fields latently legitimize certain opinions as superior to others. How does one treat, for example, the opinion of somebody who rarely participates in the everyday hard work of a common space's maintenance? And do those who participate more frequently than others have the right to decide against the opinions of others?

The main argument of those who accept forms of concentration of power in groups of individuals involved in a movement's initiative is efficiency. Quick or coherent decisions, they say, need to be taken by representatives, who, of course, should be elected democratically. The squares movement experience has shown that an obstinate insistence on direct democracy can also create coherent decisions and an efficient distribution of tasks collectively agreed upon. The Spanish 15M movement, for example, was organized on the basis of daily open assemblies which would vote on proposals formulated by thematic commissions with titles such as 'power', 'action', 'coordination', 'logistics', and so on (Hughes 2011: 412). Of course, institutions of expanding commoning have to deal with difficulties arising from a change in scale. This is a very well-known problem of direct democracy. If, however, power dispersion remains a guiding principle and is established through institutions that give form to a de-centring re-centring dialectics, then questions of scale become questions focused on the organization of different levels of participation.

Autonomous Zapatista municipalities and Juntas de Buen Gobierno offer a relevant, very interesting and inspiring example. As we know, Zapatistas never chose to base their emancipating struggle on indigenous Maya fundamentalism. They chose neither to accept the 'reality' of self-referential traditional societies excluded from Mexican civil society nor to struggle for an independent Maya state (Stavrides 2010b: 121). Autonomy meant for Zapatistas self-governance of Zapatista communities and the creation of a second level of autonomous institutions which interconnects and coordinates community decisions and activities through the Juntas de Buen Gobierno. Zapatistas attempt to limit the possibilities of an accumulation of power to community representatives by insisting on a rotation in 'government' duties (with very short rotation cycles). This possibly limits efficiency, if efficiency is measured by managerial standards, but effectively educates all the people in community self-governance (ibid.: 126–7 and Esteva 2014).

Comparability and translation form potential links between strangers and therefore create possibilities of exchanges between them. Egalitarian sharing may support an always-expanding network of exchanges that is open to newcomers. What those three characteristics of emergent open institutions of commoning establish is forms of sharing that defy enclosure and take equality both as a presupposition for collaboration and as a promise for a just society. There is perhaps one more social relation that expands and also transforms egalitarian sharing: the gift. In most anthropological approaches, gift exchanges are shown to be based on explicit or latent obligations that enforce (or euphemize) asymmetries of power (Mauss 1967, Godelier 1999, Peterson 1993). There can, however, be forms of offering which essentially transgress self- or group-centred calculations and possibly hint at different forms of togetherness and solidarity. In conditions of harsh inequality (including differentiated access to knowledge and poorly developed individual abilities resulting from class barriers), commoners of expanding commoning need to realize that they often need to offer more than they expect to receive, to speak less and hear more than those who are not privileged speakers and to contribute to common tasks without demanding a balance among individual offers (De Angelis and Stavrides 2010: 23).

Protest camps in many parts of the world were actually sites of commoning practices that encouraged gift offering. In the occupied Tahrir Square in Cairo, for example, food offering was part of a process that extended socially important habits of hospitality, usually connected to the realm of the family house, to the appropriated public space. Maybe this is an essential part of the process of converting an occupied square or a protest camp to a collectively crafted home (Feigenbaum et al. 2013: 43, Alexander 2011: 58). Food offering, thus, contributed to forms of sharing in and through space that 'enable alternative forms of circulation and distribution, and encourage forms of relationality different from capitalism (in both its welfare and neoliberal renditions)' (Mittermaier 2014: 73). Solidarity is both a prerequisite of egalitarian sharing and a set of practices that create equality through offering.

As we can see, institutions of expanding commoning do not simply define modes of collective practices but also, importantly, forms of social relations through which collective subjects of commoning are being shaped. Compatibility, translatability, power sharing and gift offering are indeed forms of relations between subjects of commoning that encourage commoning to expand beyond the limits of any closed community. This is why expanding commoning necessarily activates processes of identity opening. In order for subjects of commoning to be shaped through comparison, translation, shared mechanisms that prevent power accumulation, and gift gestures that help in diminishing existing inequalities, those subjects have to be open to new definitions of what is considered as common. We can actually contextualize differently Rancière's understanding of politics as 'a manifestation of a "we" that restages the scene of the common' (Rancière 2009a: 121). Expanding commoning always activates and develops a manifestation (and, of course, a production) of a 'we' that restages the scene of the common, 'the objects that belong to it and the subjects that it counts' (ibid.). Belonging to this kind of 'we' means being able to consider the possibility of employing new practices for restaging the 'scene of the common' and, thus, recognizing new subjects that are being shaped by their inclusion in the expanding commoning process.

Expanding commoning involves specific and characteristic processes of subjectivation. It constantly invites 'newcomers' and thus transforms the community from which commoning radiates as well as those who are not simply attracted by and integrated into it but who essentially become co-producers of a modified common world. The phrase 'restaging the scene of the common' implies perhaps that the process of redefining what is common is always a process of both material and immaterial transformations. Giving new meaning to existing practices and goods becomes just as important as inventing new practices and products. Newcomers, thus, may upset dominant taxonomies and dominant role distributions even in communities and so-cieties that tend to become homogenized through commoning. Expanding commoning orients commoning practices away from homogenization – which necessarily encloses and keeps 'others' outside – and directs actions towards constant nego-tiations with others as potential co-commoners. Expanding commoning feeds on differences but does not simply tolerate or recognize differences. Expanding commoning always invites different groups or individuals to become co-producers of a common world-in-the-making.

Institutions of expanding commoning establish the common ground on which such encounters may take place. They are not simply forms of openness to contingency; they are mechanisms which give shape to potential transformations by ensuring that commoning will continue to be a set of practices of sharing that treat commoners as equals but different.

Clearly the perspective of this book aspires to be political rather than economic. Alternative economies and forms of solidarity economy indeed go well beyond a mere alternative model of production and consumption. They generate and encourage social relations based not on exploitation but on mutual support. One should not reduce those forms to an allegedly 'fair trade', although so-called fair trade networks of distribution are often based on ethical codes and agreements which lessen exploitation and certain inequalities. A solidarity economy may directly involve forms of organization of production and consumption that attempt to organize the creation and distribution of common goods and services through forms of association and collaboration based on sharing practices.

Perhaps we need, however, to disentangle commoning from an imaginary of emancipation in which economic reasoning prevails. One needs to respect and support ideas of developing a parallel economy, and people all over the world often develop those ideas and relevant practices in order to survive in harsh conditions of the utmost exploitation. One can even suggest that the 'circulation of commons' or the 'multiplication of commons' which 'can only arise from the circulation of struggles' (De Peuter and Dyer-Witheford 2010: 47) may be the essential characteristics of such a developing parallel economy. In order, however, to be able to envisage anti-capitalist or post-capitalist perspectives, one has necessarily to focus explicitly on alternative forms of social organization. And those forms can of course include work relations, or, generally, production relations, but should not be reduced to them.

It seems that the work of E. Ostrom, which has undoubtedly offered important arguments to those who try to oppose the logic of aggressive individualism, limits its praise for the commons to economic reasoning. Ostrom studied 'common-pool resources' extensively and developed theoretical proposals about their effective management (Ostrom 1990, Ostrom et al. 1994). Her main arguments are in support of collective management of the means of a community's or a society's subsistence. She does not question, however, the assumption that societies always treat or have treated those means as resources. Different cultures in different times give different meaning to natural elements that the current society recognizes as resources. It makes a lot of difference if people think that they do not simply have to calculate the outcome of their various acts of production but have also to acknowledge the results of acts of sacrifice (for example in acts of ostentatious expenditure or in expiatory rituals). Gift-exchange socialities, the shared gratifications of friendship and solidarity, ideas (such as patriotism) and affects (such as love) also have the power to defy self- or group-centred calculations. The very concept of 'benefit' (individual or collective) is culturally and historically determined. And it is open to struggles that contest it, transform it and connect it to different shared values and meanings. Even the allegedly innocent term *access* (which is employed in problematizing the management or governance of resources) more often than not presupposes a prevailing scarcity principle that shapes human behaviour and demands. Using the term to describe the opportunity to share knowledge enclosed by those who profit from its uses hides the fact that the production and circulation of knowledge is not an economic process (and is not subject to the logic of scarcity). It is the capitalist logic of transforming everything to economic entities and reducing human creativity to economic-benefit-oriented work that creates a knowledge economy (an economy of knowledge). It is not, of course, enough to disentangle knowledge from economic reasoning to open it to commoning. It is equally important to free knowledge from practices of domination in which knowledge is performatively declared as a source of power. The term *access* may even hide these aspects of knowledge enclosure that have survived and continue to thrive in capitalism ('sacred knowledge' guarded by 'priests', elitist knowledge guarded by connoisseurs, etc.)

Societies are being structured through geometries of power, and it is those geometries that commoning should challenge. Domination is being imposed and legitimized in every field and at every level of social life, production of goods obviously included. Perhaps going beyond capitalism would mean taking away from the economy and economical reasoning the power to dominate all the other systems of social structure. Creativity, play, passion and experiments in social relations that are not the means to something else but themselves the ends of social common life are modes of social organization that may describe a way out from the predominance of the economy. This predominance, after all, seems to characterize a small part of human history. This is how we can understand commoning not as an alternative economy but 'as an alternative to economy' (Esteva 2014: i149). Commons can indeed be 'the cell of the new society' (ibid.: i147) not only if common is 'the cellular form of society beyond capital' (De Peuter and Dyer-Witheford 2010: 44 and Dyer-Witheford 2006) but if commoning is to be a process of sharing both resources and power. Commoning, thus, may possibly develop not simply as an ever-expanding network of alternative economic relations but as an ever-expanding network of equalitarian forms of social organization, an ever-expanding network of alternatives to economocentric reason and to exploitative power relations.

### Common space as threshold space

Common spaces are those spaces produced by people in their effort to establish a common world that houses, supports and expresses the community they participate in. Common spaces, thus, should be distinguished both from public spaces and from private spaces. Public spaces are primarily created by a certain authority (local, regional or state) which controls them and establishes the rules under which people may use them. Private spaces belong to and are controlled by specific individuals or economic entities that have the right to establish the conditions under which others may use them.

Common space can be considered as a relation between a social group and its effort to define a world that is shared between its members. By its very conception such a world can be stable and well defined, completely separated from what is kept outside and the 'outsiders'. This is indeed the kind of world that can be contained in an urban enclave: enclaves can be secluded common worlds, as in the case of a *favela*, or of a gated community.

Common space, however, can also be a porous world, always in-the-making, if we consider the relation that defines it

as dynamic both in terms of the formation of the corresponding group or community and in terms of the characteristics of
the common world itself. Common space, thus, may be shaped
through the practices of an emerging and not necessarily homogeneous community which does not simply try to secure its
reproduction but also attempts to enrich its exchanges with
other communities as well as the exchanges between its members. Common space may take the form of a meeting ground, an
area in which 'expansive circuits of encounter' intersect (Hardt
and Negri 2009: 254). Through acts of establishing common
spaces, the discriminations and barriers that characterize the
enclave's urbanity may be countered.

From the the perspective of reappropriating the city, common
spaces are the spatial nodes through which the metropolis becomes again the site of politics, if by 'politics' we may describe
an open process through which the dominant forms of living together are questioned and potentially transformed. This is how
a group that almost ignited the Gezi Park struggle – in defence
of a park that was meant to be destroyed by the government's
plans in Istanbul, Turkey – described the collective experience
of reappropriating the metropolis: 'The struggle for Gezi Park
and Taksim Square set a new definition of what public space
means. Reclaiming Taksim has shattered AKP's [the governing
party] hegemony in deciding what a square is supposed to mean
for us citizens, because Taksim is now what the Resistance wants
it to mean: our public square' (Müştereklerimiz 2013). Interestingly, the group's name may be translated as Our Commons.

The prevailing experiences of urban enclosures and the dominant imaginary of recognizable identity-imposing enclaves
colonize the thought and action of those who attempt to reclaim

politics. We need to abandon a view that fantasizes about un-contaminated enclaves of emancipation (Stavrides 2009: 53 and Negri 2009: 50). Threshold experience and the threshold metaphor offer a counter-example to the dominant enclave city (Stavrides 2010b). Rather than perpetuating an image of this city as an archipelago of enclave islands, we need to create spaces that inventively threaten this peculiar urban order by upsetting dominant taxonomies of spaces and life types. Spaces-as-thresholds acquire a dubious, precarious perhaps but also virus-like existence: they become active catalysts in processes of reappropriating the city as commons.

Threshold spatiality may host and express practices of commoning that are not limited to secluded worlds shared by secluded communities of commoners. Thresholds explicitly symbolize the potentiality of sharing by establishing intermediary areas of crossing, by opening the inside to the outside. As mechanisms which regulate and give meaning to acts of passage, thresholds may become powerful tools in the construction of spaces which escape the normalizing urban ordering of the city of enclaves.

Thresholds may appear as mere boundaries which separate an inside from an outside such as, for example, in a door threshold, but this act of separation is always and simultaneously an act of connection. Thresholds create the conditions of entrance and exit; thresholds prolong, manipulate and give meaning to an act of passage. This is why thresholds have been marked in many societies by rituals which attempt to control the inherent potentialities of crossing. Guardian gods or spirits dwell in thresholds because the act of passage is already an act that brings into a potential connection an inside and an outside. Entering may be taken as an intrusion, and exiting may convey the stigma of ostracizing.

Thresholds acquire symbolic meaning and are often shaped in ways that express and corroborate this meaning. Societies construct thresholds as spatial artifices which regulate, symbolically and actually, practices of crossing, practices of bridging different worlds. And those practices may be socially beneficial or harmful. Societies also use the image and the emblematic experience of thresholds to metaphorically invest meaning into changes of social status which periodically and necessarily happen to their members. Passing from childhood to adolescence, from single to married life, from life to death, from apprenticeship to the status of the professional, from trainee to warrior, and so on, are cases of supervised social transformation that mould individuals. Societies often understand these changes as the crossing of thresholds: initiation procedures guarantee a socially 'safe' crossing by directing neophytes to the 'other' side (Van Gennep 1960: 15–25).

As the anthropologist Victor Turner has observed, threshold crossing contains an inherent transforming potential which is not necessarily bound to the rules of social reproduction. People-on-the-threshold experience the potentiality of change because during the period of their stay on the threshold a peculiar experience emerges, the experience of *communitas* (Turner 1977: 96–7). People who have lost their previous social identity but have not yet acquired a new one linger on the threshold of change 'betwixt and between' (ibid.: 95), almost reduced to the common characteristics shared by all humans. Social differentiation may appear quite arbitrary during such an experience. A kind of equalizing potentiality seems to dwell on thresholds.

Liminality, the spatiotemporal quality of threshold experience (Turner 1977 and 1974: 197), is a condition which gives people the opportunity to share a common world-in-the-making in which differences appear as pre-social or even anti-social.

Turner thinks that 'there are … two major models for human interrelatedness' (Turner 1977: 96). The first one refers to the hierarchical set of relations which characterizes societies in general and which is most of the time organized as a system of 'politico-legal-economic positions' (ibid.), a 'structure', in Turner's terminology. 'The second … is of society as an unstructured or rudimentarily structured and relatively undifferentiated comitatus, community or even communion of equal individuals' (ibid.). Turner names this *communitas* to distinguish it from *community*, which for him is an 'area of common living' (ibid.). Communitas, therefore, is an exceptional collective experience which happens in cases in which people lose, don't pay attention to or consciously bypass, ignore or challenge forms of distinction that separate them. This may indeed happen in the ritual context of rites of passage. It may also be the product of experiences connected to 'liminoid' phenomena, those phenomena that share the same 'anti-structural' expressions as the phenomena of ritual liminality. Connecting to Sutton-Smith's idea that 'anti-structure represents the latent system of potential alternatives from which novelty will arise' (in Turner 1982: 28), Turner considers liminoid phenomena – in which he includes charivari, fiestas, wearing masks at Halloween, etc. – as the 'seedbeds of cultural creativity' (ibid.). Although he did not choose specifically to connect liminoid phenomena with collective acts of transgression, Turner thought of the experience of communitas as equally present in those phenomena. In a somewhat alienated form, the feeling of communitas persists in mass entertainment experiences as well as in the so-called 'high art' collective contemplation (when, for example, one goes to the museum, to the opera, to the cinema, etc.). Whereas, however, these forms of communitas unite individuals without supposedly highlighting their cultural or social differences, they often end up being mere simulations of communitas experience: the mass audiences are often united in their common fantasies and their common consumer appetites (sports and games audiences included). What a discussion on the equalizing experience of communitas can offer to a problematization of the commoning practices is the means to understand a community of commoners as a community which develops in its members a feeling of the sharing of qualities which are common to all. And this feeling liberates people from their anguish to prove that they are better and stronger, et cetera because of their neighbours. In such a context, communitas may be taken to represent not a feeling of belonging to a specific closed community but a feeling of becoming part of a community that is potentially limitless.

Initiation threshold spaces are defined through the ritual practices which bring them into existence. Such threshold spaces are under society's surveillance, and any form of communitas is carefully limited to an ephemeral initiatory existence. However, in thresholds which give ground to and shape institutions of expanding commoning, communitas is experienced as an always-in-the-making community of participating commoners. These people do not experience the potentialities of equality by being ritually reduced to a common degree zero of humanness (as do the initiated in rites of passage). Rather, they construct through their acts a community of equals because they choose to define at least part of their life autonomously and in common. Emergent communities of creators and users of city space: isn't this a prospect that transforms city space to common space, to space-as-commons?

In what follows, an attempt is made to study practices of urban commoning and to discover in them potentialities that hint at different forms of social relations and organization: can commoning practices offer us glimpses of a different future, of a just and emancipated society?

As we will see, in many cases common spaces give ground to prefigurations of such a different future. Common spaces, however, as well as commoning practices should not be taken into account only because of such inherent potentialities. In today's hierarchical, divided and often harshly partitioned predominantly urban societies, real people attempt every day to control at least fragments of their lives themselves. Explicitly organized struggles for common spaces and for the strengthening of commoning practices of collaboration (in recuperated sites of production, for example, or in less ambitious neighbourhood garden initiatives) are not the only important sources of inspiration for opening passages to a different future. Lots of small, even mundane, initiatives exhibit the power commoning has to shape habits and acts of sharing as well as bonds of solidarity. Commoning practices become reinvented in today's metropolises in acts of collective everyday survival. Commoning practices also erupt in attempts to secure channels of communication and exchange that are not regulated solely by the destructive rules of exploitation. Everyday forms of encounter and collaboration indeed take shape in and through commoning without even declaring themselves to be an alternative to the existing social relations.

Institutions of expanding commoning may or may not be present in all of these implicit or explicit commoning practices. Such practices sometimes struggle to manage themselves, to become repeatable and recognizable, to establish collective identities and to circumscribe collectively agreed-upon stakes and targets. But commoning practices are necessarily caught in an antagonistic social context which supports dominant capitalist command and forms of capitalist usurpation of the commons. We have to carefully study common spaces not as pure expressions of a different culture but as necessarily hybrid collective works-in-progress, in which glimpses of a different future emerge. Commoning in those spaces may fall into the trap of enclosing itself (reversing, thus, those potentialities) or may strive to go beyond capitalist capture. Commoning, thus, is not anti-capitalist by essence but may activate and express attempts to go beyond capitalism.

Part two

# Inhabited common spaces

Chapter 3

# Shared heterotopias: learning from the history of a social housing complex in Athens

Commoning may characterize communities which, especially in periods in which their very existence is threatened, tend to become closed common worlds: in such worlds some people may even lose their previously established privileges when practices of community survival tend to make all share the same fate. This happens, for example, during a natural or man-made disaster that creates forms of sharing and togetherness between those who suffer (Solnit 2009).

However, although communities under such circumstances may appear to be almost naturally inclined to enclose themselves for collective self-protection, in some cases crisis conditions encourage practices of community opening and create spaces of osmotic sharing.

Rebecca Solnit describes the cases of the San Francisco and Mexico City earthquakes in which existing urban communities did not aggressively try to survive by fighting with other communities or individuals who also claimed the same scarce (due to the disaster) resources but actually opened their boundaries and organized their participation in new networks of encounter and mutual support (ibid.: 148). 'The quake marked the rebirth of what Mexicans call civil society' (ibid.: 143). This term was used to include all those networks of sharing that were created 'from below' in the absence of government support for the quake victims and included 'relief brigades' and 'cleanup crews' in the first days after the disaster (ibid.: 143). Soon housing rights movements and neighbourhood initiatives for feeding and sheltering the new homeless were to follow. The organized Zapatista communities which slowly emerged after the 1994 uprising adapted a slogan that had been created in those days of the 1985 earthquake: 'We are the civil society.'

Maybe we can learn something important about the practices of expanding commoning if we study more closely the history of a social housing complex in Athens which was constructed in 1935 in order to accommodate refugees from Asia Minor after a devastating war. Inhabitants of this complex belonged to specific uprooted urban communities and arrived in Athens economically and emotionally ruined. Their communities had been dismantled and their common worlds shattered. But they remained attached to their shared cultural habits and values while in search of a new urban collective identity in a 'foreign' city. As we will see, those refugees neither simply adapted to their new housing environment, nor did they choose to barricade themselves in a poor but seemingly secure enclave meant to contain a culturally and socially homogeneous urban community. In their everyday practices they developed osmotic relations with adjacent neighbourhoods and the city and became catalysts of expanding commoning: their habits and open sociality influenced a lot of their neighbours. In crucial periods of this complex's history, rich exchanges and encounters created an expanding shared world.

The inhabitants of these buildings were stigmatized as 'others', coming into Athens as refugees from Asia Minor. How were they able to perforate the borders of their seclusion? How could they

invent spaces of negotiation, spaces that mediated between differing cultural traditions?

The concept of heterotopia can describe a collective experience of otherness, not as a stigmatizing spatial seclusion but
rather as the practice of diffusing new forms of urban collective
life. In search of potentially emancipating urban practices, we
may thus find heterotopic moments in the history of specific
urban sites. Can we locate such moments? And can we describe
them as thresholds, in social time as well as in social space, opening towards an alternative culture of space-commoning?

### Urban thresholds and heterotopias

The porous rocks of Naples offered Walter Benjamin an image
for a city's public life: 'As porous as this stone is the architecture.
Building and action interpenetrate in the courtyards, arcades
and stairways' (Benjamin 1985: 169). Porosity seems to describe,
in this passage, the way in which urban space is performed in
the process of being appropriated (Sennett 1995: 56). It is not
that action is contained in space. Rather, a rich network of practices transforms every available space into a potential theatre
of expressive acts of encounter. A 'passion for improvisation',
as Benjamin describes this public behaviour, penetrates and
articulates urban space, loosening socially programmed correspondences between function and place. Porosity is thus an
essential characteristic of space in Naples because life in the city
is full of acts that overflow into each other. Defying any clear de-
marcation, spaces are separated and simultaneously connected
by porous boundaries, through which everyday life takes form
in mutually dependent public performances. Thus, 'just as the
living room reappears on the street, with chairs, hearth and altar,

so, only much more loudly, the street migrates into the living room' (Benjamin 1985: 174). Porosity characterizes above all the relationship between private and public space, as well as the relationship between indoor and outdoor space.

For Benjamin, porosity is not limited to spatial experience. Urban life is not only located in spaces that communicate through passages ('pores'), but life is performed at a tempo that fails to completely separate acts or events. A temporal porosity is experienced while eating in the street, taking a nap in a shady corner or drinking a quick espresso standing in a Neapolitan café. It is as if acts are both separated and connected through temporal passages that represent the precarious, fleeting experience of occasion. Everyday occasions thus seem to shift and rearrange rhythms and itineraries of use (De Certeau 1984: xix).

Porosity may therefore be considered as an experience of habitation, which articulates urban life while it also loosens the borders which are erected to preserve a strict spatial and temporal social order. In our need to suppose a founding act for architecture, we usually imagine humans delimiting a territory by marking boundaries. In the rich complexity of city life, however, architecture becomes above all the art of creating passages. Georg Simmel, the well-known dissector of early modern metropolitan experience, points out that 'the human being is the bordering creature who has no border' (Simmel 1997: 69). For Simmel, the bridge and the door become the archetypal artefacts that concretize an essentially human act, the act of separating and connecting simultaneously. As the door presupposes a separation between inner and outer space only to transcend it, so the bridge defines the banks of a river as separated and not merely apart in order to concretize the possibility of crossing.

This interconnectedness of an act and a will of separation with an act and a will of connection can be taken to epitomize the double nature of a porous border: a borderline, transformed to a porous membrane, separates while connecting bordering areas (as well as bordering acts or events).

Thresholds both symbolize and concretize the socially meaningful act of connecting while separating and separating while connecting, the act that Simmel considers to be a characteristic human ability (ibid.: 66). Thresholds are constructions that are present both mentally and materially. This is why thresholds not only ensure the act of passage, but also serve as representations of the act of passage (we say we are on the threshold of a new era, etc.). And these representations, as we know from anthropological research, are explicitly involved in crucial ritual acts (Van Genepp 1960).

We can include in the category of social artefacts that symbolically and literally regulate the act of passage all those spatial arrangements that perforate boundaries. We may also include all those areas marked by human crossings that attribute to space characteristics of passage. All such spatial artefacts that are either materialized in constructions that endure time (gates, stairs, squares) or temporarily created through use (such as the route of a pilgrimage or a quest, or the ephemeral appropriation of a street by a feast or a demonstration) can be considered thresholds. Either created by stones or bodies in action, these arrangements exist to indicate the importance of the act of passing from one condition to another. Thresholds separate while connecting areas that are distinct but also interdependent. The social meaning of a crossing act is indeed to leave a condition that is familiar and to enter a condition that is essentially 'other'.

By regulating passages, thresholds indicate a potential movement towards otherness.

Otherness is, after all, a relational term. Approaching otherness is therefore an act involving both spatial and temporal passages. This can give new meaning to Harvey's assessment: 'The relations between "self" and the "other" from which a certain kind of cognition of social affairs emanates is always … a spatiotemporal construction' (Harvey 1996: 264).

In contemporary metropolitan experiences, urban thresholds define the quality and meaning of spatial as well as social borderlines. In today's partitioned cities (Marcuse 1995, Marcuse and Van Kempen 2002), thresholds are rapidly being replaced by checkpoints, control areas that regulate encounters and discriminate between users. Residential enclaves can define recognizable urban identities. The suburban areas of American cities, the shanty towns in Latin America or Asia, the gentrified residential areas of many European cities or the immigrant ghettos all over the world all possess visible urban identities. Public space contained in these areas is eventually separated from the rest of the city, and its use is essentially restricted to the members of the corresponding community of residents. If this may be considered as common space, regarding its use rather than its production, then it is enclosed common space or common space deprived of its inherent dynamism of expanding. It can even be described as 'corrupted common space', to borrow a relevant term from Hardt and Negri (2009: 171).

Urban identities are exhibited in spaces where a common feeling of belonging dominates every experience of being in public (Sennett 1993). Spatially and conceptually framed identities therefore correspond to the experience of partitioned urban space. Inside homogenized urban enclaves, potentially shared space becomes trapped in the form of an *identity based com-mons*' (De Angelis 2012b) which prevents it from expanding to include 'outsiders'.

Benjamin, seeking to redeem the emancipating potential of modernity, offered a way to reclaim the power that thresholds possess to mediate actions that open spatially (as well as socially) fixed identities and encourage chance encounters. According to his reasoning, threshold awareness could have provided op-portunities to defy the dominating myths of progress that had re-enchanted modern urban experience. Such awareness char-acterized the *flâneur*, this ambiguous hero of modernity, who 'stands on the threshold of the metropolis as of the middle class' (Benjamin 1999: 8).

Thresholds can perforate the unity of urban myths as well as the unity of history, considered as the site of 'homogeneous empty time' (Benjamin 1992: 252). Thresholds mark occasions and opportunities for change. Thresholds create or symbolically represent passages towards a possible future, already existing in the past. Recognizing such thresholds, the *flâneur*, and the inhabitant as *flâneur*, can appreciate the city as a locus of discon-tinuities, as a network of crossroads and turning points. In the unexpected connections realized by these thresholds, otherness emerges, not only as a threat but also as a promise.

Today's partitioned city is not of course the nineteenth-century metropolis. Threshold awareness, however, may reveal encoun-ters between differing social groups and also between different life courses. Literally or symbolically perforating the perimeters of enclaves might mean comparing and connecting those sep-arated as others. Threshold experiences actualize the mutual recognition and interdependence of identities. The prospect of a 'city of thresholds' (Stavrides 2010b) might represent an alternative to the city of enclaves. In such a perspective, becoming aware of the power of thresholds to compare spatially performed identities is already a step towards a culture of mutual involvement and negotiation. Instead of facing otherness as clearly marked in space, one is encouraged to cross boundaries, invent in-between spaces of encounter and appreciate situated identities as open and developing.

When we confront spatial experiences that tend to actualize in time and space this precarious prospect of a city of thresholds, we can speak of heterotopias – places where differences meet. With the notion of heterotopia, Michel Foucault described those 'counter arrangements', those spaces that are absolutely other compared to the normal spaces they 'reflect', representing them, challenging them and overturning them (Foucault 1993: 422). Heterotopias are real places, existing in real societies and inhabited in ways that deviate from what these societies consider and impose as normal. This deviance may, however, be either constitutive of groups of people considered as other (people in prisons, in psychiatric clinics or in rest homes) or characteristic of a temporary period of crisis (usually marking crucial transformations of social identities, as during young people's military service).

According to Foucault, 'heterotopias always presuppose a system of opening and closing that isolates them and makes them penetrable at one and the same time' (1993: 425). These 'other places', therefore, are being simultaneously connected to and separated from the places from which they differ. We could consider this characteristic of heterotopias to be an indication of their relational status. And we could name as thresholds those arrangements that regulate the relationship of heterotopias with their surrounding spaces of normality. Heterotopias can be taken to concretize paradigmatic experiences of otherness, defined by the porous and contested perimeter that separates normality from deviance. Because this perimeter is full of combining/separating thresholds, heterotopias are not simply places of the other, or the deviant as opposed to the normal, but places in which otherness proliferates, potentially spilling over into the neighbouring areas of 'sameness'. Heterotopias thus mark an osmosis between situated identities and experiences that can effectively destroy those strict taxonomies that ensure social reproduction. Through their osmotic boundaries, heterotopias diffuse a virus of change.

'Heterotopias are linked for the most part to bits and pieces of time' (Foucault 1993: 424). We could thus understand their status as historically ambiguous. It is at specific historical conjunctures that specific spatiotemporal experiences can be recognized as heterotopias. Heterotopias can become the places of an emerging new order that will turn the experience of otherness into a new rule of sameness (Hetherington 1997), or they can contain moments of rupture in social and spatial history.

Heterotopias may be reduced to the thresholds that connect them to the rest of social space-time. We can speak then of heterotopic moments, moments of encounter with socially recognizable otherness, that become possible because of acts of perforating normality's perimeter. Heterotopias assume a threshold character, being both present and absent in a different time, existing both as reality and potentiality.

In the diverse histories of urban porosity, heterotopias may represent moments in which otherness manifests itself in established inhabitation practices in the form of emerging counter-paradigms to urban normalization. These counter-paradigms, always ambiguous and sometimes still bearing the traces of the prevailing culture, may become either demonized (confronted with attempts to delimit and control them) or seductively metastatic, insinuating themselves into different established common worlds.

In a study of commoning practices that tries to explore the emancipating potentialities of sharing, the concept of heterotopia may become unexpectedly useful. Heterotopias, as we have seen, may be understood as sites of osmosis and encounter, as areas in which different identities may meet and become mutually aware of each other. Comparison thus becomes a crucial characteristic of heterotopic conditions. Heterotopias are sites of comparison: adjacent spaces are being compared while being separated and connected at the same time. Identities become comparable by being present in a place that gives them ground to share, a place that is not identified by or with any of them.

We need, of course, to distinguish heterotopic performances of otherness that put emphasis on relationality and comparison from fashion-like performances of otherness. What characterizes the spectacular proliferation of lifestyles and consumerist aestheticism is the emphasis on individualist values and the promotion of performances of illusionary uniqueness. Most publicity images try to convince 'you' that 'this product' was specifically 'made for you': wearing it, drinking it, watching it, and so on makes 'you' unique, 'yourself'. Staged heterotopias of fashion and lifestyle showcases attempt to capture the power heterotopic moments have to gesture towards deviation and liberating novelty by converting it to a tamed exhibition of personal taste and to individual fantasies of distinction. Stereotypical otherness is not relational otherness but otherness captured in the taxonomies of dominant roles. The fact that in the so-called postmodern period such taxonomies appear more diverse or less apparent does not change their normalizing role. A proliferating discourse on diversity and heterogeneity misses (or intentionally hides) the dominant practices of normalization. Normalization is not simply homogenization but, as we have seen in Chapter 1, a process of subjecting the potentialities of otherness to models that shape behaviour according to prevailing power relations.

A social centre, a self-managed factory or an occupied public space may become the locus of a radiating heterotopia. But they may equally be trapped into the model of an autonomous enclave of otherness, as we will see in Chapter 9. A social housing area, a public park or an outdoor festival may possibly become punctuated by heterotopic moments. It all depends on performances of otherness that create or use threshold spaces as instances of encounter and as a means to establish comparisons through mutual involvement. A department store, a amusement park or a gentrified neighbourhood promoting 'alternative' lifestyle products and services are not heterotopias but mere showcases of merchandized, 'tamed' and carefully staged otherness.

If the expanding inclusiveness of a community is activated through comparisons which open the circle of commoning to new potential participants, then heterotopic qualities may become important catalysts in such a process. Heterotopic spaces and times open the boundaries of communities without reducing encounters to a homogenizing procedure. Heterotopias do not circumscribe otherness but actually make otherness visible, actively comparable and thus potentially translatable. The moment heterotopias become the places of a new 'ordering' process (Hetherington 1997) and their power to generate comparison and thus create common ground without reducing different identities to this common ground, they become annexed to new imposed taxonomies of social practices and roles. It is heterotopias, considered as always-open urban and social pores, which keep the process of expanding commoning always going. Exactly because the prospect of expanding commoning retains its power as equalitarian sharing by opening a community of commoners to newcomers, it needs to activate forms of approaching those 'outside' the already-established circle of sharing. Commoning, if it is to avoid being trapped in new forms of enclosure, needs to open itself to otherness. Expanding commoning gains its power from this always-risky, often unpredictable, sometimes dangerous but always-intense encounter with an 'outside' that may threaten but also enrich an 'inside'. Expanding commoning is the risk that commoners have to take if they don't want to become themselves agents or victims of enclosure.

What follows is a history of urban porosity that has marked the housing complex in Athens already mentioned. Through instances of urban porosity, I will trace not only chronicles of past acts, but also possibilities for future ones. And in the exceptional periods when porosity seems to impose itself as a counter-paradigm, perhaps it will be possible to discern, in this fragmented history of specific urban experiences, heterotopic moments. It is during these periods that the so-called Prosfygika area of Alexandras Avenue temporarily became the locus of a potentially 'other' public culture oriented towards the creation of common space.

## A collective experience of urban porosity

The year 1922 marks a crucial turning point in modern Greek history. An increasingly dominant nationalist ideology, focused on 'liberating' Greek people then living in Turkey, culminated in the disastrous expedition of the Greek Army into Asia Minor. The *Entente* Coalition (Russia, England and France) seems to have encouraged such an expedition after the Sèvres Treaty (1920), or at least did nothing to prevent it. The Turkish Army, part of the National Revolution headed by M. Kemal Atatürk against the Ottoman state, won this war, an outcome marked in Greek history as the 'Asia Minor disaster'. After the war, a treaty was signed specifying a large-scale population exchange to be supervised by the League of Nations (Svoronos 1972).

Some 1,200,000 Greeks, mostly from cities on Turkey's Aegean coast, had to leave their homes and be transported to Greece, deprived of all their possessions. Turks from the Greek mainland, mainly peasants, had to follow the opposite route (Vlachos et al. 1978).

The state's policy was to keep almost half of the refugee population around major cities, so as to control them and to 'integrate' them into the local economy. Those who were allowed to stay in Athens had to build their houses on empty public land, mainly outside the city, using whatever building materials they could find and with almost no money. Shanty towns with no roads or public facilities emerged around Athens and Piraeus. Uprooted people tried to live in a country that appeared more hostile to them than they had ever expected.

Of course, these settlements provided Greek industries and handicraft workshops with low-wage labour. This is why many people considered the refugees a threat to their jobs, and to their well-being. Refugees were demonized as invaders who would destroy the city's public life. Forced to cross a threshold in a period when it separated rather than connected two neighbouring countries, they were allowed neither to return nor to feel at home in their new destination. These people were actually not allowed to belong anywhere. Moreover, the Greek government aimed to ensure that poverty and discontent would not cross the borders of the shanty town: refugee settlements were spatially and socially formed as ghettos.

People coming into Athens from Asia Minor were mostly city people. They had a highly complex urban culture, so their life, even though almost completely destroyed, followed forms of sociality that were sometimes far richer than those of surrounding neighbourhoods. Refugees slowly re-established a public life based on community rhythms, making their small shops or houses into meeting places to accommodate a rich tradition of collective festivities, music and oriental cuisine. Their way of life invited other city people to share new experiences of urban companionship. Slowly the refugees converted the sanitary zone that was erected around them, those literal or symbolic walls of prejudice and status (Marcuse 1995: 249), into a porous membrane that allowed their culture to diffuse into the city. Instead of representing an unwillingly invading other that stood on the threshold separating two opposing neighbouring countries (Turkey and Greece), the refugees thus came slowly to be recognized as people who dwell on a threshold that connects two cultures sharing many common values and habits. In spite of opposing nationalisms, cultural porosity was to emerge once again, rooted in a history of cultural exchanges amongst different peoples in the Balkans and Asia Minor. After all, this region was and is still a threshold connecting as well as separating 'East' from 'West'.

After a long period of emergency, during which most of the funds of the Greek Refugee Rehabilitation Committee were used in rural rehabilitation, the responsibility for social housing development was shifted to the Technical Department of the Ministry of Welfare. Almost ten years after the Asia Minor exodus, a slum clearance project produced a series of model settlements (Vasileiou 1944: 80–90, Vlachos et al. 1978: 118, Morgenthau 1930).

The Alexandras building complex, built during the years 1934–5, was among them. The thirties represent a crossroads in the urban history of Athens. In 1929, a new law which established floor ownership in apartment buildings opened the road to rapid commercialization of residential development. In the same period, however, some of the best examples of social housing were constructed in Athens, designed by Greek architects working with the Technical Department. Those buildings constituted an alternative model of housing, contrasting with the packed multistorey buildings of private housing that were soon to engulf all Athenian neighbourhoods.

The Alexandras complex is distinctive in its abundance of open space between the buildings. Although apartments were relatively small (most of them with two rooms, a kitchen and a small bathroom), all of them had ample sunshine and ventilation. These buildings were among the first to concretize the new spirit of Modern architecture in its programmatic manifestos and works on social housing. In 1933, the International Conference on Modern Architecture (CIAM) culminated in the Charter of Athens, epitomizing the objectives of the Modern Movement

(Mumford 2000: 91–103 and Conrads 1971: 137–46). Quality mass housing was one of the major goals. It is not by chance, then, that when Greek architects were encouraged to participate in the design of refugee housing complexes, they employed concepts and models from the Bauhaus School to produce houses appropriate for the new standards of living. Not being the direct result of market laws which had completely reduced housing to a commodity, these buildings could have set an example to follow in the rapid urbanization of the post-Second World War years.

The Alexandras building complex was characterized by a rational layout. It consists of eight blocks totalling 228 apartments of two types. Uniformity is absolutely characteristic. An effort to provide the essential household facilities in a minimum space makes the plans of these buildings representative of the Modern Movement's obsession with efficient minimum spatial standards. Socially, however, those buildings were once again a place where the refugees were to be secluded. No care was taken about the remaining open space, no initiatives were given for the complexes to be incorporated into the city. These complexes were both physically and symbolically set apart from the city, surrounded as they were with amorphous public space easily read as a separating zone.

A kind of deviation from 'normal' urban life must have been attributed to such residential areas that appeared morphologically and functionally different from every other residential neighbourhood in Athens. Although symbolically quite effective, separation was not based on a layout that tried to impose physical segregation. Formless outdoor space was left to surround and contain the blocks. A loose space, with no defined uses, sometimes even without trees, characterized the Alexandras complex as well as most of the other refugee building complexes. Residents, who had to confront a hostile and unfriendly environment, nonetheless appropriated loose space through private and common activities that could not be contained in the buildings. A rich and evolving common life burst out of the buildings, transforming outdoor space into an ambiguous network of small courtyards, pavements, tree-shaded areas, improvised playgrounds and meeting places (Stavrides 2002b:142–3).

In direct contrast to the rational and function-oriented design of the buildings, outdoor space was not marked by absolute boundaries. Most of the basement apartments were extended in small private courtyards, which were either circumscribed by low walls and fences or integrated into a recognizably communal outdoor space. In this latter case, private and public uses were not clearly demarcated. Visiting, small feasts and everyday encounters between neighbours wove the fabric of a diverse and porous urban environment. Terraces, where common laundry facilities were situated, became minuscule stages of an everyday theatricality where mostly women met. During the winter, staircases were transformed into noisy play areas absolutely integrated into the life of the buildings. The 'passion of improvisation' which Benjamin found in pre-war Naples came to characterize the activities of residents, who became highly inventive in inhabiting their standardized and minimum sized houses. Improvisation appeared to mark their ability to collectively appropriate threshold spaces, converting them into lived spaces. The staircase was not simply used to cross an in-between area. Rather, much of everyday life came to take place in the stairways, as well as in front of doorways, in the pavement areas and in the empty space between the kitchens of facing blocks, which was constantly being crossed.

Activating in-between areas as crucial public spaces means creating urban sites with no clear boundaries. A permeable membrane, a porous membrane, was thus crafted through everyday use. Analogous practices developed in most of the refugee housing settlements throughout Athens and Piraeus (the nearby port city). As Hirschon observes in her anthropological study of such a refugee neighbourhood, 'the pavement became a quasi-private area; it became an extension of the home in full, public view: the community and family commingled … The notion of public and private space in this locality clearly overrode simple physical, spatial boundaries' (Hirschon 1998: 190). Balancing between the sometimes conflicting forms of sociality connected to family and neighbourhood respectively, life unfolded by converting spaces, which, like the pavement, acquired a threshold character, to common spaces. Not simply annexed to a family's private milieu but also not simply remaining as public city spaces, those urban areas became spatial artifices of an expanding communal life.

### Heterotopic moments

On one side of the building complex stood one of the most infamous prisons in Athens. A large multistoreyed building was used to detain common lawbreakers as well as political prisoners until it was demolished in the mid 1960s. People living in the nearby buildings of the Alexandras complex remember how friends and relatives gathered outside the neighbouring wall of the prison, communicating with the prisoners by shouting or receiving notes. People also remember how during the German occupation they used to look from the terrace of their building into the prison courtyard, trying to gather information about the detained patriots of the resistance. They recite stories of young boys and girls daringly approaching the high walls to collect the messages the patriots used to throw from the windows, usually messages to announce that they were to be executed the next morning. And of course nobody will forget the image of a small black cloth hanging from a cell window to indicate that one of the cell's inhabitants had been executed that day (Papavasileiou 2003).

Through such collective experiences, the Alexandras Prosfygika inhabitants formed a kind of hidden solidarity, participating in their own way in the resistance. An impossible osmosis of the prison space with the outdoor areas of the complex was realized through acts that symbolically perforated the separating wall. A recognizable osmosis between different families in such a period of tacit solidarity and mutual help formed the basis of those qualitatively different social bonds that characterized the community during the years of the German occupation (1941–4). Due to the active involvement of the Alexandras complex residents, those buildings were part of liberated Athens months before the Germans abandoned the city while retreating.

One can imagine this period as punctuated by heterotopic moments. Solidarity seems to have transformed the already-osmotic relations between private and public space into mutually recognized common uses of both private and public spaces, producing, thus, metastatic common spaces. Many residents used to share their poor everyday food supplies, and families used to help each other in taking care of the children or cooking. Out of an extremely precarious situation, and because of the growing appeal of the left resistance movement, a communitarian culture that was distinctively urban manifested itself in the refugee neighbourhood.

In the years that followed, this culture was literally blown to pieces by British canons and aeroplanes as well as by Greek government troops in the incidents of December 1944. During the so-called Battle of Athens, the Greek Popular Liberation Army (ELAS), the major anti-occupation resistance movement, was opposed to British policy in the area, which denied the popular will for post-war democracy and social justice. British politics resulted in a massacre on 3 December 1944, when a huge peaceful demonstration was attacked by royalist troops, sparking a long and devastating civil war (Svoronos 1972). Members of ELAS fought a decisive battle in defence of the Alexandras buildings that were attacked by the above-mentioned forces. Many men decided to side with the fighting guerrillas, while women and children took shelter in a nearby football stadium. As if to dramatically symbolize the osmotic space between the houses, holes were made in the inner walls of adjoining apartments. Those passages enabled the defenders to move from one apartment to another. The Battle of Athens was only a dramatic prelude to the civil war which came after. People living in the buildings in those days of December still remember the romantic young fighters who sought in vain to defend the dream of a just society (Tsougrani 2000).

A 94-year-old inhabitant of Alexandras Prosfygika, who has spent years and years sitting by his window because of a serious disease of his knees, recalls: 'People used to walk differently in those years [during the 1940s and 1950s], they used to look at you differently, they used to say good morning' (Tzanavara 2000). Overlooking one of the streets between the buildings, which used to be a dirt road, this old man was using his window during the post-war years as a 'box in the theater of the world' (Benjamin 1999: 9).

Urban porosity for this man could not be experienced actively in inhabiting public space. He could, however, appreciate the characteristics of an osmotic public culture, feeling the way his window was integrated into a network of thresholds, as opposed to the screen character of windows in modern big cities.

Since the late sixties, these buildings have from time to time been the focus of successive governments who promised a park in place of a degraded housing area. The pressure produced a precarious situation for the inhabitants, who in most cases were hesitant to spend any more money on house maintenance. Common porous spaces, terraces, staircases and pavements started crumbling. The municipality of Athens did not maintain the vast surrounding open space, which could have been transformed into an urban green area. Instead this area became a large informal car park for people using the nearby hospital or watching a football game in the large football stadium facing the complex. This land is also used every day by those who work in the Supreme Court building (erected on the site of the former prison) and in the Athens police headquarters, located on the next block.

Shapeless open spaces such as the one between the Alexandras Prosfygika buildings used to be important informal public spaces in pre-war Athens. Children used them in their games, grown-ups in their walks, younger ones in their exciting journeys into adolescence. Outdoor loose space was, however, demonized by middle-class morality. The word used to name such places was *alana*, and the people who in the middle-class imaginary were only worthy to wander there were called *alania*, a word that became synonymous with 'vagabond'. The alana was, however, a rich and porous urban space, always in the process of being transformed through use, especially in low-income neighbourhoods.

Alanas were actually spaces of commoning in pre-war Athens. People informally appropriated leftover empty spaces between the buildings and temporarily converted them into ad hoc common spaces. No authority had authorized the informal uses of alanas and that is why those spaces appeared as threatening no-man's-land in the middle-class cognitive maps of the city. The Alexandras refugees had appropriated the alana-like space between the buildings in a more systematic and habitual manner than the occasional wanderers or the playing children. They had integrated this space into a rich network of in-between spaces, a network of common spaces which were shared by the inhabitants' community.

Dispossessed and marginalized people are forced to live in hard conditions in which space is either not enough or inappropriate for a decent everydayness. They often try in informal and inventive ways to compensate for this lack. As Blomley suggests, relevant acts should make us acknowledge the 'possibility of a collective property interest of the poor' (Blomley 2008: 325) recognized as socially just. Even though Alexandras Prosfygika inhabitants didn't actually own this outdoor area (which remained the property of the Municipality of Athens, excluding the streets, which are the property of the Greek state), they should have had the right to claim the area collectively as an integral part of the complex. Instead, the ad hoc use of the area as a car park was the result of an aggressive attitude by people who thought that the area had no owner and that they could use it according to their own interests. This of course became possible because the municipality never really looked after those spaces. From 2000 to 2010, when the immense pressure on the residents to sell their houses culminated, this deliberate abandoning of public spaces by the authorities which were obliged to look after them was an additional factor which contributed to the buildings' devaluation.

Today's parking area has destroyed the alana character of the complex's open space, transforming it into an inert urban setting. People come and go with only the aim of finding a place to leave their car, sometimes becoming extremely frustrated since this area is now very near the city centre and crowded with multistorey buildings.

The car park users are participating in an individualized appropriation of public space. Their practices of temporary appropriation are simple acts of space grabbing (often recurrent) and actually blocking and degrading the in-between outdoor space's common uses.

We can think of these space-grabbing practices as practices of 'emptying' public space, as practices of blocking the potentialities of alana-like space which would transform it into an urban threshold. Alanas were never empty spaces. They were part of a neighbourhood's diversely used shared space. Alexandra Prosfygika's outdoor area was also not an empty space. Actually, it was emptied as soon as it was filled with parked cars. If 'terrain vague' is more than urban void, then this area was a terrain vague, as 'expectant, imprecise and fluctuating' as Solà-Morales claims such spaces to be (Solà-Morales 1995: 122). But a 'terrain vague' may become the site of commoning not only if it becomes 'filled' with a specific urban use but if it is inhabited and shaped as an urban threshold (Stavrides 2014: 57–8).

During recent years the inhabitants of the buildings were once again demonized as feared others. Otherness was identified this time with stigmatized urban poverty and marginalization, emphatically represented in the image of derelict and deserted buildings. Most of the inhabitants had become owners of their apartments, having paid off state mortgages under very favourable terms. A lot of them, however, in fear of imminent compulsory expropriation, sold their apartments to a public property development company (KED). Others had either abandoned their houses or had rented them to contemporary immigrants and refugees or other low-income people. Some inhabitants, though, remain, descendants of the Asia Minor refugees, claiming their right for a better future in a place where the past was generous, no matter how hard. Today, the area appears to be almost abandoned, symbolically as well as literally 'out of order'. In the heart of Athens, this building complex represents a kind of downgraded housing area that belongs to the past – for many, a collectively repressed past.

However, a new set of experiences of urban porosity has recently emerged, scattered among the devastated everyday life of the buildings, resulting from initiatives taken by those who resist the demolition of the complex. A residents' coalition, with a few determined and active members, has managed to combine its forces with architects and teachers from the School of Architecture at the National Technical University of Athens (NTUA). Volunteer and ecological organizations have contributed to this struggle that started in 2000. Through public appeals, demonstrations, exhibitions, happenings and discussions taking place in and around the buildings, these residents and activists from the left and anti-authoritarian movement have shown that this housing area represents an anti-paradigm to Athens's housing history (Vrychea 2003).

Participating in a course focusing on social housing, students of NTUA School of Architecture have shown through differing proposals that a revival of the area can be achieved through regeneration plans that respect the history of the buildings and learn from the informal uses of their inhabitants. In those student projects, the rich variety of extensions offers an architectural vocabulary that gives form to additional spaces for small apartments, encouraging at the same time osmosis between collective and private uses.

Celebrating the prospect of reviving a rich space-commoning culture, a two-day festival was organized in 2003. This same year, because of the 2004 Olympic Games programmed to take place in Athens, the government placed extreme pressure on the inhabitants. The Council for Modern Monuments made a controversial decision to support the government's main target. This decision proposed the preservation of only two out of eight buildings in the complex, considering them worth preserving as an example of a modern housing project. Sampling of course has nothing to do with the essentially paradigmatic nature of this building complex. Such a decision can neither preserve the porous condition of its urban space nor its potentially heterotopic character.

The two-day festival aimed to show through exemplary acts of re-inhabiting a different concept of social housing that was and can be concretized in the Alexandras Prosfygika. Different groups of young activists and students of architecture organized temporary squatting in empty apartments now belonging to the government-run KED. Exhibitions presenting the housing problems of Athens and a history of the refugee settlements and struggles were organized. Prototypical children's areas and environmental awareness exhibits were housed in appropriated empty apartments. The prospect of an osmotic relationship between public and private uses was also explored by improvised constructions in outdoor space, obstructing parking uses and encouraging various acts of collective appropriation and companionship. A small deserted coffee kiosk that used to be a neighbourhood's meeting point was reconstructed and reused ad hoc. An improvised stage was constructed in one of the open spaces. Musicians as well as performers had the opportunity to communicate with the residents and all those who used the area daily and were unaware of its potentialities as a public urban space. Many people, including numerous remaining inhabitants, had the opportunity to experience an essentially heterotopic organization of space.

All these festive and paradigmatic acts attempted to regenerate a porous common space. They tried to show that the history of those buildings has transformed them to potential sites of an osmotic common life. Staircases were to become again spaces of life and everyday improvised encounters. Windows were transformed into doors, establishing a direct communication between basement apartments and the outdoor spaces. Balconies were used as temporary boxes overlooking theatrical sketches in the public space: balconies which at the same time are miniature stages of individuality that differentiate the uniform appearance of the façades.

The festival culminated in a large feast, which was enjoyed even by the patients of the neighbouring hospital. An active group of doctors supported the idea of converting some of the empty apartments into a free guesthouse for the patients' relatives, who come from all over Greece to this public anti-cancer centre.

This festival demonstrated that the preservation of this building complex cannot and must not take the form of a museum-like renovation of the buildings. What is worth preserving is not the memories attached to the buildings, but the passages that can connect these memories with the present.

## Memories of porosity

We can perhaps understand the history of these buildings as being perforated by moments of heterotopic potentiality. Rather than a continuous chain of events culminating in the present, this history is more like a discontinuous and shifting flow influenced by critical turning points. We can understand those turning points as temporal thresholds, periods that seem to disconnect past and future only to establish new, unpredicted links.

A housing complex absorbs history through its porous walls. Memories seek out traces; mostly, however, memories interpret and reinterpret traces. What the festival sought to establish is exactly this memory of turning points, this memory of fertile discontinuities in history. Refugees in the Alexandras complex, people-on-the-threshold, have witnessed a history of threshold moments, both in the micro-history of their places as well as in the macro-history in which their homes were directly involved. Monuments, on the contrary, represent marks in a national narrative obsessed with continuity, marking the road from 'glorious ancestors' to the present (Boyer 1994: 343).

The history of this refugee housing complex is connected with ruptures in the homogenized narrative of Greek official national history which crucially shapes Greek society as a fantasized common world. The refugees interrupted national history and caused conflicts and collective hostility. Packed in their modern buildings they were both outside the city and outside the prevailing urban ethos. However, they managed to perforate the separating spatial and temporal membranes. The German occupation, the liberation of Athens and the civil war that followed were major ruptures in modern history that were mended by the dominant ideology of post-war discriminatory democracy. In the Alexandras Prosfygika the marks of these ruptures remain, representing thresholds in the past and indicating an alternative future. Life could have evolved in a different direction, if the refugees had been allowed to develop their own distinct sociality in a modernist environment transformed through use. A rich public and private life found ways to produce spatial experiences of differentiation, as well as communality, deflecting the homogenizing modernist vocabulary. Those buildings could have become an experimental prototype for modern urban concepts in the city of Athens. Instead, they were allowed to crumble, waiting to be wiped out by the market version of collective housing, the Athenian private development 'boxes'.

The refugees of Asia Minor were people who had to wait for a long time on the threshold, trapped between the world they were forced to leave and the one that they were seeking. These people, perhaps more than anyone else, were in a position to understand how important it is for the city to include and not separate. Their ambiguous and discontinuous life in the refugee settlements can indeed indicate the possibilities of an osmotic urban experience.

The Alexandras Prosfygika inhabitants could have developed a closed community in search of mutual protection and attempted to preserve a threatened collective identity. Instead of that, they opened their community and developed forms of urban commoning that welcomed others. Their use of available shapeless public space with inventiveness and persistence created a common space that was not identified with the building residents' community. In their own way they supported practices of expanding commoning which included neighbours, relatives from other refugee complexes and settlements, and friends from all over the city. Their culture was a cosmopolitan one even though frictions and hostilities between ethnic minority groups or different religious communities developed during certain periods in their homeland (Asia Minor) due to dominating national rivalries.

What happened in the Alexandras complex is perhaps indicative of the overall changes in Greek society activated by Asia Minor refugees between the two world wars. Most of those refugees who came from important and flourishing cities were not ready to accept that their form of integration into Greek society would be in village-like enclaves of urban misery clearly separated from the rest of the city.

A shared culture and memories of a common world (even when severely shaken) can play an important role in shaping practices of commoning. The sometimes desperate effort of collective survival does not necessarily lead a community to barricade itself in. What those refugees have taught us is that crucial and urgent needs in conditions of devastating poverty can possibly create opportunities for expanding commoning so long as commoners share values and aspirations that transcend their life conditions in a certain period.

Could the present-day inhabitants of the complex profit from the experiences and acts of the 1922 refugees? Probably yes.

Some of them are immigrants from various parts of the world who found shelter in the complex either by occupying empty apartments (which had been bought by KED and remained unused after the demolition plans were cancelled by the Supreme Court's decision) or by renting those which still belong to private owners. Through the participation of activist squatters, who also use some abandoned apartments, today's immigrant inhabitants have developed forms of sharing and cooperation and even managed to expel from the complex some who were involved in mafia-like practices (including drug dealing). Unfortunately, surrounding hostility as well as a culture of fear spread among most of the so-called 'illegal' immigrants prevents them from attempting to expand the commoning practices they tacitly develop. Maybe a kind of 'separatist' militant orthodoxy among the involved activists has also not helped in opening the circles of commoning, although those activists offered much in establishing inhabitants' assemblies and organizing collective kitchens in the outdoor common space (which is always to be reclaimed from the parked cars). But, after all, expanding commoning is always a possibility to be created jointly through shared needs and shared dreams.

Chapter 4

# Housing and urban commoning

## Urban movements and urban commoning

There is ongoing discussion about social movements, often focused on their defining characteristics (Pickvance 1995, Giugni et al. 1999, Coy 2001, Tilly and Wood 2012). Are these movements constituted through and by specific collective demands: are these movements, that is, demand-centred? Or do these movements potentially constitute social laboratories in which new forms of social relations are tested? There seems to be a crucial political problem underlying such theoretical discussions: do social movements belong to those mechanisms that contemporary societies develop so as to channel the redistribution claims of different social groups, or is it perhaps that in social movements the seeds of a different society find fertile ground?

Probably such a political dilemma cannot be solved simply through canonized methods of reasoning. Different social movements in different periods of capitalism's history have created very different opportunities for collective actions which reach beyond the limits of the society. What has been and continues to be very interesting, however, during the last decade of the twentieth century and the first of the twenty-first, is that social movements have acquired a central role in transforming the life conditions of popular classes but also their aspirations for a different future. Zibechi has proposed the term 'societies in movement' (Zibechi 2010: 11) in order to capture a series of phenomena that go beyond typical social movement action: he urges us to think about the ways in which various forms of collective action, developed at various levels of social life by the popular classes, promote changes or ruptures in power relations.

The discussion on social movements tends to focus on activities organized around a collective demand, and it is in this context that forms of organization are being studied and classified. The proposed term 'societies in movement' shifts attention to the ways in which everyday survival strategies of the subordinate classes de facto acquire the power to produce changes when, out of need and as a result of an imposed political programme, these strategies tend to become coordinated and collectively pursued. This might possibly give an answer to the political problem connected to social movement action. When a society is in movement, then forms of movement action tend to become inherently politicized. It is not because, as the well-known rhetoric has it, people's conscience is raised to a level of understanding the mechanisms of society, but because people see in practice that different values and social relations can give them the opportunity to take their life in their hands and make it better. Politicization might possibly mean, in this context, becoming aware of the power a collective develops when it is organized horizontally and through bonds of solidarity. Societies in movement provide the ground for the development of movements which politicize the everyday life of 'those below'.

Urban movements are social movements which explicitly express urban demands and often enter into practices connected to urban rights. Urban movements, thus, shape opinions and aspirations that focus on the definition and use of such rights.

There is a long and ongoing debate on the political implications of the kind of collective action and the forms of organization specifically attributed to urban movements (Castells 1977 and 1983, Pickvance 2003, Hamel et al. 2000). What, however, seems by now an almost obvious observation is that 'they are key to social construction of conflict within the city' (Hamel et al. 2000: 1). Urban movements may be considered, thus, as movements that are involved in urban conflicts. They do not only struggle for a specific, historically defined urban right but they also use the city as a means to establish, define and perform such a right. Remembering Lefebvre's discussion on the right to the city (Lefebvre 1991 and 1996), we may even discover urban movements that claim such a right in ways that show that the city is not merely a context of rights but the means and the stake of an all-encompassing effort to collectively shape a common world. In this case, urban movements emerge through the confluence of political struggles which directly challenge political power and hegemony. As we will see, the homeless movements in Brazil may be considered as such a kind of urban movement because they struggle to create in and through city-space communities that challenge metropolitan models of coexistence.

Brazilian urban movements can offer a very inspiring example of movements that grow in a 'society in movement'. Their demands and especially their forms of organization do not simply express the everyday needs of the popular and excluded classes. Those movements learn from the ways people fight for survival in their everyday life. And those movements tend to integrate the traditional practices of ad hoc solidarity (as we will see in the case of *mutirão,* a form of mutual help developed between families) into their organized collective actions. Solidarity, then, a crucial element of a future emancipated society, is not discovered ideologically, as an alternative value, but is distilled from the everyday experiences of small and large urban communities. Obviously, not only solidarity grows in these everyday struggles for survival. It is, however, a movement, deeply rooted in these communities, that can fertilize solidarity actions against any prevailing and often hopeless atomism.

Urban movements, when and if they grow out of a society in movement, tend not only to appropriate city spaces, temporarily or more permanently, explicitly or in less obvious ways. Urban movements actually transform or even produce parts of the city, either because they explicitly attempt to produce new spatial arrangements, as in a self-constructed settlement, or because their actions mark specific public spaces, as in a demonstration or street action. What is more important in those movements, however, is that they in a way build upon a crucial characteristic of the societies in movement from which they stem: the creation of common spaces. These are spaces for common use created and supervised by a corresponding community. As we will see, they are produced in common and differ from private spaces as well as from public spaces.

Commoning, to use a term coined by P. Linebaugh (2008), is a process which characterizes both the everyday strategies of societies in movement and the movements which politicize these strategies. Commoning is not a contingent phenomenon in modern large cities. Differing from the production of common goods and services characteristic of traditional non-urban communities, contemporary commoning is a metropolitan phenomenon: what Hardt and Negri term 'artificial common', 'that resides in languages, images, knowledges, affects, codes, habits and practices ... runs throughout metropolitan territory and constitutes the metropolis' (Hardt and Negri 2009: 250). In this context, 'the multitude of the poor ... invents strategies of survival, finding shelter and producing forms of social life, constantly discovering and creating resources of the common through expansive circuits of encounter' (ibid.: 254). Commoning, thus, is a process of production and distribution of knowledge and the experiences of those who try to cope with the harsh conditions which characterize their life in large cities.

Commoning is an inventive process, a process that involves creation, a process that produces new forms of social life, even though it appears as the result of adaptive practices. Commoning even offers the opportunity for new 'forms-of-life' to emerge, if by using this, Agamben's, term we attempt to follow his theorizing of an emancipated social life as pure potentiality oriented towards living considered as a goal in itself and not as survival regulated by dominant power (Agamben 2000). The important point in this reasoning is that commoning potentially creates shared experiences and knowledges that overspill capitalist norms. Popular classes, excluded and marginalized, are forced to devise ways to survive, and in the process discover forms of social relations which deviate from dominant models. This is how, for example, extended families become transformed from social reproduction nuclei to micro-communities of solidarity and production/use-in-common (Zibechi 2010: 39–40).

On the level of the everyday experiences of the urban poor in Brazil, the city becomes the very ground of a constant 'struggle for rights to have a daily life ... worthy of a citizen's dignity' (Holston 2008: 313). What Holston understands as 'insurgent citizenship' is a series of such struggles against the predominant inequality and citizenship differentiation which characterizes contemporary Brazilian society. Insurgent citizenship, however, does not manifest itself in acts and demands focused on the redefinition of contested public space only. These demands are articulated 'with greatest force and originality ... in the realm of *oikos*, in the zone of domestic life taking shape in the remote urban peripheries around the autoconstruction of residence' (ibid.). This kind of 'politicization of the *oikos*' (ibid.: 312) produces the ground on which urban social movements in Brazil develop mobilizations focused on the right to the city. In a society in movement, 'insurgent citizenship' creates through targeted struggles new forms of appropriating and using the city and thus belonging to society. Insurgent citizenship is not necessarily a process oriented towards radical social change or collective emancipation. It plants, however, the seeds of collective action and commoning in the heart of the private realm, of the household. The 'politicization of the *oikos*', thus, is not only a means to develop demands and gain rights but also an emergent process of redefinition of family relations and spatial arrangements inside the house. Movements have propelled this process by giving to it the momentum of collective inventiveness. This is how houses become more complex arrangements, more open towards the community and less hierarchical. Let us not forget that Brazilian society directly maps social inequalities in the layout of housing complexes and apartments. As Caldeira observes, the 'closed condominium' has become the dominant model for the middle- and upper-class dwelling buildings in the 'city of walls', São Paulo (Caldeira 2000: 257). The resulting 'aesthetics of security' tends to spread throughout the city, conferring status value on the fences even in self-built houses in the peripheries (ibid. 293–5).

São Paulo perhaps represents the limiting case of a whole array of divided cities in which class, tribe or culture not only differentiate people but actually constitute the basis of segregating spatial distinctions. Gated communities tend to become a dominant form of housing for the urban upper-middle classes. But the form of closed, controllable and 'safe' housing areas seems to effectively infest the urban imaginary of the middle or lower classes too. Politicization of the *oikos* implicitly or explicitly clashes with these forms of 'corrupting the common', to paraphrase Hardt and Negri. Urban communities, which fence city public space (as streets and parks) inside the walls of their controlled-access enclaves, indeed define a common space for their inhabitants. But this kind of space would be better described as collectively privatized space, space which repels strangers and discourages 'felicitous encounters' (Hardt and Negri 2009: 254). In a way that is directly reminiscent of the fencing of common land by early capitalist agricultural enterprises, in gated communities 'the common is corralled as property' (Hardt 2010: 349).

Commoning appears on various levels of organized collective actions. In Brazilian urban movements and especially in the homeless movements, a first step in the collective production of commons, in and through the city, is the organizing of land occupations. Whether it is landless peasants who organize to occupy large plots in cities or urban homeless people who organize to occupy empty unused buildings, those movements mould out of an agglomerate of families a community-in-the-making oriented towards commoning. In this step, commoning has to do with creating a community of solidarity and appropriating the occupied land as a common resource under rules imposed by the emerging community of commoners.

The next step is to organize through collective decisions and acts the form of cohabitation (the settlement or the parcelling of empty apartments). In this process new forms of common are produced. First of all, common knowledge is created and shared, knowledge concerning building techniques and dwelling needs and procedures. Urban movements consider a crucial point in the practices of cohabitation the sharing of knowledge as well as the mutual support of all who participate in the creation of their temporary 'homes'.

The forms and the processes of occupation have direct influence on the commoning practices. As a member of Brigadas Populares (a *Sem Teto* – literally 'Without Roof' – movement in Belo Horizonte) has observed, there was a significant difference between land and building occupations in terms of constructing a community of cohabitation.[1] An apartment building carries, because of its form, a spatial arrangement logic, which can easily make families focus their attention on their own occupied apartment microcosm. Families tend, in such cases, to withdraw from the practices of commoning which create common spaces, common ways of space management and maintenance and, of course, common forms of organization in order to defend the occupied building.

Land occupations make people confront from the beginning the problem of building a family shelter with the necessary help of others and the emerging community. Autoconstructed settlements thus seem to grow out of an awareness that commoning is necessary, helpful and gratifying and not only ideologically preferable. An ethics of commoning therefore develops side by side with actual practices of commoning.

A lot can be said about the importance of commoning in the creation and arrangement of the settlement on occupied land. Just to take an example, in the settlement of João Candido in the periphery of São Paulo, a common space was created for the community of the settlers to use.[2] This space comprised an open area for assemblies at the centre of the settlement and a larger-than-average barrack used as a 'community centre', facing this open area. At this centre, children of the settlement were offered lessons, various commissions had their meetings and general assemblies were also held. Typical of such urban movement initiatives was the organization of commissions specializing in services necessary for the functioning of the community: a security commission, collective cooking commission, childcare commission, unemployed support commission, et cetera.

The difference between settlements like the one in Joao Candido and unorganized ad hoc settlements, especially those of the developing *favelas* in the periphery of São Paulo, is striking. People in organized occupations, as in the João Candido settlement, take care of the settlement and not only of their 'home'. Facilities for collective use are created (for example water tanks, rubbish collection points, community stoves, etc.). The arrangement and maintenance of 'streets' in this settlement is also indicative of practices of commoning. The street is not a necessary 'residual' space but a space formed through collective decisions and collective work.

In cases where a movement had succeeded in making the local state accept its housing demands, a new level of potential commoning was created. Let's take as an example the case of União da Juta in Sapopemba, São Paulo. Due to the continuous efforts and acts of the corresponding homeless movement Sem Terra Leste 1, the State Government of São Paulo was to agree on offering the land for the settling of 160 families. The movement did not agree with the state authorities on a social housing programme to be executed by the local state and private constructors. They managed to impose a different procedure for the planning, building and administration of the project which directly involved the future inhabitants organized as a community. The role of USINA (Centro de Trabahlos para o Ambiente Habitado) was very important in this context. Specializing in participative planning, this organization became the movement's architectural and planning collaborator. Important aspects of commoning developed in the process: drawing from the rural tradition of *mutirão*, a form of mutual help developed between families, USINA has proposed ways of participation in the design and construction of the housing complex that were based on the common work and abilities of the community members.

As one of the USINA reports explicitly sums it up: 'In the case of urban "*mutiroes*", the pedagogical process of social change begins with the people's organization in the struggle for land and access to public funding; it continues with the collective definition of projects and is finally consolidated in stonemasonry' (USINA 2006: 17).

It took several years for the project to be completed (1992–8). People now live in those houses they have built themselves, participating in all the stages of the project by taking decisions collectively. An association of inhabitants, organized in the form of a community of commoners, is now responsible for the management of the housing complex which includes a community centre, a community nursery for sixty children and a community bakery.[3]

Although they do not strictly speaking belong to an urban environment, the MST (Movimento dos Trabalhadores Rurais Sem Terra, Landless Workers' Movement) agricultural villages (*agrovilas*), which were created on occupied land, have a general layout depicting the prevailing commoning procedures out of which these settlements grew. 'Houses are grouped together in one area rather than on each campesino's parcel of land' (Zibechi 2007: 122). This creates a settlement with common services and resources as well as the opportunity to integrate communal buildings into the settlement. As MST supports distinct alternative training and education programmes for its members, communal buildings can house such activities too (as in the case of the Filhos de Depi *agrovila* near Viamao, Porto Alegre, on which Zibechi reports). *Agrovilas* thus become small community laboratories in search of a different society.

Directly influenced by the MST experience, a homeless movement (MTST) developed an experimental model of cohabitation called '*assentamentos rururbanos*' (rurban settlements). According to Souza, 'The core of this strategy lies in an attempt to build settlements for urban workers at the periphery of cities, in which people could cultivate vegetables and breed small animals, thus becoming less dependent on the market to satisfy their alimentary basic needs' (Souza 2006: 382). Although this strategy was abandoned as unsuccessful, it really contains a very interesting fusion of a commoning subsistence process with an attempt to overcome the intensity of the city–village antithesis.

The process of commoning, which characterizes, as we have seen, Brazilian urban movements on the various levels of their initiatives and practices, has important results in the corresponding forms of production and use of space. It is not

enough to describe the produced space between the 'houses' of
the settlements, the occupied apartments or the apartments of
the self-administered *mutirão* housing projects as 'public space'.
A new kind of space as well as new forms of 'performed' or
'practised' space emerge out of the constructing and inhabiting
practices of the organized 'commoners'. We could term this space
'common' in order to distinguish it both from private and from
public space. In common space, in space produced and used as
common, people do not simply use an area given by an authority
(local state, state, public institution, etc.). People actually mould
this kind of space according to their collective needs and aspirations.

Common space is shared space. Whereas public space, as
space marked by the presence of a prevailing authority, is space
'given' to people according to certain terms, common space is
space 'taken' by the people. A community of common space users
develops by appropriating space and by transforming it into
potentially shared space. Rules about how this sharing is to be
performed develop in the process of creating space as common.
But there is an important difference between these rules and the
ones imposed by an authority overseeing public space. These
rules are made and remade, and therefore remain contestable, by
various groups and persons who negotiate their presence in such
spaces without any reference to a predominant centre of power.
In order for common space to remain common there must be
developed forms of contestation and agreement about its use and
character which explicitly prevent any accumulation of power.
Especially, any accumulation of situated, space-bound power.

Common space that is developed through such movement
action is in-between space, threshold space. Whereas public

space necessarily has the mark of an identity, *is* (which means *belongs to* an authority), common space tends to be constantly redefined: common space *happens* and common space is shaped through collective action.

Common space is thus space created and recreated constantly by a community which is organized through processes of participation of its members, considered as equals. This therefore has to be a community in movement: a community created in a society in movement through the catalytic activities of social urban movements. A community in movement is a community which is not oriented towards practices that create and defend a secluded microcosm, even if this microcosm presents itself as a 'liberated' stronghold. A community in movement, thus, is characterized by an 'always alert and always generous disposition towards the common' (Zibechi 2010: 136). Alert indeed, because keeping the process of commoning alive means fighting against any accumulation of power. In the *mutirão* construction experiences, for example, careful attention was paid by the inhabitants' association to a rotation of tasks. Participation is a process which produces and educates at the same time. Even the most difficult target, the elimination of differences between manual and intellectual work, was pursued in these collective experiences (USINA 2006: 33).

Generous indeed, because commoning is not simply a balance of giving and taking. Sometimes some have to offer more, whether because they know more, they are more capable, or they simply have been more lucky than others in their family life. Generosity is the propelling force of sharing-as-commoning if the corresponding community indeed moves towards collective emancipation and equality. Because what commoning essentially creates is new forms of collective subjectivation. Through the creation of common space, people change themselves and their communities.

'The wisdom hidden in the threshold experience lies in the awareness that otherness can only be approached by opening the borders of identity, forming – so to speak – intermediary zones of doubt, ambivalence, hybridity, zones of negotiable values' (Stavrides 2010b: 18). In common space, differences meet but are not allowed to fight for a potential predominance in the process of defining, giving identity to space. If common space is shared space, then its users-producers have to learn to give, not only take. Common space can thus essentially be described as 'offered' space. Space offered and taken the way a present is. True, the offering and acceptance of a present can mediate power relations. But the commoning of space presupposes sharing as a condition of reciprocity (De Angelis and Stavrides 2010: 23). Commoning can thus become a form of offering which keeps roles interchangeable.

## Social housing and the quest for common space

A potential research area for locating the forms that common space may take if considered as a crucial element of cohabitation is the planning and production of social housing. The term 'social housing' can perhaps be an inadequate term if the aim is to include all kinds of 'housing provided for people on low incomes or with particular needs by government agencies or non-profit organizations' as the Oxford electronic dictionaries suggest. But we can take it as an umbrella term that can describe housing projects in which habitation standards and spatial qualities are shaped, at least programmatically, by social welfare logics and not by profit expectancies.

It is interesting to observe how, at least after the visionary declarations of the Modern Movement in architecture (Conrads 1971), social housing was literally reinvented as an architectural and urban planning object which necessarily included a specific focus on the inhabitants' shared space. Spaces of common use were explicitly designed in social housing projects, and their relation with private as well as city public spaces was always an important design problem. Depending on the sociocultural context, spaces of common use acquired different weight in the planned and actual life of the corresponding complexes. The results, however, concerning the social meaning and function of common space, considered as space of shared use among the complex's inhabitants (or any subgroup of them), need to be compared with a view to exploring the connection of those spaces with practices of urban commoning.

The 1920s and 1930s constitute a period of important relevant experimentations, mainly in Europe. It is clear that the socio-economic context of these experimentations played a decisive role in shaping policies of support for workers and people living on low incomes. It was a time in which the city itself was treated as the laboratory of a new society. Weimar Germany's Berlin and Frankfurt, Red Vienna and Soviet Russia's big cities were to become crucibles of an emerging new architecture that produced important new ideas and buildings. Housing was at the centre of such visionary architectural experiments, quite different perhaps in terms of their magnitude, their pragmatic and utopian aspects and their implementation but sharing the same belief that urban space can actively shape a different 'new society'.

What follows, of course, attempts neither to produce a detailed appraisal of modernist architecture's social visions nor to explore the role of mass housing design in shaping important areas of major modern cities. Focusing on the sociocultural urban contexts already mentioned, this chapter will try only to locate the possible emergence of a concept of common space in the housing projects designed and produced with the explicit aim of establishing forms of communal life quite distinct from those corresponding to rural life and to traditional communities. German architects 'called for a "new community", spiritual and social, in which architecture supported by the revolutionary government would act as a powerful educational force among the citizens of the new state' (Miller Lane 1985: 41).

How, in this context, was common space conceived? It seems that the crucial characteristic of common space was to be located in the very form of space that the new urban communities would identify as their own, shared in different ways between their members.

During the Weimar Republic period in Germany (1919–33), two important factors contributed to a flourishing discussion and praxis connected to the problem of housing. The first was the acute need for new and affordable homes after the devastating war period, and the second was the increasing influence of modernist architects' ideas both on the newly elected Social Democratic government and on the public.

Bruno Taut, the visionary modernist architect who was to become the chief designer for one of the greatest Berlin housing cooperatives, spoke in his numerous publications about a 'social ideal' that would be a kind of 'socialism in an apolitical sense, above politics' (Miller Lane 1985: 48). Taut explicitly asked architects to help people realize that they could become 'organic members [*Glieder*] of a great architectural structure' (ibid: 49) which would house this organic community of the future.

Walter Gropius, the architect and founder of the famous Bauhaus architecture school in Weimar's Dessau, also explicitly referred in his early writings to a coming community that would be expressed and housed by a new architecture. His ideal was deeply inspired by the unity of arts and crafts in the building of great medieval cathedrals, and he even attempted to imagine the social role of architecture in the process of creating 'the freedom cathedral[s] of the future' (ibid: 49).

Social housing, then, during the Weimar period was produced not only in response to a shortage of affordable housing but also to show paradigmatically what a planned welfare city might be like. This is why most of the projects designed and constructed in these years were located on the periphery of big German cities, being 'heavily influenced by the British garden city movement' (Urban 2012: 11). Ernst May's New Frankfurt was conceived, thus, as a network of large housing neighbourhoods with a distinctly suburban character that would prefigure a new model for the city. What he himself named his '*Trabantenprinzip* [the idea of a city divided into semi-autonomous nuclei]' (Tafuri 1990: 206) was a planning principle that aimed at producing parts of a future city which would contain not only houses but also important public and municipal buildings such as churches and schools as well as other community facilities (Miller Lane 1985: 102).

What May managed to plan and constructed in Frankfurt, Gropius envisaged establishing as an urban planning gesture of considerable magnitude in his project for a 'cooperative city' on the outskirts of Berlin (Tafuri 1990: 222). Both seem to insist on the idea that the future communal city should preferably be constructed on land previously not built on and through a completely new architecture. The choice, however, to create these new housing areas outside the existing big cities already imposed important characteristics on the designed common space. In the new housing neighbourhoods (*Siedlungen*), people would share communal facilities and outdoor space which could not become part of the city's network of public spaces and public buildings.

Essential to the modernist innovative logic of social housing planning was the idea of minimum dwelling (*Existenszminimum*). The urgent need to cut down costs and to develop construction techniques based on speed and standardization forced planners and architects to reduce the space of individual houses and to devise typologies with limited variations. These needs, connected to the choice of developing new forms of communal life, produced various proposals for transferring certain functions of the house to communal facilities and buildings, for example recreation and laundry, but also communal meals and health and childcare. We can actually trace the different paths followed by Russian constructivists, German Bauhaus architects and Viennese municipal architects along the same line of producing common space as space of shared everyday uses. The crucial differentiating point is the degree of autonomy attributed to the constructed or proposed new urban housing structures.

New Frankfurt was conceived of as a series of suburban nuclei. Autonomy was thus an explicit planning target, but could only be established at the expense of keeping the new areas separated from the rest of the city. The idea and the experience of a cohabitation community was based on the shared class characteristics of the inhabitants and the use of common facilities which, supposedly, created bonds of sociality and shared habits. Common space was explicitly established through planning and was meant to functionally bind the inhabitants who shared common similar needs which they could not satisfy individually. Modernism's prevailing functionalist logic seems to have almost equated sharing with need. The new spiritual and social brotherhood would thus be the result rather than the prerequisite of a rationalized and efficient planning focused on the hygienic and productive promises of a functional 'garden city'. This kind of community, however, (and the common space created for it) would be a socially uniform community kept apart from the rest of the city and thus unable to link to the other potential or existing common and public spaces in the city.

Supposedly expressing the rationality of 'liberated work' (Tafuri 1990: 214), working-class and cooperative *Siedlungen* were meant to provide images 'of a possible alternative to the capitalist city as a whole' (ibid.). Their planning, however, reduced them to precarious urban enclaves with no power to influence the rest of the city by establishing expanding networks of commoning.

What perhaps created an anti-enclosure dynamic in some of these social housing projects was a planning innovation that changed the character of the open space between the buildings. Departing from the model of housing neighbourhoods with buildings arranged alongside the street or around an inner shared court (a layout predominantly used during the nineteenth century), modernist planning introduced the idea of free-floating buildings (often tall) with large open spaces between them. Depending on the project, this kind of planning might possibly create osmotic boundaries for the complex's common space. For example, the 'finger plan' (Miller Lane 1985: 90), which places buildings perpendicular to the surrounding streets, potentially opens the space between the buildings to general access. Such shared spaces may be gradually integrated into the network of city public spaces, especially since those pre-war social housing complexes have by now become part of the city's dense fabric.

The case of Red Vienna differs in a significant way from the corresponding German cities' housing projects, in a way that directly affects the character of common space included in the social housing complexes. As Eve Blau shows, Social Democrats decided 'to build urban *Gemeindebauten* rather than suburban *Siedlungen*' (Blau 1999: 172). Thus, the municipality of Red Vienna decided to build housing inside the limits of Vienna and not on the outskirts of the city. Instead of designing autonomous or semi-autonomous urban islands, Viennese architects and planners had to find ways to insert large building complexes into the existing urban tissue. The typological choice made seemingly followed an already-established housing neighbourhood type in which buildings were arranged around an inner court. The city-building office's guidelines, however, encouraged important innovations in this typology that had crucial impacts on the uses and forms of each complex's shared communal space. The 'Red *Höfe*' had communal facilities in the courtyard areas, buildings for a communal laundry, a kindergarten and, in one case, a central collective kitchen and dining room (ibid.: 213). The central courtyard, which had dimensions comparable to a small city square, had access both to communal and to private spaces (ibid.: 228) and thus became the main common space for the buildings' inhabitants. What is important is that although this courtyard was clearly separated from the rest of the city's public space by doors and passages often of monumental proportions, direct access and use of the courtyards was (and still is) possible for 'outsiders'. Compared to the traditional Viennese housing courtyard, then, these common spaces were more open to public use (ibid.: 230). However, one cannot miss an overall spatial arrangement that gives the impression of a potentially enclosed community which explicitly marks its presence in the city through a recognizable spatialized collective identity. It was in the turbulent period which followed that these complexes had to be not only interpreted but also actually experienced as 'red bastions' by the workers-inhabitants in their resistance against the Nazis (Zednicek 2009: 15).

Common spaces both in Red Vienna and the Weimar Republic's cities were indeed spaces planned for and offered to the residents in the hope of introducing or encouraging communal aspects into their everyday life. One can even take these planning acts as 'pedagogical' in terms of the development of a communally organized new society. Inhabitants, however, for reasons having to do with historical context but also with deeply embedded cultural habits, did not seem prepared in all cases to follow the architecture's inherent potentialities. Women, for example, were offered facilities that would relieve them of certain everyday burdens or, at least, give them opportunities to share those burdens. Were the mechanical common laundries common spaces that helped in working-class women's emancipation by giving them the chance to socialize and become visible as workers themselves (working in private household maintenance)? Blau suggests that *Gemeindebauten* blurred 'the boundary between public and private living space, between housework and work performed outside the home, between family and larger community' (Blau 1999: 215). This indeed produced a fertile ground for the development of osmotic relations between the inhabiting practices focused on private space and those focused on the communal and public space. We cannot actually speak, however, of practices of commoning which tended to overcome the boundaries of a situated homogeneous community, even though these communities were projected as prefigurations of an emancipated future society.

The housing policies that were developed in Soviet Russia during the same period after the 1917 revolution were obviously even more connected to the building of a new society. Right from the first days after the revolution, architects, planners, elected workers' representatives and officials got involved in a fierce exchange of ideas and proposals in search of the city and housing spaces that would not only prefigure but also create the coming communist society. This fermenting period of engaged modernist art and architecture productions would come to an almost abrupt end as the Stalinist era violently imposed a different political as well as cultural perspective. Starting from the experience of ad hoc-created housing communes in the first years after 1917, a huge debate unfolded on the meaning, the qualities and the form of space to be shared by cohabitants considered as the 'test-bed for trying out new ways of organizing life' (Khan-Magowedov 1978: 343).

State ownership of urban land together with centralized planning at various levels of economy and land use created a different context for housing policies from those in Red Vienna and the Weimar Republic. What made it possible, however, for innovative and promising ideas about common space to be formulated was the visionary quest for a different community of cohabitants who were to develop a new kind of communal life in and through the new architecture.

An important new housing type which was developed during the 1920s from such a perspective was the so-called *dom-kommuna* (communal house). According to Anatole Kopp, this is 'an urban element functioning as a small autonomous commune in relation to a whole series of services and facilities' (Kopp 1970: 130). More specifically, the *dom-kommuna* was considered, according to the constructivist group of architects OSA, as a 'social condenser' (Thomas 1978: 272 and Kopp 1970) and as a spatial structure through which the transformations of social life in the form of a collectivist organization would take place. The idea of social condensers in fact connects the urgency of housing production to the design of new architectural types meant to shape new everyday habits for the inhabitants. Such innovative design proposals were meant to concretize in spatial arrangements new collective habits scrupulously studied and even 'measured' by architects deeply immersed in the functionalist efficiency logic but also inspired by the political project of producing the 'new man'.

The *dom-kommuna* was not simply a large apartment house with some added communal facilities. It was a building/community in which people would share spaces that used formerly to be considered part of individual apartments (kitchens and dining rooms, laundry equipment and rest areas), as well as spaces and facilities formerly connected to the public life of a whole city (recreation areas, libraries, nurseries, workers' clubs, etc.). Common space, thus, in the 'communal houses' was going to be of various kinds and forms and was in many different ways connected to city space and to the private cells. As the research progressed during the 1920s, this architectural type evolved through an expansion of the communal or common parts of the building at the expense of the private ones. The architect T. Kuzmin, among many other experts, proposed a kind of 'super-collectivization of life' that was based on a very strict, army-like spatiotemporal organization of everyday life in such communal houses (Kopp 1970: 152–5). As Kopp neatly remarks, this was 'a house so "communal", that it ceased to be a house' (ibid.: 144).

Research on the *dom-kommuna* housing type ended abruptly at the beginning of the 1930s. It was even ridiculed and condemned by Party decisions that equated it with the most extravagant and utopian proposals advanced by architects with views similar to Kuzmin. But the motivating ideas of the *dom-kommuna* as well as its experimental realizations have shown that a redefinition of the relation between public and private space in a housing complex is not only possible but can also create new kinds of communal space. The idea of the 'social condenser' already contains a belief that spatial forms of organization can catalyse, encourage, accelerate and even inspire changes in social life. 'A new life demands new forms' (ibid.: 145). Common spaces acquired a crucial role in giving shape to this new life. What was debatable, however, was whether these spaces should belong to an autonomous building-community or become part of a network of spaces that could be extended throughout the existing cities or implemented in the newly created ones.

One of the mistakes of the Soviet avant-garde planners seems to have been that they believed that new cities could be designed and constructed by using the *dom-kommuna* as a repeatable building block. Indeed, however, 'city planning was more than architecture on a large scale' (Thomas 1978: 276). We really cannot know if the Soviet cities would have been more common-oriented if the ideas of planner advocates of the *dom-kommuna* type of housing collectivism had prevailed. We know, however, that after the 'defeat of modern design' (ibid.:

275, also Kopp 1970: 235), from 1930 on, architecture was more connected to a monumentalizing praise of the 'Socialist State' than to a search for spaces of collective emancipation. From the mid 1920s a new model of housing was already starting to emerge. As Khan-Magowedov observes, 'The closed system of the communal house was being replaced by large dwelling complexes made up of sectional housing, shops, children's facilities, canteens etc.' (Khan-Magowedov 1978: 346). From this to the last days of the USSR there was a long road of city-planning decisions that shaped many urban environments (some of them presented as new model cities). It seems, however, that an important shift in planning during the 1930s favoured the design of public spaces and facilities at the expense of potentially communal spaces. Public spaces were meant to be used by inhabitants of large complexes but were more identified with the state than with a potential community of inhabitants.

Perhaps what the early modernist Russian architects failed to understand is that common space has to be more of a catalyst for new social relations than a ready-to-use mould in which those relations would be forced to take shape. The planners of the post-1945 USSR were too much directed towards establishing functional urban environments in the service of a state-controlled productive machine obsessed with development and the East–West antagonism. Common space, fragile and context-sensitive as it is, could have been a very important empirical as well as theoretical invention of architects as well as of active inhabitants during a period of social experimentation in a potentially post-capitalist society. 'Social condensers' and '*dom-kommuna*' prototypes are, nevertheless, valuable experiments and ideas in search of common space's attributes and qualities as well as in search of inhabiting practices that may be oriented towards a collectively organized common life.

It is in this context that Red Vienna, the Weimar Republic's cities and the early Russian urban experiments become comparable. The search for a new life which is oriented towards communal habits and towards the development of new communitarian links between people was connected to architectural proposals meant to encourage, sustain or even create this process. What in all cases seems to be crucial is the lack of active participation of inhabitants in the process of devising architectural solutions, as well as in the process of transforming common spaces through use and collective forms of appropriation. Common space may potentially come into existence only when people actively shape it and are shaped by it, and only when they keep on creating sharing practices in it and through it. Common space is more a kind of spatiality that may emerge through sharing than a container which will shape a wished-for community. Common spaces, which either force this community to come into existence or produce spatial boundaries to such an emerging community, are bound to give ground to new forms of enclosure. Inventive architectural solutions can contribute invaluably to the dynamics of common space creation. But architecture alone cannot guarantee that designed spaces will become commoned spaces, spaces of commoning and spaces-as-commons.

## Urban communities reinventing themselves

Research that was recently conducted into the present condition and spatial characteristics of social housing complexes constructed in Athens may add interesting findings about the role of planning and design in the creation of common spaces.

This research explicitly aimed at locating different forms of relationships between public and private space and how these forms have developed over the years of their use.[4] Social housing in Greece has two distinct characteristics that differentiate it from similar projects in other European and in Latin American countries. First, a very large proportion of the complexes built were designed for refugees of Greek origin who came to Greece especially after the great population exchange of 1922. Second, in all cases inhabitants were not meant to be tenants (renting the apartments from a state social welfare organization) but owners. From the very beginning of these programmes in the 1920s, people entitled to these forms of social support were given property titles provided that they bought their apartments, at very low prices and through very cheap loans.

These two distinctive characteristics implicitly triggered the inventiveness of inhabitants who in all cases had to live in very small apartments and with limited facilities. The refugees, who came mostly from the urban populations of Asia Minor, had a rich culture of urban public life. They thus soon transformed their social housing ghettos, stigmatized as areas of poverty and immoral behaviour (Athenians were rather conservative compared to the refugees in terms of their views about public culture and everyday socializing habits), into neighbourhoods rich in communal life.

Refugee neighbourhoods developed into areas of commoning inventiveness especially through a dense network of exchanges between inhabitants. As Hirschon observes, this network had an 'in-built contradiction … since actions of giving and receiving entailed an inequality of status' although 'neighbourly relations were equalitarian and universalistic' (Hirschon 1998: 172). It

seems that women were those who mainly ensured that neighbourhood life provided the group with solidarity and mutual
support without the household boundaries becoming blurred or
unrecognizable (ibid.: 173).

Commoning, thus, was a multilevel and multifarious process, which created areas of shared uses and recognizable habits.
Those areas were not, however, meant to define and symbolize closed communities but were treated by the inhabitants as
threshold spaces, spaces in which they could meet with people
from the rest of the city and create an open publicness. Refugees
overflowed the boundaries of their urban ghettos and influenced, through their open and inclusive cosmopolitan urban
culture, Athenian public life.

The fact that both the refugee inhabitants and the inhabitants who acquired access to social housing apartments built
by the Workers Housing Organization (OEK, a state welfare organization) were owners has made possible numerous ad hoc
interventions in the built complexes. Rich diversity characterizes their ways of extending the apartment's space, for example by
transforming balconies into additional rooms, or by projecting
parts of the family's life to places of common use such as cor-
ridors, open spaces or terraces. The results in many cases are
similar to those mentioned by Benjamin in his famous essay on
Naples: the apartment becomes 'far less the refuge into which
people retreat than the inexhaustible reservoir from which they
flood out' (Benjamin 1985: 147).

Commoning practices of course often clash with individual interests. Especially in OEK's complexes, in which no
pre-existing networks of cultural homogeneity are present,
shared class belonging is not enough to encourage inhabitants'

solidarity or joint initiatives for the transformation and maintenance of common space. As we were able to discover in the aforementioned research, commoning tends to become in those cases a practice of protecting and maintaining common property by decisions that exclude 'strangers' and 'others' from a well-defined community of users/inhabitants. The identification of common space (or any good understood as common) with a closed community essentially changes commoning to a practice of collective privatization. Porosity should be an important characteristic of common space, and it is through osmosis that exchanges between common space users can take place. Porosity is both a precondition and a performed result of practices of space-commoning.

Commoning not only transforms public space while creating common spaces. Commoning directly influences the form of private house spaces. A latent social change which accompanies the development of urban movements is observable in the way households change: both internally by becoming micro-communities of commoners and externally by developing new kinds of relations between them and the communal organization. The changing role of women is central in this process (Zibechi 2007: 246). According to Zibechi, women often influence popular struggles not as explicit leaders but by supporting and extending existing networks of cooperation which are being built through everyday exchanges between neighbouring households. These everyday acts of information and services exchange weave the fabric of sociality, and women have a central role in this. In such a context, new family forms emerge which contribute to the 'creation of a domestic space that is neither public nor private but something new' (Zibechi 2012: 39).

As in the everyday solidarity networks developed in the Asia Minor refugee settlements already mentioned, women in Latin America have used their presence in specific public spaces (such as the open-air market) to enhance or even build networks of dissident action and movement initiatives. They thus liberated themselves from a dominant taxonomy of gendered roles which attributed to women only responsibilities and rights connected to the realm of *oikos*.

A comparison between the spatial logic of a self-built urban settlement in Chile and that of the social housing complex which has replaced it (mentioned in Zibechi 2007: 209–11), is revealing in this context. People in the settlement used to produce their space by inhabiting it. Moreover, they collectively recognized their common area as porous, permitting an osmosis between private houses and common space (the external boundaries of the settlement were, however, rather rigid and recognizable as representing the limits of the community's power). Those same people, when forced to move to the newly built social housing complexes, lost a feeling of belonging to a defined community. Space had become fragmented and rationally divided into quantified areas of private and public use. This is how, according to Juan Carlos Skewes, the researcher Zibechi mentions, 'a transfer from a feminine domain to a masculine world' is effectively imposed (ibid.: 211). Popular classes base their survival, especially in periods of crisis or in countries in which the state ignores them, on the improvising inventiveness of household or family networks. And it is these networks that at times support the inventiveness of the struggles of 'those below'.

Commoning creates subjects of action. Not simply in the well-known way in which acts define actors. Commoning changes the way collective identities are constructed and performed. As people collectively produce commons, they create themselves. A collective identity, then, is not the identity of a community of belonging. If a community in movement is a laboratory where forms of common are invented and tested, if a community in movement invents itself as it invents its spaces and institutions, then this community is a community-in-the-making. It cannot be summarized in a name or an identity.

Such a community produces and diffuses the common. If 'the institutions of the common are the organizational force of the collective appropriation of what is produced by all of us' (Roggero 2010: 370), then communities in movement are in a constant process of organizing: forms of organization are being tested, not because innovation or efficiency is sought for, but because the means are always projected on the ends. Not fixed identities, then, but perhaps strongly defended collective values: equality, solidarity and common responsibility. And these values have actually grown in the everyday practices of societies in movement.

Testing, experimenting and identities-in-the-making – there is a term which can probably capture the dynamics of commoning: 'inventiveness'. People participating in communities of commoning, people as commoners, have to invent forms of survival. People have to live and people want to live even though a decent life is denied them. This vital force creates movement in societies. But this is not enough. People have to devise ways to live. People try to find help and try to take advantage of every available means.

There is a long discussion about the tactics of the powerless. De Certeau (1984) speaks about those tactics as ways to make use of space and time by employing a shared practical wisdom or *metis*, the ancient Greek term associated, for example, with the cunning of sailors, hunters and athletes as they have to face context-specific difficulties and opportunities (Detienne and Vernant 1991). Observing the practices of inhabitants who appropriate and transform the public spaces surrounding their housing blocks, R. Sennett suggests: '[t]he work of improvising street order attaches people to their communities' (Sennett 2009: 236).

These crafts of the poor have deeply influenced the practices of communities in movement. People have carried into their movement this collective wisdom and this ability to improvise by making use of what is available. This inventiveness is transmitted throughout the metropolis by subaltern channels of communication, by the spread of rumours and tacit knowledge which implicitly moulds models of action and patterns of practices (building crafts focused on '*bricolage*', recycling, etc.). And people always learn how to modify models, how to improvise according to recognizable motifs, how to discover and correct and how to 'make better'. This kind of sharing of knowledge and experience supports the emergence of commons. Knowledge and experience become forms of commons.

Communities in movement oriented towards the common develop when inventiveness is practised collectively. The *mutirão* tradition is necessarily linked to this kind of inventiveness. People augment their capacities by sharing resources and by helping each other (all help, for example, one family at a time in the harvesting of the family's crops or in building the family's house).

People who invent in common create, use and inhabit invented spaces. Miraftab goes so far as to claim that '[i]nvented spaces are those ... occupied by the grassroots and claimed by their collective action, but directly confronting the authorities and the status quo' (Miraftab 2004: 1). Inventiveness, in this context, involves a kind of creation which is expressly emancipated from the rules of public space production and use.

Often the state or local authorities tend to criminalize the creation of 'invented spaces' of citizenship which emerge in actions focused on rights connected to decent living conditions (Miraftab and Wills 2005). Oppression, direct or not, often tends to separate these actions from the lawful acts of 'invited' participation (mostly aimed at legitimizing already-decided policies).

Through the practices of commoning, people literally reinvent community as a form of social coexistence. As Zibechi explains in his analysis of the Aymara movement in Bolivia which we have already encountered, 'The Aymara did not simply migrate from rural areas to El Alto with a "community consciousness" that they "revived" upon arrival. On the contrary, they created another type of community – they re-invented and recreated one' (Zibechi 2010: 18–19).

Communities in movement are not replicas of pre-existing rural communities nor do they simply employ the extended family social bonds, which indeed form part of the accumulated experience of the participating people. Communities as equalitarian and commoning social organizations are continuously being created: crafted by and through acts of inventive commoning.

People in their everyday survival struggle actually reinvent spaces of common use, sharing them with others, creating them collectively as able urban craftsmen. Collective inventiveness flourishes in societies in movement, but it is in the communities in movement, collectively crafted, that this inventiveness acquires the power to develop forms-of-life oriented towards an emancipating society. Extending and reappropriating the production of the common gives power to the communities of commoners as these communities create themselves.

Chapter 5

# Metropolitan streets as contested spaces

## The modernist dream of rationalized traffic

It was in the middle of the nineteenth century that the city streets became a tool for transforming big cities, a tool for interventions with political targets, hidden or not behind the rhetoric of decongestion and unobstructed circulation of goods and people. The word 'circulation' evokes a metaphor which was going to have serious consequences for the legitimization of such interventions as well as for the manipulated collective imaginary which supported them. In the same way that blood circulation is considered as the most important condition for the sustaining of life, circulation in cities appears to be the grounding precondition for the sustaining of urban life. And exactly as the circulation of blood is characterized by a hierarchy of vessels which distribute blood throughout the human body, so it is with the city streets, which should be categorized into main and secondary arteries which develop in a capillary-like fashion in order to sustain and 'feed' the city (Sennett 1994: 324–38).

This organic metaphor, which considers street movement as a precondition for city life, matched absolutely with the growing feeling that industrial cities had been sick and in urgent need of 'therapeutic' interventions. It was this approach that became predominant in both the discourses and the ideas which have been developed in interventions decisively connected with the birth of modern urban design. However, urban therapeutic logic (Donald 1999) did not borrow from an imaginary attached to the empirical understanding of illness which is an important part of everyday medicine. Everyday medical practices contain important instances of regulated improvisation as doctors often get involved in tentative searches for symptoms, in trial-and-error experiments when treatments fail, and in idiosyncratic approaches to each patient's individuality. Although these practices are often considered to be outside the prevailing canon of medical protocols, they are always there because medical knowledge is far from being absolutely certain, fixed and context-free. On the contrary, the medical imaginary that was evoked in and transposed to urban therapeutic interventions was that of a confident doctor with unlimited faith in medical knowledge who already knows what to do: planning interventions based on this imaginary rarely questioned diagnoses and assigned treatments, even though urban bodies were at least as complex and as unpredictable in their reactions to treatments as human bodies are. Planning in both its meanings (design and programming), considered as a project of curing city life through rationalized control of urban 'functions', did not profit from the inventive wisdom of everyday medical practice which always puts into doubt the possibility of an absolutely certain and conclusive knowledge of any disease. It was this ignorant confidence that guided urban design and planning in its search for a universally valid language which would be able to express the main characteristics of urban 'health'. And this language was indeed discovered (or, rather, rediscovered in a different historical context) in the supposedly universal language of geometry.

Baron Haussmann, in his famous urban interventions in Paris, actually concretized both the predominant urban therapeutic imaginary and the employment of geometrical rationalization of city layout as a form of urban cure. A revealing detail of his overall project was that '[t]o make the actual streets of the plan, Haussmann constructed tall wooden towers up which his assistants – whom he called "urban geometers"– ascended, measuring out straight streets with compass and ruler to the old walls of the city' (Sennett 1994: 330). Geometry was present both in the discursive practices and in the working methods of the urban interventions.

According to Benjamin, Haussmann was nicknamed by his contemporaries an 'artist-demolitionist' (Benjamin 1999: 128, E3,6) and his projects were dubbed 'strategic embellishment' (ibid.: 12). Both terms capture a legitimized contrast between means and ends in Haussmann's project: a decisive and accurate hand of a strong and determined man who nevertheless works for a universally recognized goal, namely beauty and a well-calculated blow against proletarian neighbourhoods in the city centre in the name of a longed-for urban unity, possibly nuanced with Saint-Simonian utopianism overtones (Donald 1999: 46). Haussmannian city-order utopia was formed as a project of redesigning public space and had a role in the reproduction of bourgeois hegemony.

Everybody was supposed to be able to walk on the wide boulevard pavements. And anybody could supposedly use the pavement cafés. However, social inequalities were directing people's expressive acts on this new public stage. The poor were the dazzled spectators in performances of wealth and elegance given by the rich. As in Baudelaire's poem 'The Eyes of the Poor', this mutual act of seeing and being seen is charged with the asymmetries of social status. What Marshall Berman describes as a modern 'primal scene' already contains a major contradiction: 'The setting that makes all urban humanity a great extended "family of eyes" also brings forth the discarded stepchildren of that family' (Berman 1983: 153). Behind the illusion of a new, inclusive space that is open to all, behind the new setting of a democracy based on a generalized visuality and exposure, lies a hegemonic project that excludes those who cannot hide their misery. In a democracy of anonymity the poor were offered an alternative to fantasized social ascent: the chance to hide their true social and economic condition, the chance to deceive through the manipulation of their appearance. If the boulevards created a new kind of public space this was the ceremonial space par excellence: displays of wealth and power were socially effective because they were projected onto a spatial arrangement that was meant to be the culmination of a bourgeois recuperation of the city centre. More than the aristocrats who could reproduce their dominance by organizing only occasionally their presence in public, the bourgeoisie needed to expose in public its economic power and thus to legitimize its rule. But this legitimization was dependent on the staging of a certain democracy of equal chances.

The boulevards were undoubtedly expressing a new public culture. And they could emphatically present this culture as democratic and inclusive. They could even present this culture as natural, obvious and indisputable. The boulevards naturalized a presentation of society as an agglomeration of individuals who, as in the experience of the crowd, could be different and anonymous. This process 'depoliticizes' the street experience. Instead of becoming the public space in which social antagonism is expressed and demands are collectively made, the boulevard is meant to become a phantasmagoria of a brand-new world of promises and peaceful progress. Sharing space in boulevards would mean participating in a fantasy of well-being oriented towards an always-better future.

Publicness and the art of being in public were shaped in the boulevards through the hegemonic project of presenting an explosively divided society as a united whole in pursuit of the modernist dream of eternal progress. It is in this ideological context that a model of urban order was effectively shaped in the form of an effectively regulated mobility in the city. The dream of the pacified city is from these times onwards connected to the rational and never-broken control of traffic. Social chaos is still being depicted nowadays as a city circulation system out of order.

The fantasy of urban order expressed in the form of a geometrical street layout that would 'allow the most efficient circulation of goods, people, money, and troops' (Donald 1999: 46) was the fantasy of Haussmann but also the dream of modernist urban planning. After all, 'Le Corbusier admired Haussmann as a surgeon who had tried to decongest the arteries of Paris' (ibid.: 57). What seems to be very persistent in this fantasy or ideal (meant to change urban reality) is the idea of complete separation of movement flows. The pedestrians were to be completely separated from the vehicles.

During the years between the First and Second World Wars, Le Corbusier (1970 and 1987) contributed decisively to the clarification of modernist architecture's vision of the future of cities. In a formulation that would have important consequences in reconceptualizing the role of the streets, he maintained that the modern street is 'a sort of stretched-out workshop' (Le Corbusier 1987: 167). In direct correspondence with his view that architecture and urban planning should learn from the way engineers formulate and solve problems of machine functioning, Le Corbusier insisted that the street is essentially a machine for the effective, fast and precise regulation of circulation (ibid.: 131).

In Le Corbusier's vision, vehicle circulation arteries are very wide and are arranged in an orthogonal grid. The most important of them are to be suspended above ground level and thus become absolutely separated from pedestrian movement (ibid.: 168). Emphatically favoured is the straight-line design of streets as opposed to the site-specific irregular street pattern that is characteristic of historical cities (ibid.: 207–11). His dream was to build the future cities from scratch, in flat places devoid of geographical and historical particularities (ibid.: 220).

It is interesting to note that an important debate between prominent German-speaking architects and planners on the character of city streets which unfolded in the 1890s already prefigured modernist hymns to the rationality and efficiency of straight streets. Defenders of 'crooked streets' were arguing in favour of a 'harmonious cityscape' that created feelings of 'cosiness' and 'intimacy'. Their counterparts were accused of defending 'boring' streets in which 'anonymity', 'indifference' and 'uniformity' were bound to prevail. Straight streets would correspond to a 'geometric man' belonging to an 'abstract mass' (Frisby 2003: 76). In this debate the connection of street form to distinct modes of social interaction is more than apparent. What was at stake then and continued to be at stake in twentieth-century modernism is the forms of appropriation of the street by individuals, masses or communities in the process of contesting their character as public, communal (connected to the closed neighbourhood communities which Haussmannian projects attacked) or common spaces.

The modernist programmatic separation of the world of pedestrians from the world of vehicles appeared to be promising a
city that was to be offered to pedestrians. Functional solutions
of this separation were supported not simply by a rationalizing
approach that would optimize the work of the city-machine but
also by an ideology of freedom expressed as a freedom of unobstructed movement both for cars and for walkers. In a later
chapter we will see how deeply this ideology has affected the
imaginary of emancipation. In the context of this chapter it is
important to note that the modernist street layout offered images
of a completely tamed streetscape, devoid of conflict and clashing uses. It was these converging and different, even clashing,
flows, however, which made the streets lively public spaces. Intersections, apart from being areas of possible traffic congestion
and of circulation flow discontinuity, were places of great social
value by becoming nodes of commerce and social interaction.
Informal and formally organized practices converge in places in
which movements intersect and various forms of encounter are
bound to flourish.

Pavements and pedestrian areas in direct connection with
flows of vehicles and goods, are spaces in which various activities
that might introduce conflicting interpretations and uses of the
city unfold. Thus, 'as shared spaces that people transverse by ne-
cessity, sidewalks have provided arenas for negotiating exclusion
and inequality' (Loukaitou-Sideris and Ehrenfeucht 2009: 85).

Le Corbusier's city-park with its high-rise buildings which
were supposedly providing more open-air ground space for a
community of pedestrian users created what we could describe as
'cities without qualities' (compare Musil's 'man without qualities').
There would be no contested areas in such cities, no unpredictable

intersections and no unregulated encounters. Circulation defined as one of the four basic functions of the city according to
the modernist epitome of urban ordering, the Charter of Athens
(Conrads 1971), is considered as a discrete, localizable and repair-
able part of the city-machine (Mumford 2000: 90).

An example of what kind of extreme outcomes may result
from this logic of attributing to streets the role of regulators of
urban order is the urban interventions of Mussolini's fascist
regime during the pre-war years in Italy. The construction of
huge monumental avenues in major cities was meant not only
to ensure unobstructed and separated movement of vehicles and
pedestrians but also to create the setting for the parades, ceremonies and public spectacles organized by the regime (Atkinson
1998: 24). The effort to regulate pedestrian movement reached
almost absurd levels of suppression as 'jaywalking was outlawed
and the police enforced a one-way system upon the narrow
pavements of central Rome' (ibid.: 19).

Haussmann's ideal of the city as a 'cleaned' and ordered urban
environment, Le Corbusier's fantasies of a flawless city-machine,
and Mussolini's paroxysmic urban autarchy share the same genealogy. In all of them, city streets represent a world of social
disorder that needs to be controlled through planning policies
and authoritarian interventions in a direct clash with practices
that appropriate the street as a possible common space.

### Gentrification rhetoric and the 'shared space' approach

Contemporary city and traffic circulation problems have con-
siderably changed in consequence of important structural
transformations in capitalist societies. What is being described
as globalization and the advance of global cities is a complex

set of economic and cultural phenomena which were and are being conceptualized either through terms that indicate a crisis of modernity and modernism ('postmodernity', 'supermodernity', etc.) or through terms that name a society different from industry-based ones ('post-industrial', 'post-Fordist', etc.). A critical appraisal of the relevant debates is obviously beyond the scope of this chapter. What is helpful, however, in trying to understand an important shift in the ideals and practices of urban planning interventions is to keep in mind that those structural and cultural transformations put the modernist imaginary into severe crisis. The city itself could no longer be presented as a world-out-of-order which might be fixed; rather it was seen as a multilayered and conflictual reality which would have to be treated as a challenge requiring the devising of context-specific tactics of intervention. From this perspective, public space, and specifically streets, became the focus of important interventions in city centres which were supported by widespread diagnoses of urban degradation. Such interventions depart from the modernist imaginary of a new city designed from scratch and the corresponding rhetoric of a rationalization of city functions. Whereas modernist planners took for granted that what they described as urban chaos needed important organizational and regulatory interventions (and in their most extreme statements they said that this was not possible in maze-like historical cities), after-modernist planners emphasized diversity and surprise as important characteristics of a new kind of urban environment. In place of rationalization, zoning and clear legibility of urban functions, it was organized contingency, mixed uses and a rich communication-focused urbanscape that were praised.

As we will see, this change of approach helped to shape at least two different sets of urban policies in terms of redefining the meaning and role of public space and streets. The first is by far more dominant than the second and has already left its mark on important big cities all over the world. It is characterized by interventions that attempt to regain control of degraded city areas and redefine a kind of publicly used space that generates private profit in conditions of protected consumption. Local authorities or states have an important role in shaping the targets and the processes through which these areas are to be planned in direct connection to the logic of urban enclavism, as we have already seen. Gentrification interventions are predominantly policies of redefining the character of urban public space and extending its implicit or explicit privatization.

Less ambitious in its goals and a lot less able to influence, so far, the shape of urban centres is an emerging set of policies and ideas that attempt to create what is termed 'shared space'. This kind of public space programmatically departs from the dominant model of 'traffic segregation' which was initially proclaimed as the quintessence of modern road design. Putting emphasis on inclusive public space and the mixing of uses, the 'shared space approach' shares with gentrification planners the will to redefine public space by favouring difference and diversity and also a keen awareness that mass communication strategies fundamentally shape today's cityscapes. Both approaches criticize and construct urban images as a means to establish or corroborate identities of urban places which may directly or indirectly support market economic activities. But these approaches differ greatly in the forms of space sharing they create. Whereas gentrification often creates a simulacrum of 'common space' by carefully planning the collective consumption of space (and not only consumption through space), the shared space approach creates certain kinds of space-commoning, although such commoning is based more on individual responsibility than on collective inventiveness and collaboration.

Let us first examine, then, the gentrification logic. What Neil Smith has proposed to term the 'revanchist city' (Smith 1996) captures a dominant approach towards the city developed by the ruling elites which is characterized by an effort to regain control of the city's crucial public spaces and especially the city centre. According to Smith, such policies directly aim at replacing liberal capitalist politics of public control – which were more tolerant of deviant behaviours and minorities – with neoliberal zero tolerance. This shift may indeed constitute a form of revenge against all those who acquired rights during the liberal period characterized by important mass movement struggles. But it also crucially includes a redefinition of public space by neoliberal governments in an effort to reclaim the city for middle-class interests, including renewed opportunities for profit and secure urban consumption.

Gentrification may be publicized through rhetorics of diversity and plurality but it is essentially a highly selective set of interventions that establish strict rules of public space uses. Gentrification is explicitly connected to displacement acts directed against all those who are stigmatized for their misery or their 'unruly' behaviours and especially against those who inhabit areas that may become 'developed' in the interest of real estate investors. Gentrification, thus, is a specific set of policies that shapes the revanchist city as both an aggressively homogenized urban order and a rhetorically shaped world of individual opportunities and safe consumption of differing lifestyles.

Undoubtedly, city-centre renovations potentially create a field of unpredictable public behaviours. These behaviours may even create ad hoc common spaces through the appropriation of certain parts of public street spaces, no matter how temporary this can be. However, it is not the creation of pedestrian zones that characterizes mainly gentrification projects. Gentrification policies are predominantly devoted to ensuring an urban environment as secure as it may be and as deeply immersed as it can be in consumption culture. Constant surveillance is a necessary part of the gentrification setting: it can be accomplished not only through mechanisms of control but also through the very form of spatial arrangements. Le Corbusier's anathema of the old 'donkey street' (Le Corbusier 1987: 6–12) with its labyrinthine layout is just one of the modernist contributions to the design of streets that are exposed to total visuality (and therefore control). Gentrification architecture did not only use the straight line which Le Corbusier considered 'the proper thing for the heart of a city' (ibid.: 10). Scenic layouts and picturesque winding roads also became tools for organizing and disciplining urban uses in gentrified areas. Spatial form becomes a means to fix those uses and to eliminate surprises in the organized consumption of space. A planning view which favours an overlay of differences (Sennett 1993: 166 and 202) or gives 'narrative properties to space' (ibid.: 190) may very well create staged spectacles of tamed and predictable public life, contrary to Sennett's suggestions that such approaches are necessarily connected to a 'humane city' (ibid.: 202).

Too much is at stake in a gentrification venture to allow space to be used or be appropriated by 'deviant' users. Unauthorized street merchants, beggars, 'illegal' immigrants or skaters and graffiti 'villains' are chased out of the gentrified neighbourhoods either by police controls or by ingenious uses of public furniture and lighting. Curved benches which do not allow somebody to sleep on them, random grass watering to discourage temporary appropriations by homeless people and lighting that exposes to cameras every bit of allegedly dangerous or deviant action: these are just some of the means used to establish a safe setting for encouraged behaviours and to avert those that upset spatial and social order. M. Davis goes as far as to describe such environments as 'sadistic street environments' (Davis 1992: 232–6).

Gentrification projects vary greatly, of course, but dominant classes support these projects everywhere in the world in order to reclaim city centres or, generally, to regain control over parts of the city in which the 'dangerous classes' predominate and threaten public security as well as prevent rich profit investments. At the far end of this logic is, of course, the 'zero tolerance' policies epitomized in mayor Giuliani's administration in New York, which have since become the dream of many big city mayors, for example A.M. Lopez Obrador of Mexico City, who completely changed the rules of public street uses in the city centre. During Obrador's administration, street vendors, who used to play a crucial role in the life survival strategies of the poor, were expelled from their centuries-long selling spots and their practices were criminalized.

Collective and individual identities are performed in gentrified public or quasi-public spaces in ways that tend to reproduce and corroborate stereotypical behaviour. As many researchers

show (Zukin 1995, Sorkin 1992, Smith and Williams 1986), gentrification is promoted and established in city space through
policies heavily dependent upon the manipulation of images.
Public space is designed to be used, recognized and appreciated
through images that are connected to marketable urban identities. The resulting visualization of public culture dominates
over the construction of city inhabitants' identities. Trapped in
taxonomies of image types, identities are thus performed without really been affected by the contingencies and challenges of
encounters. Gentrification projects mould not only space but
also the collective identities of 'gentrified' users. People are encouraged to enter an exclusionary urban scenery that redefines
the city as the locus of a collectively referred-to proper identity. Cleaned from the impurities constantly generated by social
antagonism, this identity condenses widely publicized images
and forces people to act in and through those images which
stage a form of carefully manipulated publicness. Obviously
these projects are very far from providing opportunities for
common space to emerge. Nevertheless, gentrification projects
often employ a peculiar common-space rhetoric that actually tries to present public space as being reclaimed by decent,
law-abiding, at times successfully creative but always-insatiable
users-consumers.

No matter how often diversity, freedom of movement and
individuality of use are called upon, gentrification manufac-
tures enclosed identities and defines enclosed urban settings of
collective consumption. Even in cases in which gentrification interventions are meant to transform a city through extensive city
branding projects, and the new collective identities appear as inclusive and plural, an overarching manufactured 'city patriotism'

reduces differences to harmless variations of the dominant models. The 1992 Barcelona Olympics provides a valuable example. The construction and redesign of many public spaces as well as large-scale urban renewal interventions were combined with an equally large-scale public rhetoric on the part of the local authorities which presented the city as the symbolic and inhabited locus of a collective identity of which citizens should be proud. As the campaign slogans condensed it: 'Barcelona, everybody's goal' and 'Barcelona, more than ever' (Albet i Mas and Garcia Ramon 2005: 236). The so-called Barcelona success story carefully hides from view some really alive public spaces which were replaced by sophisticated design gestures, the displacement of Roma camps near the seaside, the radical transformation of the popular housing area of Barcelonetta, also near the sea (part of which remains as a sightseeing island with small enclaves of a different public culture), and of course the replacement of the rich harbour life (with all its contradictory characteristics) by a zone of leisure activities. Admittedly the seaside interventions have offered to the city an access to the sea enjoyed by many inhabitants and tourists (Busquets 2005: 392–5). City patriotism, however, prevailed as an imposed collective fantasy which continues effectively to subordinate cultural and social differences to an always-expanding touristic phantasmagoria.

The 'shared space' approach was initially formulated through focused research on the problems connected to traffic and especially on the ways traffic has destroyed the city streets' character as spaces of multiform public uses. According to this approach the solution to these problems depends heavily on 'the integration of traffic into the social and cultural fabric of the built environment'

(Hamilton-Baillie 2008a: 169; see also Hamilton-Baillie 2008b). Although such a perspective arose from a technical, empiricist search in pursuit of efficient and quality road planning, it has a straightforward view on what are the social implications of different models of traffic management. Directly opposing the 'segregation principle' (ibid.: 164) according to which it is imperative to separate cars completely from pedestrians, this view experiments in creating urban traffic landscapes of mixed use and planning tools that encourage the active entanglement of drivers and pedestrians in shaping the use of reclaimed street and square spaces. Instead of dividing, this view integrates worlds of movement which can differ in form, speed, means, et cetera (Methorst et al. 2007, Moody and Melia 2013).

The very logic behind the shared space idea is that people have learned to negotiate their place and their trajectories in urban settings and that when they are allowed to interact freely they know how to avoid accidents and find ways to coexist as street users. Eliminating signs or spatial arrangements that separate and control, this approach develops planning proposals that aim at resolving 'potential conflict through informal protocols and human interaction prompted by clues from the built environment' (Hamilton-Baillie 2008: 171).

Probably these ideas have a kind of genealogical connection with attempts to invent 'traffic calming devices' (ibid.: 167 and Vahl and Giskes 1990) but they reach well beyond that. They take shape through an undertheorized but specific approach to human interaction that privileges negotiations and the employment of 'informal social protocols' (Hamilton-Baillie 2008: 166). 'The rationale of shared space is that no one has priority of access or usage; it is an egalitarian space' (Jensen 2013: 15). According to this approach, when people are left to negotiate freely with others they will find their way of dealing with different priorities and stakes especially because they themselves will assume responsibility for the negotiations rather than ignore each other by being obliged to obey signs.

What kind of space is the shared space shaped through these practices of negotiation? One is tempted to see in these practices a kind of 'traffic commoning'. Aren't performed negotiated crossings, after all, instances of shaping traffic in common? Indeed, but we should not forget that space as well as vehicle and pedestrian flows are shaped by planners and not the people themselves. What people are allowed to do is to move in these spaces (either as drivers or as pedestrians) by learning to use a less movement-defining spatial form that is less restrictive than the usual segregation-and-control paradigm. People cannot intervene in the materiality of space, and people are not asked to participate (as a local community) in the site-specific definition of the stakes connected to the social and cultural integration of traffic. The community evoked in shared space is a rather vague abstraction of real communities, as is the abstraction of informal protocols. Real existing communities develop shared priorities and shared skills as well as, of course, conflicting approaches to the uses of urban space – a polemic over the common, to recall Rancière.

The shared space approach considers users as responsible individuals who out of an almost inherent courtesy or ability to calculate risk and optimize personal trajectories are able to negotiate their way effectively and harmlessly. All those attributes and potential abilities are developed in specific sociocultural contexts. Maybe it is a paradigm fit for Northwestern types of society (and sociality), although it remains to be proved that it not only works but also contributes to the reproduction of informal protocols. After all, informal protocols exist only in and through practice.

Furthermore, assuming that people negotiate 'freely' is also assuming that they can equally make risk assessments and that they are in equal positions. However, pedestrians, cyclists and car drivers neither have to face the same dangers nor do they enter negotiations as in an ideal democratic deliberation in which views are considered as equal. In a metropolitan context, the shared space approach may very well run the risk of unwittingly supporting a street law of the jungle (Methorst et al. 2007: 12).

It is interesting to compare the shared space examples with examples of ad hoc management in places and societies in which a very inventive spirit of constant negotiation is developed in everyday urban settings of what Westerners call traffic chaos. How do people negotiate their way in Cairo, Nairobi or Mumbai for example –not because traffic lights or zebra crossings or road signs do not exist but exactly in spite of them?

The experience and practice of matatu driving and using is highly indicative in this context. Matatu cars are small private vans that are a popular and cheap means of transport in Nairobi (Kenya). There is a distinct matatu culture there, especially influenced by youth subculture trends (Wa-Mungai 2010: 376), which makes the matatu presence in the streets more than a circulation symptom. Mostly poor people use matatu regularly, and lots of them identify with the drivers' inventive abilities to almost heroically find a way in the dense and always-unpredictable traffic of downtown Nairobi. Matatu crews (comprising the driver and a highly active co-driver who collects tickets and shouts or whistles to attract the attention of potential customers) even used to be fashion trendsetters for the Nairobi youth (ibid.)

The matatu is a private minibus, there is no doubt about it. But at the same time it constitutes a potential catalyst in the creation of common space, both inside it and outside it as it moves in a traffic-congested urban environment. Rules of use exist but are not imposed by a certain authority – they result from the accumulated negotiations between drivers, co-drivers, passengers and pedestrians who all belong to a community in which these roles may be interchangeable or, at least, easily recognizable and acceptable. Micro-communities may take shape inside this loosely defined community, like, for example, a community of those who regularly use a specific matatu line, or the community of those drivers who share the same service and parking station.

What makes matatu a commoned space and a commoning catalyst is the very process through which people collectively create rules of sharing. There is even a distinct set of matatu culture terms which define practices and actors involved in urban everydayness (Wa-Mungai 2009: 273). In the shared space approach, common space seems to be *offered* to people from above. What is more, people do not act as a collectivity even if this collectivity sometimes is assumed by planners as an abstract socially meaningful and binding context. Shared space is nearer to a liberal utopia of negotiations between free individuals, who due to the ethical superiority of freedom will necessarily take the best decisions and thus avoid any mischief.

However, the shared space approach is a valuable testing ground for evaluating practices of shared use of space by comparing the differences created not only by the rules but also by the forms of rule production and implementation. Common space, precarious and precious as it is, cannot be given to people by a certain authority nor can it be planned. Common space is actually a process of space creation that unfolds through practices of commoning. And if these practices are to be sustained well beyond the boundaries of capitalist society, they will have to be collectively inventive and always welcoming to newcomers.

## Streets as potential sites of commoning

In direct contrast to the politics of urban regeneration, which almost as a rule aims at reclaiming the city centre for the middle and upper classes, important urban practices develop which struggle to use the streets as subsistence terrain for the poor. Throughout the world, these practices shape behaviours and habits which produce 'unauthorized' meanings and uses for the streets, the pavements, the junctions, the residual spaces around and below highways, and the leftover spaces of urban peripheries.

As AbdouMaliq Simone describes it, in contemporary Africa urban control is based on a management of urban populations which looks a lot like the management of refugees. Policies tend to ensure a 'right to place – that is, the sheer ability to live in the city and survive ... but not the right to the city – that is, the right to use the city as an arena to actualize and/or transform specific aspirations' (Simone 2008: 114). In this context, 'the apparent provisionality of African urban life' (ibid.: 104) is expressed in practices that take advantage of urban points of intersection, of urban flows of trade and exchanges, by 'maneuvering the relation between social spaces, visual fields, symbolic resources, concrete objects and linguistic materials' (ibid.: 105).

Are these practices of the weak and the dispossessed being developed in common? Do everyday improvising skills create individual trajectories or confluent tactics? These questions are important in order to understand the possible ways through which street practices create ad hoc common spaces.

Streets may become common spaces especially when street trade or neighbourhood markets create conditions of living together in which individual survival practices interweave to create formal or informal support networks. Neighbourhoods may become, in this context, important collective reference nodes (ibid.: 109) in which the exchange of services and goods is recognizably spatialized.

Urban communities obviously differ from traditional communities (this, as we have seen, is true for urban Aymara communities in Bolivia too). However, in Africa, as in many cities of the global south, urban neighbourhood streets develop into crucial commoning spaces by providing not simply the ground but also the emblematic images that represent, support and reproduce ways of action, habits and forms of communication. In this context, the street is more than a spatial support of the circulation of people and goods. The street becomes a means to shape shared habits, everyday rhythms and forms of regulation which, nevertheless, remain open to everyday negotiations and individual tactics. This subtle creation of commoning rules and institutions 'from below' and through constant renegotiations unfolds in many market streets in which various levels of informality mix and interweave. Formal rules and planning policies are in many cases simply direct attacks on the potentiality of such emerging common spaces. They usually seek to establish 'the tidy, modernist city-image of politicians' dreams' (Brown et al. 2010: 677) which amounts to a controllable public space.

'Associational life in Africa is built around overlapping obligations, responsibilities, customs and traditions that determine reciprocity' (ibid.: 678). Street trading, which many governments attempt to exorcise (either by criminalizing it or by directly and brutally suppressing it), is actually a set of practices that explicitly treats the street as a livelihood asset. However, street traders also weave, in and through the streets they use, important networks of solidarity and collective culture which may support and give ground to common needs, aspirations, values and habits.

The social context of course differs but in many places throughout the world, family ties and relations of kin become crucial 'mechanisms for securing access to space and other recourses', as in the case of African street trade (Brown 2006: 52). Thus, 'In Ghana it was common for women to "inherit" a trading space from another family member' (ibid.: 185). Street trading appears today in all metropolitan areas of big cities, whether these cities belong to the so-called First, Second or Third world. Actually, this distinction between 'worlds' seems today to describe different layers of urban life coexisting or clashing in every such city. And street trading does not have to do only with practices of temporarily appropriating public space. Often, hidden networks of communication and exchanges interconnect the private realm of poor households with appropriated public space so that communities of vendors and neighbourhood communities overlap or even coincide.

The social capital that street traders accumulate and share supports common livelihood strategies but also creates common worlds and common claims and struggles. Family, kinship, religious, ethnic or professional networks may be expressed in associational ties, both informal and 'formalized'. What all those associational practices have in common is their direct adherence to specific spaces and spatial trajectories. Space, and the street in particular, is the locus, the means of expression and the stake of such practices.

Street-commoning, thus, may be produced by various kinds of associational communities. Some of them may be a lot more closed and impenetrable than others. The street economy in inner-city Johannesburg, for example, is based on the predominance of Nigerians organized as a hierarchically structured support network which can exhibit its presence in the street and participate in various forms of 'pirate economy' (Simone 2008). Creating a common sociality in the city, Nigerians can both reinforce their presence as an ethnic group and, more important, navigate their common course as a multi-levelled community between informality and formal trade, between legal and illegal practices (ibid.: 362). In the same city, another kind of regulated street-commoning based on hierarchically organized street traders' communities is organized by the so-called Johannesburg's 'block captains', who 'informally control the pavements of the inner city' (Brown 2006: 51).

Street-commoning supports forms of subjectivation that may possibly corroborate dominant social role taxonomies but also deviate from their normalizing grids. By learning to negotiate in the streets, either as traders or as street users and neighbourhood members, many people throughout the world learn not only how to survive but also how to be, how to express themselves and how to assume or lose socially meaningful identities. Excluding the affluent urban elites who have no contact with the mixed world of metropolitan streets and who either fly above the city (in helicopters as in São Paulo) or travel barricaded in armoured cars, all other people have to deal in differing ways with street practices.

What makes street traders and hawkers so inventive is the fact that their lives depend on their ability to seize opportunities, to attract attention where and when this will become favourable and to optimize their assets and their knowledge of urban life. Street traders develop, thus, ways of negotiating their presence in the streets but also their relations to potential buyers as well as to potential competitors. In the gentrified streets of world metropolises, dominant policies succeed in organizing street life in role taxonomies that stage diversity only to extinguish or mask social antagonism. However, outside the heavily controlled enclaves of urban normalization, streets become areas of contestation. Only focused research on specific cities may reveal the complexities of the relation between rules imposed on spaces of urban renovation and practices which transform, bend or defy those rules throughout periods of intense political or social struggles. Christina Jimenez offers us an exemplary study of the Mexican city of Morelia by following the way street vendors organized both their claims and their associations in the nineteenth century in order to negotiate their right to be in public space. Their negotiations with state and local authorities, as she shows, employed in different periods the rhetoric of street and city modernization as well as the hegemonic discourse of early post-revolution governments (Jimenez 2008).

Loukaitou-Sideris and Ehrenfeucht have carefully studied the history and life of sidewalks in five major US cities to document and support their theoretical arguments about the need to retain 'conflict and negotiation over public space' (Loukaitou-Sideris and Ehrenfeucht 2009). Carefully focusing on collective and individual rights which are being curtailed by policies of security and 'homogenization', they conclude: '[A]s residents and urban designers and planners, we need to be more vigilant to ensure that sidewalks remain accessible and open, even if this means some potential danger and conflict' (ibid.: 272).

To know how and where to be is already an art that exceeds the mere observation of rules and etiquettes. People in the street have to perform not simply themselves but those selves that may profit from the street's opportunities. An informal theatre of the weak (Stavrides 2002a), an inventive manipulation of buyers' expectations or of the attention of passers-by, is using the streets as ephemeral stages in which shared meanings and stakes are created or are being lost and found again. Performances of approach, of aggression, of seduction or of probing negotiation unfold on the street stages. This is how people may reconfigure possible common worlds but also themselves.

Just observe a Nigerian street vendor in Athens. Selling cheap electronic gadgets, he will present himself as a modern young man. He will learn to address young people by using recognizable catchwords, preferably English ones, and by displaying a shared technological enthusiasm. See him selling 'traditional' craft items from his country. He will reinforce his 'exotic' look, he will talk about luck, good health or legendary African beauty and even evoke a bit of African 'mysticism'. Just a person who knows to change masks? No, this is, rather, a complex set of practices and expressions through which an immigrant moulds himself or herself in the process of finding ways to be in another country. Identities become themselves both the locus and the stake of negotiating encounters.

Talking about life in Naples during the inter-war period, Walter Benjamin (in a work he himself says he wrote with Asja Lacis) observed a 'passion for improvisation, which demands that space and opportunity be at any price preserved' (Benjamin 1985: 170). Edensor uses the same word, 'improvisation', to describe ways of behaviour which unfold in the Indian bazaar (Edensor 2000: 136). As he suggests, the contemporary city offers a series of stages on which different roles may be performed but variety is not unlimited: 'most performances are "regulated" improvisations' (ibid.: 124).

In the city streets of contemporary metropolises, practices of individual improvisation are an integral part of everyday role performances. When those practices become, however, the means to construct collectively arranged street common spaces, then we can talk about forms of commoning which shape common identities. We need to understand the construction of common worlds and the unfolding of commoning practices as processes which directly influence the stability of pre-existing identities and possibly contribute to the creation of new ones. Theatricality in public performances may describe these inventive (either adaptive or dissident) acts which create spaces of negotiating encounter between different people. If theatricality is the socially learned skill to become other and not simply an art of deception or disguising imitation, then through theatricality people can create bridges to otherness (Stavrides 2010b: 81–91).

Does common space possibly acquire the characteristics of a stage? Yes, if people try to create it not out of an already-existing feeling of community or communality but in the process of discovering possibilities of sharing between different groups and individuals too. As we will see in the next chapter, this was the case in the square occupations of 2011. To be able even to approach others and to possibly establish common ground, people or individuals need to be inventive in their ways of expressing themselves and understanding the expressions of others. A visit to otherness through the construction of an intermediary self, a self that is not simply an impersonation but an extension and transformation of an identity-in-the-making, is valuable from the point of view of exploring and expanding commoning. We definitely need to distance ourselves from the view that presents commoning as a necessarily homogenizing process. Commoning, if it is to remain a dynamic set of practices that overspills all kinds of enclosures, should remain open to otherness. Common spaces may become stages on which negotiations and bridges to otherness develop as people learn to become others without losing themselves to otherness. A visit to otherness, as in the intricate and inventive styles of street negotiations, becomes, thus, not a mere tactic of deception but an active contribution to identity formation. To share means, from this perspective, to be able to create bridges and thresholds to otherness rather than to enclose in and through space already-established common identities.

We can possibly think that such an everyday inventive theatricality contributes to the emergence of common spaces by creating 'the virtual space of the other' (Féral 2002: 98). This space concretizes a spatiality of in-betweeness. And such a threshold space, in which differences are offered a stage to exchange approaching gestures (Stavrides 2010b: 90–1), is a space-in-the-making, a potentiality of space. Virtuality expresses the most important quality of this process. Encounters *may* happen and differences *may* meet. But, what is more important is that space should remain in this dynamic condition of virtuality if it is to support such possibilities of exchange and encounters. Virtuality actually corresponds to the dynamic character of space-commoning which is oriented towards expanding beyond the boundaries of any established communities of commoners. In order to be open to newcomers, commoning has always to test its boundaries and transcend them by creating, activating or taking advantage of such 'virtual spaces of the other'.

One can focus on the individual tactics and skills that become visible in performances of theatricality in everyday encounters. But one can also focus on the conditions under which everyday actors collectively construct the ephemeral or more permanent stages on which they perform. It is not necessary to assume that such acts of stage construction or stage definition are conscious or deliberate acts. A collective frame of reference is formed through myriads of individual micro-acts which tend to develop collectively recognizable modes of behaviours. We can even assume that this process leads to the formation of practice codes. For example, Anderson studies the characteristics of the 'code of the street' in the black neighbourhoods of inner-city Philadelphia in an effort to trace everyday tactics of gaining respect and protection employed by young marginalized people (Anderson 2000). Well beyond the formative explicit rules that we usually attribute to a code of behaviour are the expressive and inventive individual and collective practices which shape such a code. Codes of this kind may thus be considered as common worlds that support common spaces and are supported by them. And these codes may be as strict as the rules and institutions developed in a closed community of commoners (more or less hierarchical or not) or as open as the rules and institutions of an expanding community of commoning which needs to readjust and reconfigure the very process of its self-management.

The more the construction of common spaces as minuscule stages is regulated by a non-admissive community, the more this process tends to evolve to an enclosure of practices and habits. On the other hand, acts that expand commoning are neither totally unexpected nor absolutely innovative. They rather have the characteristics of a musician's improvisation within a music ensemble, as Sennett suggests (2009: 237).

There is a hidden order behind the appearance of the visual (and functional) 'mess' of the stoops of the tenement buildings of New York's Lower East Side. People use the steps in ways that are based on improvised acts and gestures which develop according to this collectively recognized hidden order. 'Improvisation is a user's craft' (ibid.: 236). This craft is shared and keeps on producing spaces to be shared. But if we choose to focus on the community of users rather than on the individual user-craftsman, then we can observe how such a community emerges as the sometimes contingent, sometimes habitual confluence of various micro-communities. Only if we abandon the idea that comes from the musical improvisation metaphor according to which there should be some kind of formal rules and consistency underlying improvised acts can we possibly capture the inherently negotiable character of an expanding commoning process. Micro-communities, as we will see in the next chapter, which examines the squares movement, may coordinate practices that unfold in them too but they may also explore the boundaries and opportunities created by practices that retain their relative independence. The idea of an overall synthesis will sometimes look like an order introduced from outside to a process which evolves either through political experimentation (in the case of squares) or through everyday micro-tactics. Maybe we can learn from the hawkers' choreographies (ibid.: 237), but also from the matatu drivers' improvisation acts, that common space is not necessarily an ordered space but rather an always-emerging patchwork of fragments of order reconfigured by inventive actors. An expanding community of commoners need not be envisaged as a well-organized machine that can integrate new parts into its always-improving functioning; rather, it can be understood as an artifice of collective *bricolage* which people always mend, and even enjoy in doing so, and which is being shaped and used according to their needs and dreams.

Chapter 6

# Occupied squares, societies in movement

## A legitimacy crisis?

We can't yet agree even on what name should be given to a series of phenomena that erupted almost unexpectedly throughout the world from 2011 and on. Was it an occupied squares movement, a worldwide set of collective acts of civil disobedience, a series of consecutive uprisings against undemocratic regimes or simply mass mobilizations against unjust economic policies? Maybe it is too early to try to distil out of these phenomena a common cause or common aspirations. It is important, however, to see them both as a result and as an aspect of a socio-economic crisis that is sweeping the capitalist world. What these phenomena clearly show is that capitalism has lost the power to promise a better future for all. And this happened exactly when ruling elites thought they had managed to reach the heavens of the absolute capitalist utopia: the heavens in which money begets money without any interference of often disobedient and unpredictable real people as well of always-problematic production procedures. The arrogance and power of bankers and stockbrokers is symptomatic of such a paroxysmal utopianism.

'Those below' have to be reintegrated into a system which, caught in its own paroxysmal utopia, thought it could do without them. As so many social eruptions and statistics show, people are losing their faith in a system which presents itself misleadingly as a mechanism of potential wealth distribution to which they expect to have access.

Collective disappointment, either explicitly expressed in riots or implicitly expressed in solitary depression, poses new problems of governability: it seems that two crucial tasks are laid before this necessary 'return to politics' for the governing elites. The first is to ensure that people continue to be defined by social bonds which constitute individuals as economic subjects, as subjects whose behaviour and motives can be analysed, channelled, predicted upon and, ultimately, controlled by the use of economic parameters and measures only. The second task is to ensure that people continue to act and dream without any form of connectedness and coordination with others. Collective actions and aspirations, especially those that produce common spaces, are to be blocked.

In a period of crisis these two priorities in population governance aim at producing individuals who share with others only fear.[5] Fear about everything that keeps on destabilizing their life conditions and plans. At the same time, each one alone has to believe that he or she 'will make it'. And that can possibly happen only at the expense of any other's opportunity to make it too.

Cracks and ruptures manifest themselves, often violently, in the ambitious yet precarious edifice of this governing model. Outraged and rebellious people enter again the field of politics and acquire visibility and power to transform implemented policies. And out of these collective acts, public space acquires new meaning. It is as if people reclaim space as a locus of dissident acts, a locus separated from the dominant mediatic space of simulated participation. It is as if people explicitly or implicitly redefine the meaning of space sharing and of publicness.

It is certainly too early to say that the dominant policies have entered into a crisis of no return, even though history travels with an amazing speed these days and indications of a deepening of crisis proliferate. We can, however, observe in various parts of the world two interconnected series of phenomena that deeply affect what we could diagnose as a crisis of legitimacy.

The first series includes phenomena that have to do with the role of information and communication in destabilizing collective faith in the system. From the Latin American movements and uprisings (such as the *Argentinazo* or the people's massive protests in São Paulo) to the Arab revolutions (especially those in Tunisia and Egypt), including the 'indignant' square occupations in European cities and the North American Occupy movement, communication and information exchanges through social media and interactive communication devices have played a very important role in moulding collective action.

The second series includes phenomena that have to do with community- oriented or community-inspired actions that, often quite distinct from neocommunitarian neoconservative ideologies, create or even reinvent communities-in-the-making. These are often unstable but always metastatic and expanding communities in movement.

Both series of phenomena converge in practices of redefining and reappropriating public space; both contribute to the emergence of common spaces. And both series of phenomena are characterized by forms of hybridization, the mixing of incompatible and often opposing elements in the creation of 'unauthorized' combinations.

According to Homi Bhabha, hybridity characterizes a specific form of agency, 'subaltern agency'. As he suggests, 'subaltern agency emerges as relocation and re-inscription' (Bhabha 2004: 227). We can attribute these two characteristics, re-inscription and relocation (understanding them not only metaphorically but also as descriptive terms), to a series of urban practices that are focused on the collective reinvention of public space as common space. These practices, which may well be characterized as subaltern, create, use and disseminate information through the new communicative media already mentioned, but they are not practices of information exchange only. These practices 'mark' the city through the information exchange they make possible.

'Reinscription' can invoke the material results of these practices on the city's body. It is a process of marking out specific places through inscriptions that not only disseminate information (as in the case of wall writings or graffiti) but also connect places and create shared points of reference for specific emerging collectivities that recognize them. This happened, for example, during the December 2008 youth uprising in Athens,[6] when a 'migrant' stencil art spread all over the city centre and condensed the uprising's messages into emblematic images. Some of these markings of the city's body were short-lived while others survive: inscriptions over other inscriptions, messages and traces in combat with other traces. A reinscription process, indeed, can effectively transfer the feeling of a city in movement, a city in turmoil. Similar reinscription acts spread in Tunis and Cairo during the 2010–12 Arab uprisings and in Barcelona, Athens, Madrid and other European cities due to the 'squares movement' in 2011.

'Relocation' has to do with one very important characteristic of information dissemination: these new urban practices of public space appropriation and collective dissent use information exchanges with the aim of potentially coordinating those who participate in the exchanges. Information is not a flow, in this context, but an arrow directed towards potential receivers and returned as a promise of mutual involvement.

One of the early examples of such practices was the case of the '*pasalo*' mobilizations in Barcelona and Madrid on 13 March 2004. During the 'night of the short messages' people exchanged through the internet and by SMS a message that would overthrow a government: 'Liars murderers. Your war our dead. *Pasalo* (Pass it on).' This message was circulated the day before general elections and accused the government of systematically hiding from the people the real reasons for the bomb explosions which had killed 200 persons in three suburban trains. Huge demonstrations occupied the central squares in Barcelona and Madrid, which were defined by the messages of protesters as meeting points.[7]

In this process, information ('they are not telling us the truth') addresses people as potential actors. Information acquires a power to mobilize people through sharing and participation. The city thus is not simply the background or the medium through which information spreads but an active element in the transformation of information to a call: defined meeting points punctuate the city's body and organize a network of locations connected by a common cause, a common will for action. A fragile and migrational set of common spaces is thus developed. To borrow and recontextualize De Certeau's beautiful phrase, '[a] *migrational*, or metaphorical, city thus slips into the clear text of the planned and readable city' (De Certeau 1984: 93). This process can be described as a series of relocation acts which support expanding social movements. Spaces and actions are redefined by being connected in new ways. Analogous urban inventive forms of coordination developed during the Athens December, the Tunisian 'Jasmine revolution', and the squares '*indignados*' actions.

Rumours and gossip used to be forms of information exchange, which, in traditional societies, participated in the reproduction or refashioning of existing social and personal relations. These were communities which pre-existed face-to-face interactive 'media', and community values or general hierarchies were rarely questioned. In contemporary societies, however, interactive technologies mediate the creation of communities of collective action that are not necessarily communities of people sharing a common identity or common values. These communities of collective action are communities in movement, communities developed through common action and the sharing of an emerging common space.

The occupation of Syntagma Square in Athens in 2011 was an act directly inspired by the Spanish squares occupation and the news which came from the Arab uprisings. Alternative media played a crucial role in this. But, more important, it was through a call on social media (which literally came from five young people) that Syntagma Square became unexpectedly filled with 30,000 anonymous protesters. It was 25 May 2011 and thousands of people flooded the central squares in thirty-eight cities all over Greece. The initial call spread via Facebook at an amazing speed, managing to mobilize all these people, something the radical left had failed to do three months earlier by using the typical forms of mass demonstration initiatives.

It is not that opportunities are created by interactive media. It is that through the processes of reinscription and relocation, shared information and shared meeting points bind people.

In a curious reversal, the reterritorializing of politics happens through the active mediation of de-territorializing communication technologies. Communities become located in urban space and develop by redefining and reappropriating their surroundings.

## Common space in the squares

Communities in movement 'secrete' their own space almost as snails and seashells secrete the substances through which their 'home' is being constructed. This is not the public space as we know it: space given from a certain authority to the public under specific conditions that ultimately affirm the authority's legitimacy. Nor is it private space either, if by this we mean space controlled and used by a limited group of people excluding all others. Communities in movement create common space,[8] space used under conditions decided on by communities and open to anyone who participates in the actions and accepts the rules which were collectively decided upon. The use, maintenance and creation of common space does not simply mirror the community. The community is formed, developed and reproduced through practices focused on common space. To generalize this principle: the community is developed through commoning, through acts and forms of organization oriented towards the production of the common.

To get a clearer view of the importance of space-commoning for the creation and support of communities in movement, let us look more closely at the example of the Syntagma Square occupation. 'A view from afar' would describe this occupation as a meeting point for protesters, just in front of the parliament building, to denounce harsh, unjust and undemocratic austerity measures. Of course this view in not wrong: it just misses what is new in this occupation-protest. Syntagma Square developed into a network of connected micro-squares, each one with a distinct character and spatial arrangement, all contained or, rather, territorialized in the area of what was known to be *the* central Athens public square. Each micro-square had its own group of people who lived there for some days, in their tents, people who focused their actions and their micro-urban environment on a specific task: a children's playground, a free reading and meditation area, a homeless campaign meeting point, a 'time bank' (a form of exchange of services based on the elimination of money and profit), a 'we don't pay' campaign meeting point (focused on organizing an active boycott of transportation fees and road tolls), a first aid centre, a multimedia group node and a translation group stand, et cetera. There were various levels on which those micro-communities were connected and, of course, all of them had to follow the general assembly's rules and decisions. However, differences in space arrangement choices and in media of expression (with the use of banners, placards, stickers, images, 'works of art', etc.) were more than apparent. Although the common cause and common target (the parliament) were dominant, each micro-square established different routines and different aesthetics and organized different micro-events during the occupation.

> The benches became the holders of the exhibits of the artists, the grass lawn was full of sleeping bags and tents, the trees supported the loudspeakers and the placards, the central fountain became the source to rinse the square from the tear gas and the paved area became a great seat for all. Therefore, the common space

created was the result of the interconnectivity and interaction of a society in motion. (Galatoula 2013)

Space-commoning was not a centralized procedure, then, although the assembly and the assembly area acquired a symbolically as well as functionally central role. Space-commoning was, rather, practised as a collectively improvised process which was marked by a centrality–dispersion dialectics: dispersed activities and micro-events but also coordinated activities. Of those coordinated activities the most important were the ones connected to the General Assembly's decision to organize massive protests on 28 and 29 June in the square. Those protests were meant to encircle the parliament building in an effort to obstruct the voting of a devastating agreement with the International Monetary Fund, European Union and European Central Bank titled 'Emergency Implementation Measures for the Mid-term Fiscal Adjustment Strategy 2012–2015'.

The mobilizations characterized by a massive participation of people in Syntagma Square as well as in organized road blocks were confronted by very aggressive police riot squads which unleashed an unprecedented chemical war against the protesters. People on and around the square did not scatter and managed peacefully to return to the square and organize an unforgettable ad hoc concert which the police did not dare to challenge. Huge open discussions organized by the Assembly on topics such as 'real democracy', 'public debt and austerity policies' and public education, et cetera were also important expressions of the occupation's collective coordinating spirit. In those unique public events, people's participation was amazingly great, and collective management of space was organized in ways that possibly prefigure a democratic and egalitarian contemporary *agora* [the ancient Greek marketplace used for public assemblies].

The square did not attempt to barricade itself either symbolically or literally, even when police aggression was imminent. All the occupied square's activities and initiatives kept the square's space open and connected to the rest of the city. In place of a public space that was routinely shaped by the intersection of incessant pedestrian flows directed to the underground station's entrance, a rich common space was created in the heart of Athens. Furthermore, a constant flow of messages which arranged meetings and spread information had kept this space connected with many other places in the city. As in the case of Madrid's occupied Puerta del Sol,

> The space-time created in the last days has one single obsession: continuity. Paradoxically, this is only possible to maintain through intermittancy. Through a physical entering-and-leaving of Sol. Keep the experience alive even though you are not present. For this reason (and so many others) the camp at Sol cannot be understood without the social networks. The continuity of the experience is achieved by deterritorializing it. (Kaejane 2011)

Space-commoning in the reappropriated squares of the 2010–12 uprisings involves the production and use of in-between spaces. Common spaces emerge as threshold spaces, spaces which are not demarcated by a defining perimeter. Whereas public space bears the mark of a prevailing authority which defines it and controls its use, common space is opened space, space in a process of opening towards 'newcomers'. Parallel to Rancière's understanding of a 'democracy to come', common space is characterized by 'an infinite openness to the Other or the newcomer' (Rancière 2010: 59). Common spaces are porous spaces, spaces in movement and spaces-as-passages.

Divisions in space, which were necessary for the creation of micro-communities (or, indeed, micro-squares), did not result in space departmentalization. Micro-squares were porous themselves, and a network of spaces-as-passages constituted a spatial arrangement which resembled a miniature city, a miniature tent city with its open-air spaces. This form of expanding and inventive space-commoning characterized all the occupied square encampments. In Tahrir Square, 'Sleeping quarters that started as mere blankets evolved into full-fledged campsites with tents, electricity rigged from street lights and supervised children's quarters' (Kamel 2012: 38). And publicly used areas and installations included a self-managed field hospital and many field pharmacies, a stage with a microphone to be used by anybody who wanted to speak in public (ibid.), kitchens for hot meals, an artists' corner (Alexander 2011: 56), and so on. In important turning points of the struggle the square even became a collectively recognized 'epiphanic space', a 'parallel capital' (ibid.: 55). A 'communal atmosphere' (ibid.: 57) transformed the square into 'a living and breathing microcosm of a civil sphere' (ibid.: 56). Cooperation both in peaceful moments and in moments of confrontation with the police and Mubarak's thugs had produced a well-organized micro-city (Abul-Magd 2012: 566) with common spaces created and arranged according to common needs and aspirations.

In the Gezi Park occupation which also took place in Istanbul in 2013, public space was transformed into a network of common spaces (Postvirtual 2013) in which no clear limits were visible between the quasi-private personal spaces of those who camped in the occupied park and the spaces for public use. A mixture of second-hand materials and objects created an anarchic, urban-like diversity which contributed to the blurring of uses. Collective identities were emphatically expressed, however, in the arrangement of different spaces, although such a cultural, religious and political compartmentalization did not erect barriers between different collectivities but, rather, established forms of encounter and collaboration even between groups that used to be very hostile to each other. Kemalists and Muslim activists, gay activists and hooligan fans, feminists and religious men devoted to family values, anarchists and leftists, Kurds and Turks through their coexistence and collaboration found unexpected common ground (Bektaş 2013: 14–15).

In the occupied public spaces of the squares movement, common spaces became live, albeit temporary, urban thresholds. Such spaces neither define people who use them nor are defined by them. They, rather, mediate negotiations between people about the meaning and use of the space they share. Common threshold spaces thus correspond to a process of identity opening which characterized the squares experience. A miniature city emerged in the form of a 'city of thresholds' (Stavrides 2010b) in which encounters and dispersed initiatives built spaces of negotiation and osmosis by collectively shaping a public culture based on solidarity and mutual respect.

Communities in movement in Syntagma and the other 'insurgent squares' were not created through organizational schemes that presupposed a centre of decision making or the absolute predominance of a central space. Spaces as well as decisions were decentralized and recentralized. So was the process of creating those social bonds-in-the-making which gave form to communities in constant remaking.

## Reinventing community

Commoning procedures understood as a dialectics of dispersion–centralization leave room for differentiated initiatives and individual improvisations. What was often described as an antithesis between spontaneous and organized acts and individual and collective behaviours (often by those of the left and the anarchist movement who considered themselves 'guardians' of oppositional politics) was most of the time the result of this dialectics. Not everybody came to Syntagma to participate in the assembly. Many came only to shout and express their anger and disapproval. Some even used laser beam pointers to perform a kind of contemporary version of voodoo magic (in a symbolically aggressive gesture they focused the laser beams as metaphoric pins on the parliament building's 'body'). On Sundays some brought their children along simply to enjoy the air of a public space that was 'different'.

To search desperately for a locatable common identity that could include these people was and still is a serious mistake. Sometimes it made participating activists of the left misunderstand completely the motives, practices and expressions of all those who participated more or less regularly.

An important methodological problem resurfaces in the description and interpretation of dilemmas stemming from the Syntagma and squares experience. Does one have to recognize in these phenomena, acts, utterances and expressions a hidden meaning? Is interpretation a process of revealing the hidden logic of these events as embedded in their form? Or do we have to rethink our categories of understanding social events and forms of collective subjectivation as we face a process which possibly redefines dissident politics and communities in action?

One example: were those holding 'their' national flags (in Syntagma, in Tunis, in Barcelona and elsewhere) simply nationalists? Was this therefore a potentially dangerous community resurfacing in a period of crisis? If this was the case then the possibility of Syntagma or Tahrir becoming an enclosed, exclusive nationalist world would have been a huge threat. But this did not happen. In the squares people used national symbols in various ways which depart from a nationalist expression vocabulary. In Athens one person 'wore' the flag as a kind of shield against those who 'sell the country' (literally, indeed). Other participants used flag waving to appeal to an injured collective dignity: 'rise up', 'wake up', 'we are here', as the Spaniards are in their squares, as should be the Italians, the French, et cetera ....

One more example: one way to judge the long discussions about real or direct democracy (in assemblies but also in smaller commissions or groups) which were predominant throughout the European squares experience was to analyse the words and ideas used. One could say that this or that kind of discourse was depoliticized, utopian, ineffective, and so on. But one could instead try to compare words, acts and forms of expression. 'Real' or direct democracy was performed in various ways in the squares. No matter what observers would say, women's participation in Tahrir Square in Cairo was a de facto practising of common space as democratic space. And people in the squares devised ways to make decisions and to defend themselves against police aggression which de facto established new forms of direct egalitarian democracy. Just after one such incident in Athens – a brutal police charge on 15 June in which the people had been chased, hit and tear-gassed –the square of Syntagma was peacefully reoccupied. Then people formed long human chains that transported, from hand to hand, small bottles of water to cleanse the square of the poisonous tear gas remains. Collective inventiveness (in order to meet the lack of sufficient water) created a democratic egalitarian solidarity. Those human chains, improvised to face a pressing situation, emblematize a community in movement which reinvents 'real' democracy in action. Sometimes those human chains took the form of circle dancing, either to celebrate a victory (as in Tahrir after the announcement of Mubarak's fall) or to exorcise fear (as in Syntagma: people danced in the square as the police were 'bombing' the area with suffocating gas grenades).

Discourses, practices and forms of expression can and should be interpreted as acts in movement. Their correspondences are sometimes strengthened, but one should not deduce a pre-existing pattern that maps their common ground. Discrepancies, ambiguities, and contradictions are necessary ingredients of a potential community in action, a community of different people who remain different but recognize themselves as co-producers of a common space in-the-making.

Who were those people? Can a social identity include all of them? Can a common ideology describe them? Can patterns of action delimit their potential collective practices?

One thing that seems to have united those people, no matter how different their country's context was in regard to the global economic-social crisis, was the collectively felt loss of power's legitimacy. In myriads of inventive expressions, people mocked power, expressed their anger against power's symbols and ridiculed individual leaders. Consensus was shown to be in a deep crisis. Both societies of simulated democratic consensus and those that are outright 'autarchic' seem to have entered today into a deep legitimacy crisis. Fear and state terror are the only means to control rebellious or simply outraged and disappointed people.

### 'We' and space-commoning

A peculiar 'we' surfaced in the squares and an ambiguous 'we' condensed, but could also evaporate, in these uprisings. Is this the 'we' that marks the emergence of new political subjects, the emergence of those who did not count before but who demand to take part (Rancière 2010: 32–3)?

Here are some examples from writings in the squares: 'We are ordinary people. We are like you, people who get up every morning to study, to work or find a job, people who have families and friends. People who work hard every day to provide a better future for those around us' (Barcelona).[9] 'We are unemployed people, working people, pensioners, students, schoolchildren, farmers, immigrants, outraged with all those who plunder our lives and decide without us' (Heraklion, Greece). From Patras, Greece: 'We call on everybody, working people, jobless people, young people, we call on society to fill St George's Square in Patras. Let's reclaim our lives.' Finally, from Syntagma: 'For a long time decisions have been made for us, without us. We are working people, jobless people, pensioners and young who come to Syntagma to fight and struggle for our lives and our future.'[10] 'We are nobody' (Syntagma Square anonymous placard).

This is a 'we' of common people, an inclusive 'we' that demands life and justice. This is a 'we' that does not name, differentiate or erect barriers. Most important perhaps, this is a 'we' that is formed in complete opposition to the 'national' or 'cosmopolitan' 'we' that the governing elites and the mainstream media attempt to impose. 'We are not responsible, you are.' 'We don't have to pay your debts,' 'We don't have to fight your wars' (*pasalo* mobilizations). 'We are not you.' Opposed to a recognizable outside, the outside that contains all those who destroy the future, there is a multifaceted 'we', a kaleidoscopic 'we' full of refractions and open to ever-new arrangements of differences.

Is it the 'we' of the multitude? Perhaps, if the multitude is characterized by heterogeneous multiplicity. But the reasoning behind using multitude to describe the crowd in the current phase of capitalism is based on the idea that the multitude emerges as the productive human force in the period of biopolitical production. The multitude, according to Hardt and Negri, 'is a multiplicity of singularities that produce and are produced in the biopolitical field of the common' (Hardt and Negri 2009: 165).[11]

In the squares and in the 2010–12 uprisings, the multitude does not present itself as a productive force, though, even if we allow the term *production* to contain almost every form of human activity, as Hardt and Negri do. True, capitalism attempts to distil out of every human activity its productive power on which the production of value and profit necessarily are based. People in the squares, however, are creating rather than producing. Hardt and Negri clearly insist that today 'labor cannot be limited to waged labor but must refer to human creative capacities in all their generality' (Hardt and Negri 2005: 105). Virno believes that 'the dividing line between Work and Action [poiesis and praxis] … has now disappeared altogether' (Virno 1996: 190), and that '[t]here is no longer anything which distinguishes labor from the rest of human activities' (Virno 2004: 102). There is, however, a movement that opposes the continuing entrapment of creative action by the logic of capital, which can be recognized in the squares' commoning experiences. Perhaps it is more appropriate to speak of a potential temporary emancipation of 'doing' in the context of an 'anti-politics of dignity' as theorized by Holloway (2010: 245–9). This precarious emancipation of doing can be directly connected to the emergence of 'political subjects' as collective subjects who do not fit into the existing social order. As Rancière insists, politics 'occurs' when the dominant social order ('police') is disrupted and thus redefined. This may happen through acts which can be considered as creative not because they produce something (tangible or not) but because they form the emergent subjectivity of the acting subjects: 'The political process of subjectivation … continually *creates* newcomers' (Rancière 2010: 59, emphasis added).

Forms of sharing and forms of encounter in public are created while being performed. Cannot these forms potentially be manipulated by dominant institutions and appropriated by the market by being turned into mechanisms of exploitation? Yes, but one should not judge only in terms of possibilities. What we can know about the present shows us instead that forms of commoning are directly opposed to the main targets of the dominant politics and to the hegemonic project of governing the crisis as well as the metropolis.

What the theory of multitude can offer us along with other attempts (including Agamben's and Rancière's) to rethink the political, is that politics is necessarily linked to processes of collective subjectivation. What these theories attempt to rethink is not simply about changes in the definition of the political subject

but, rather, about the processes of collective subjects' constitution. Agamben uses 'whatever singularities' to describe the
subjectivities of a coming community,[12] and Rancière speaks of
the 'democratic practice as the inscription of the part of those
who have no part – which does not mean the "excluded" but *anybody whoever*' (Rancière 2010: 60, emphasis added). Hardt and
Negri insist on the 'making' of the multitude as a process which
does not eliminate differences but creates common ground
among singularities.[13]

Political subjectivation, thus, can be considered as a process which moves not towards the construction of collective
identities and unified social bodies but towards new forms of
coordination and interaction based on commoning practices
which create open communities of commoners.

Probably these theorizations can only hint at the possibility of a future different society, developing ideas about forms
of collective action that can indeed prefigure egalitarian and
emancipating social relations. Is this enough today? Probably
not, and so it is urgently necessary to understand contemporary
movements and learn from their actions, discourses and forms
of organization.

One thing we know already is that these events had the power
to overthrow governments even in societies with a long past of
absolutist regimes. And we also know that these events mark the
return of people to collective action. Surely, those people cannot be described as the most disadvantaged or the marginalized
ones, even though marginalized or disadvantaged people *have*
participated in the squares or the uprisings. There is no obvious
common economic or social definition that can include all the
people in a square, though. A crisis of power legitimation unites

them along with a shared feeling of a total absence of justice. Everyone draws experiences from his or her own life that verify this prevailing injustice. In the Tunisia uprising, this feeling was expressed in a revolt against a corrupt family that had ruled the country for many years. In the December 2008 Athens uprising, this feeling was everywhere in young people's actions, because the killing of a young boy by a policeman condensed into a single act all the dominant measures, politics and ideologies that imprison youth in a predetermined future of antagonisms and disappointments. And in the squares, this feeling took the form of a collectively recognized economic injustice (imposed or, rather, accelerated through austerity measures). It seems likely that this feeling was also behind the 2011 UK riots.

All these events indicate societies in movement. And this movement goes beyond any agglomeration of particular demands that are expressed by different social groups in pursuit of their interests. In practices of collective improvisation and collective inventiveness common spaces are created in which people not only express their anger and needs but also develop forms of life-in-common. True, those forms are fragile, precarious, often ephemeral and sometimes contradictory in terms of ideological premises or values. But this collective and de facto production of common spaces reinvents dissident politics and gives new form to practices which overstep the boundaries of dominant social roles. Space-commoning practices are recapturing the 'movement of doing', to use Holloway's vocabulary, and go against the dominant classifications which constrain 'dead doing', 'within an identity, within a role or character mask' (Holloway 2002: 63).

Sharing and solidarity are not introduced as values or ideologically sanctioned imperatives but are experienced in practice, in solving practical problems and in collectively organizing actions of protest. In such a context, there is no difference between the solidarity which supports the organizing of a defence against state aggression and the solidarity expressed in the collection of rubbish in the occupied squares. Solidarity is not simply a force that sustains people in clashes with the state forces. Solidarity has become and becomes a creative force. In Chomsky's words, 'the most exciting aspect of the Occupy movement is the construction of the associations, bonds, linkages and networks that are taking place all over' (Chomsky 2012: 45). In a period of crisis this proves to be not only ethically gratifying, but also effective. People are forced to devise, to invent and to discover ways to survive the crisis. And through the squares experiences, practices of collective invention acquire the form of social experiment.

The most urgent and promising task, which can oppose the dominant urban governance model, is the reinvention of common spaces. The realm of the common emerges in a constant confrontation with state-controlled 'authorized' public space. Commenting on the Occupy movement's strategies, Marina Sitrin, who has studied extensively the *Argentinazo* uprising, suggests: 'Our point of reference should continue to be one another and the creation of directly democratic spaces, but we must also find ways to negotiate issues of institutional power while maintaining our agenda' (Sitrin 2012: 7). This level of negotiations, however, depends heavily on the development of open commoning institutions which are meant to obstruct any kind of accumulation of power in and through a commoning movement. Means should look like ends: one cannot fantasize that the struggle for an egalitarian society of sharing may win by adopting forms of inequality and enclosure. No matter how impossible this may at times seem, we can hope to approach such a society only if our common worlds and our shared practices are shaped in a constant struggle against dominant forms of hierarchical collaboration and controlled distribution.

The creation of common spaces is probably a process full of contradictions and quite difficult to predict, as the experiences of the squares movement show, but it is absolutely necessary for any effort to transcend capitalism and domination. In the common realm, crafted by communities in movement, people find room to compare their dreams and needs, to rediscover solidarity and to fight the destructive individualization imposed by the dominant policies. Behind a multifarious and plural demand for justice and dignity, new roads to collective emancipation are tested and invented. And, as the Zapatistas say, we can create these roads only while walking. But we have to listen, to observe and to feel the walking movement.

Part three

# Envisaged common spaces

# Chapter 7

# Practices of defacement: thresholds to rediscovered commons

## Collective memory challenged?

We usually understand collective memory as connected to specific sites in which a specific community of people recognizes indications of past events worthy of recalling. Collective memory, thus, uses space as a kind of repository of meaning, open to those who know how to navigate their way in an inhabited environment marked by socially recognizable indicators.

However, this understanding of the relationship between space and memory is only partial. First of all it implies a role for the members of a society or social group that defines them as mere readers of signs. Collective memory, accordingly, is considered as a process of establishing and accumulating, through education and commemorative rituals, meaningful references to a collectively recognized past.

If, however, we understand collective memory as always-in-the-making, if we understand collective memory as always contested, being a crucial arena for social antagonism, then we should try to locate the different ways in which space is employed in such a dynamic process. In his study on oblivion, Augé uses a highly indicative spatial model to describe the relationship between memory and oblivion. 'Memories are crafted by oblivion as the outlines of the shore are created by the sea' (Augé 2004: 20).

This spatial metaphor says a lot more than simply describing memory and oblivion as always separated and differentiated. If we consider the space of the beach as an intermediary space in which sea and land always struggle to define a border that changes due to weather as well as to human interventions, then oblivion and memory are a product of an ongoing process rather than two fixed recognizable areas. More than that, if memory and oblivion were to be connected to space, to space as it is socially perceived, then it would have to be space in the process of being defined, moulded and created by social actors in their contesting gestures to capture a meaningful past. We can thus use Augé's metaphor to actually describe the relationship of space and memory. Hidden in this metaphor might be a potentially interesting knowledge: memory, while being contested, not only employs space but also transforms space. If it is always a matter of struggling to define the porous border between memory and oblivion, then space too is created through a kind of heightened awareness about the role that outlines play, outlines defined again and again in practices of appropriating, inhabiting and evaluating space. And it is on the spatial as well as temporal intermediary zones (like the beach in Augé's image) that the temporary meaning of spatial outlines is at stake.

What follows is an attempt to catch the inner logic of a certain memory mechanism that gives form to struggles over the definition of such intermediary zones. Because space becomes socially meaningful in the process of being performed (Massey 2005: 189), memory is not simply deposited in space but actively reconfigures space by directly affecting spatial perception.

This particular mechanism involves acts and gestures that interfere with the meaning of public space (a crucial component of collective memory) by manipulating images that shape its perception. Such gestures meaningfully distort the image of space by partially hiding some of its characteristics or by completely transforming the appearance of buildings, sites or places. As we shall see, however, these gestures and acts do not simply produce changes but also generate memory shocks by – purposely or not – providing the ground for revealing comparisons between what was formerly visible and what became visible as a result of these acts. It will be shown that in certain cases collective memory is performed and represented through practices that reclaim public space-as-commons.

In describing this particular mechanism we can use the term *defacement*. Defacement refers to acts aimed at destroying the 'face', the expressive centre of something's or someone's appearance, by distorting it, by partially hiding the face's characteristics. There is always a kind of latent violence in the defacing gesture. And there is always a kind of confrontation with an appearance, with an image representing an identity.

Space and especially public space is predominantly perceived in the form of stereotyped images which circulate through the dominant culture-shaping media and become actualized through in situ experiences. These images mould the very appearance of a specific building or urban site and establish a strong connection with the corresponding space's identity. These images identify space. Defacing the appearance of public space would thus mean targeting the perceivable characteristics of such space that create its identifiable image. Defacing acts create memory shocks because spaces familiar or recognizable through established images are suddenly rendered strange. Defacement brings forth ruptures in urban memory, since memory is essentially connected with the socially crafted images of public space.

The anthropologist Michael Taussig, who has problematized the ritual meaning of defacement, has this to suggest: 'Defacement works on objects the way jokes work on language, bringing out their inherent magic nowhere more so than when those objects have become routinized and social' (Taussig 1999: 5). This inherent magic is nothing other than a not-realized or, rather more important, repressed meaning of objects and space that suddenly comes into view by the act of defacement. The idea is that defacement does not simply distort or hide but necessarily reveals. Defacement reveals or even demythologizes without being part of a naïve Enlightenment project according to which what is hidden needs simply to be drawn to light. Myth covers reality in a way that directly shapes or transforms it. Demythologizing or the revealing of what is kept as secret, thus, means being able to execute a rather fine and cunning procedure. The secret needs to come to light without losing its transformative power over reality. Taussig often refers to Benjamin's call to reveal the secret by doing justice to it (Taussig 1999: 2, 160, 167, 194). In Benjamin's own words, 'truth is not a process of exposure which destroys the secret, but a revelation which does justice to it' (Benjamin 1990: 31). In such a peculiar demystification process, the secret is illuminated 'by treating the secret's inherent mysteriousness, its being-as-mystery, as an integral component of what makes the revelation possible in the first place' (Surin 2001: 213).

We may reformulate Taussig's argument, emphasizing the role of collective memory: defacement produces a comparison between the past and the present status of a certain 'face' which may create a new interpretation of both past and present.

Defacement can thus generate – without, however, always intending to do so – a kind of 'profane illumination', as Benjamin would call it (Benjamin 1985: 227), which forms a new constellation of present and past. It is not that the past is illuminated by an act that happens in the present: the past becomes visible as a past connected to a present which redeems it, calls it forth and thus assigns meaning to it. This process involves collective memory as the shared ability to connect and compare rather than store and retrieve. It is not simply a matter of recalling what is being temporarily hidden from view but also a way of bringing forth layers of repressed (actively forgotten) collective experiences and activating knowledge connected with the defaced places.

The logic of the defacement mechanism is a result of the essentially contested character of both collective memory and public space. As Hénaff and Strong insist: 'public space ... is always contestable' (Hénaff and Strong 2001: 4). The defacement mechanism is influenced by specific relations of power which take shape in space and time. Halbwachs, for example, in an effort to trace the history of the early Christian community's collective memory, draws attention to the acts of 'enemies of emergent Christianity' who 'tried to deface these places [imbued with the community's memories] and to destroy signs that could help to recognize them' (Halbwachs 1992: 202). Who is defacing what and under which circumstances is crucial. Comparing differing performances of defacement we can perhaps discover possibilities of employing defacement in order to actively pursue dissident uses of urban collective memory or even acts of restaging the scene of the common (to recall Rancière). In this context, it is important to understand memory as an inventive ability to compare times and places.

Collective memory can become an important target as well as a means of commoning. The most obvious aspect of this relation is the power that collective memory has to give form and content to events in the past which the members of a community recognize as their common past. From this, however, it becomes clear that the selective character of shared memory, as already illustrated in Augé's image, has a strong performative result. What the members of a group recognize as their common past crucially contributes to their identity as a group. Collective memory, then, shapes the 'distribution of the sensible' (in Rancière's terminology) and gives form to the common world which characterizes a community.

As we will see, defacement creates sudden shocks in collective memory by bringing forth inherent contradictions hidden in the foundations of the common world. Defacement may possibly introduce explosive moments of dissident awareness into the common world and thus destabilize common beliefs about the past. However, because defacement is a public gesture, a gesture made in public and directed towards dominant images which support the certainties of established common worlds, it necessarily enters the field of struggles over representations (to recall Bourdieu's suggestions). Defacement, thus, may evoke interpretative practices that give ground to new shared knowledges. Demythologizing and revealing acts through defacement produces sudden shocks both to the commoning of memory and to the commoning through memory, shocks that may force collective memory to reinvent itself, to transform, to expand and to become open to contestation. Through defacement, public spaces, and especially officially sanctioned monuments, lose their defining stability and sometimes their attachment to a dominant authority's control.

Defacement may temporarily convert public space to common space if it triggers forms of collective reinterpretation. The very violence of its clash with dominant images may even give to defacement the power to challenge the self-sufficiency and 'obviousness' of common worlds, no matter how democratically they were expressed in monuments meant to secure and reproduce a stable image of important past events. Defacement may be a dissident 'art' but it may also be one among the 'arts' of envisioning commoning (in and through representations) as an always-open process of creating open communities of equals.

## Official acts of defacement

In 1995, a very important turning point in the recent history of Germany, an official act of defacement took place in Berlin. Commemorating the fifth anniversary of Germany's 'national unification', a gesture of monumental proportions was to create a public debate on the role of collective memory and public art (Hanssen 1998). Christo, the well-known artist, extended his almost obsessive art of wrapping famous buildings or sites all over the world to include Berlin's Reichstag building. Preceding the building's renovation in the following years, this act of wrapping was contested as essentially involving a kind of gesturing towards the Reichstag's role in Germany's history. And indeed this role is full of important parts as the Weimar Republic was proclaimed there in 1918 and as the site is connected with the Nazi seizure of power emblematically condensed in the infamous Reichstag fire.

The wrapping of the Reichstag can be considered as an act of defacement. The building was effectively hidden from view without, however, totally disappearing. The contour of the building was there to perceive. What remained then was a distorted image, an image that violently reduced the building to an immense and strange object. Some could and did say that this gesture was an offence to shared memories: even temporarily hiding the building appears as some kind of memory erasure. As if a memory site can be reduced to a tabula rasa on which to write anew. Was it a modernist gesture par excellence? Perhaps, but if we are to profit from Huyssen's interpretation, a very subtle and ambiguous modernist gesture indeed. According to his view, Christo created 'a monumentality that can do without permanence and without destruction ... informed by the modernist spirit of a fleeting and transitory epiphany' (Huyssen 2003: 46). Thus, the transitoriness of the event might have hinted towards the 'tenuous relationship between remembering and forgetting' (ibid.: 36)

What this act of defacement initiates is probably a reflective attitude towards the past. While the creation of historic monuments is an essentially selective act (Boyer 1994: 144) which defines what deserves to be remembered and what is to be left to oblivion, Christo's wrapping creates some kind of contradictory monumentality. The fact that the wrapping was temporary could have made people reconsider the absent familiar image that was temporarily out of view. It could have made them see what was no longer there by generating a kind of memory shock: memory becomes activated by focusing on a building that was covered by stereotypical images cleansed from possible traumatic collective reminiscences. 'Christo's veiling did function as a strategy to make visible, to unveil, to reveal what was hidden when it was visible' (ibid.: 36).

The wrapping event had shaken a collectively repressed image of the Reichstag. The building was there to see but only as a ceremonial place or museum. How could it be connected to those traumatic events of German history that still demand publicly shared explanations? And who is going to produce those explanations? And how can collective memory accommodate the struggle between collective guilt and collective amnesia?

The unique presence of a building-monument binds it to a role that traps memory. It somehow becomes a recognizable locus around which official history weaves threads that immobilize it to a mythical once-and-for-all appraisal of a certain past. Monuments do not even express this appraisal as interpretation. They rather emphatically convert it through their presence to a self-proven truth. What corroborates this power of monuments to 'naturalize' the past is their unchangeable presence in the visual horizon of those who inhabit the city.

Monuments acquire a certain aura, the aura which characterizes a human work (or a work of nature when the human gaze captures it) when considered unique and unrepeatable. 'The aura is appearance of a distance, however close the thing that calls it forth' (Benjamin 1999: 447).

The wrapped Reichstag surely lost its aura stemming from its unique presence in the city as a work of distinguished public architecture. The very gesture of wrapping and packaging reduces objects to common recognizable and repeatable shapes. However, although Christo's wrapping reduced or even obliterated the building's recognizable unique characteristics, it was publicized as a gesture of art. Wrapping was to be interpreted as a meaningful gesture. Meaningful gestures of such monumental and site-specific proportions inevitably create singular objects. So, the created new object, the packaged Reichstag, emerged in the visual horizon of Berliners as a unique work with its own aura, a 'transitory aura', as L. Koepnick (2002: 111–12) has suggested. This peculiar aura made the presence of the building a challenge to memory and interpretation. '[T]he project's aura called forth competing images of past and present, bringing into focus the constructedness of history, truth, and identity' (ibid.: 112).

Defacement refocused collective memory. Defacement reactivated unresolved questions about the meaning of the recent past: who has inherited this past's promises and guilt, and how? What did the building represent anyhow? And for whom? The act of partially hiding the monument, distorting its 'face' as a recognizable image which remained silent about many of the past conflicts and dilemmas, suddenly created an interpretative stake. Public discourse about the symbolism and public value of the monument erupted: who has the right to shape its current image? The memory shock created may have triggered for some a renewed awareness that the past is not over, that the past is a contested terrain on which comparisons with the present bring forth new meanings and affective approaches. Probably most of the people who had to confront such a strange, albeit temporary, transformation of their customary visual urban landscape became confronted with what Benjamin described as the 'unconscious optics' (Benjamin 1992: 230). What is seen but repressed from view can suddenly emerge as visible in the time of its defacement. Isn't this process becoming a crucial factor in the perception of space in cities where different layers of history struggle to define the present?

It is not clear which official strategy was supporting Christo's art or even profiting from the Reichstag wrapping. Aside from its tourist attraction advantages, this kind of officially encouraged defacement necessarily creates ambiguous results in collective memory. However, what makes it really difficult for this act to catalyse an emerging awareness about the past as a collectively experienced process is its emphatic orchestration as a publicly sponsored, therefore approved by the state authority, artistic practice. Memory shocks were probably diverted or absorbed by the dominant rhetoric of avant-garde art which shifted attention from history to the very whimsical, surrealistic elements of a strange (therefore considered 'interesting') artistic gesture.

Can the collective memory shocks initiated by Christo's gesture create potential experiences of memory-commoning? Could the wrapped Reichstag become a *site* of memory-commoning? The very fact that this gesture had shaken established habits of collective interpretation was not enough, probably, to completely change the character of such a public space. The transitory aura of the artistically hidden monument did not destroy the site's monumental character. It certainly indicated a crisis in interpretation, but the dominant practices of sightseeing and artistic contemplation effectively managed to preserve a controlled and explicitly manipulated publicness. Public art could have introduced elements of commoning while defacing a monument so long as those gestures were part of a shared demand for reconsideration of the past. Even if Christo's gesture initiated a crisis in public space, this crisis was already tamed in advance. It was more like a staged crisis which possibly absorbed potential demands for reconfiguring public space (its monumental aspects included) during a period in which rethinking about the past was crucial for shaping modern Germany's identity. Christo's Reichstag became a rather cunning collective memory trap: no indications for a different interpretation of the past were offered and no collective acts of reclaiming the past were expressed.

After all, the ephemeral character of wrapping, sanctioned by the state authorities, guaranteed the future return of the building to its monumental presence at the centre of the city. Defacement could have been only a trick, an imitation of crisis to avoid crisis.

A second example, less well known but equally indicative, comes from Athens. During the 2004 Olympics, various government initiatives were taken in order to 'upgrade the aesthetics of Athens' (as the relevant law N2947/2001 explicitly states). Interestingly, in a municipal programme for façade remodelling, Athens was presented as 'an old lady in need of make-up'. In this context, some buildings had to be hidden from view. In front of a social housing building facing a major avenue (characterized as 'Olympic route') a large photo placard was erected. Depicting a glorious view of Athens from one of the surrounding hills, this image explicitly presented the city as a historical landscape full of recognizable ancient monuments. Behind this image however, a very important part of the city's history was carefully hidden.

The defaced building belongs to a housing complex known as Alexandras Prosfygika (the same complex analysed in Chapter 3). Constructed during the mid 1930s this complex was part of a large programme of slum clearance that was meant to house refugees from Asia Minor. As was already mentioned, these people had to come to Greece in 1922 after a population exchange that was the result of a disastrous expedition of the Greek Army into Asia Minor. The buildings were therefore associated with a collective trauma. And they represent even today a past full of poverty and struggles connected with the difficult incorporation of refugees into Greek society.

In the derelict façade of the Alexandras Prosfygika buildings, full of 'embarrassing' traces, the past seems to have become reduced to natural history: because the history of Alexandras Prosfygika was pushed to the realm of collective oblivion, decay is easily misinterpreted as a natural phenomenon rather than as a social condition and process. There are people, however, who have struggled for the preservation and renovation of these buildings as potentially inhabitable sites of collective memory.

What the glorious image defacing the buildings did was to connect an almost forgotten public debate on the complex's historic value with a renewed awareness of its existence. Even though covering the building had a completely different intent, curiously Alexandras Prosfygika seems to have become more prominent in the act of being disguised, as if the hiding gesture emphasized the presence of the buildings. Due to such an unexpected intrusion into the realm of collective oblivion, forgotten or repressed questions may arise anew. Why are these buildings there? What has caused this decay? Who still lives there? And what about the bullet marks on the walls (traces of a decisive battle fought there in 1944 at the beginning of the 1944–7 civil war)?

As in Christo's wrapping, an official act of defacing reveals by hiding. In the case of the Alexandras Prosfygika 'screening', defacement actually reveals in spite of its aim to hide and erase, albeit also temporarily. Defacing may produce ambiguous ruptures in memory through the shock in perception created by interventions in familiar and historically 'neutralized' images that colonize everyday urban experiences. Even though in this case an obvious strategy of redirecting urban memory was planned, a repressed past faintly emerged behind the distorted image. Memory generates comparisons and is generated by them. As if to show this power of revealing comparisons, one of the inhabitant-activists secretly tore the photo placard, partially revealing to the passer-by what was hidden. Defacing the official defacement is in this case an act of corroborating and multiplying defacement's power to agitate collective memory.

As an official gesture, the defacement of Alexandras Prosfygika was more straightforwardly directed against a part of collective memory that was meant to be kept dormant if not to vanish altogether. The gesture, however, was too provocative, too expressive in terms of its objective to hide something unwanted. This is why it could more easily result in attracting attention to what was hidden. Nevertheless, the visual shock alone could not have the power to prefigure a site of memory-commoning. Perhaps the activist's gesture was a dissident act that could potentially bring to the fore the space-commoning life hidden behind the defaced Alexandras Prosfygika façade. For this to be perceived by passers-by, however, one has to presuppose that they have some kind of knowledge or at least questions about the buildings present.

**Alternative or dissident defacement and common space**
Defacement can create through a shock in perception a shock in interpretation. Defacement can participate in the ongoing – no matter how latent – struggle for the always-contestable definition of the 'coastline', areas between memory-land and oblivion-sea (or is it memory-sea and oblivion-land?). Defacement generates experiences and thoughts comparing past and present.

Can we perhaps discover performances of defacement that may contribute to struggles against official manipulations of collective memory? Can people learn from the ways in which power not only effaces traces of an unwanted past but also defaces the past in order to control its social meaning? Officially sanctioned monument-defacing gestures may attempt to redirect collective memory by manipulating the ambiguous dialectics of hiding–revealing (as in the case of the Reichstag wrapping), or it may attempt to control collective memory, carelessly ignoring the revelatory results of any gesture of hiding (as in the case of the Alexandras Prosfygika photo placard). Can defacement performances employ defacement dialectics not simply to attack established meanings and uses of public space but also to invent new ephemeral appropriations of space made possible as collectively repressed memories emerge? And do these acts of collective appropriation produce potential prefigurations of common spaces?

We may broadly distinguish between three different forms such an alternative use of defacement may take: defacing spatial form, defacing spatial texture and defacing spatial traces.

### Defacing spatial form

Defacement can be directed against the defining shape of public space. If we consider that public space is perceived as a meaningful social artefact through stereotyped images that fix and reproduce its meaning, then defacement practices directed against the recognizable material support of these images can produce collective memory shocks. This is why demonstrations and relevant transgressive practices not only produce political events but may also deface dominant street images. Demonstrations may use the asphalt as a blackboard on which to write their demands. The black functional carpet of vehicle traffic becomes suddenly an area of collective expression. So do the pavements when demonstrators rest on them.

Demonstrations can even reconfigure the street outlines as did street blockings by members of the *piqueteros* movement

in Argentina. There, jobless people used to protest by violently interrupting traffic in major avenues, paralysing the city
until they were violently evacuated. The visual, symbolic and
functional shock they produced forced society to notice them
and authorities to respond. With their ephemeral barricades,
*piqueteros* defaced the urban normality epitomized in everyday vehicle traffic. Intentionally or not, they used streets as
short-lived common spaces and they projected through them
images of space-commoning that would challenge the dominant
representations of public space. As one of them explained, 'it's a
liberated zone [the *piquete*], the only place where the cops won't
treat you like trash. There the cop says to you "pardon me, we
come to negotiate". The same policeman would beat you to death
if he saw you alone in the street' (Motta 2009: 94).

The Reclaim the Streets movement is a characteristic example of defacing the street in order to produce a new awareness of
what the street could be and used to be. This movement organized public collective acts through which it tried to reappropriate
streets as ad hoc common spaces. Through self-organized parties which abruptly invaded vehicle streets in city centres, the
image of traffic was defaced: in some cases a deliberate mild car
crash was used to start the blocking of the street. Astonished
passers-by would discover that what they routinely interpret
as a temporary misfortune in the traffic order (a car accident)
could be theatrically used as a means to deface traffic, to create
interpretative shocks and reveal hidden or forgotten possibilities
for the collective uses of the streets. As if evoking the May 1968
symbolic motto 'beneath the pavement lies a beach', which is already a defacement gesture expressed in words, the Reclaim the
Streets movement showed that underneath the predominantly

car-traffic street lies the public square. An emerging public square crafted by collective acts of defacement is a kind of common space experienced and envisaged at the same time. 'Cars cannot dance' (Ferrell 2002: 136) was one of the movement's mottoes which gained currency in Britain in 1995 and spread to many metropolises throughout the world. Participants used to transform the occupied street area by means of their carnivalesque performances into a temporary public stage (Notes from Nowhere 2003: 51–61). Memories of a different culture were thus evoked which included the communal feast and its generalized metastatic effervescence.

In all these cases, temporarily hiding from view the recognizable image of the street as a linear channel for distributing traffic creates the possibility of remembering the street as a multifarious common space. In cities where those repressed collective memories may resurface, actively defacing the street images can indeed reveal something important by hiding. Equally revealing defacement gestures can be performed in symbolic acts such as guerrilla gardening (emblematized in the famous People's Park in Berkeley created during the late 1960s and violently attacked by the police) or in the creation of community vegetable gardens in public areas destined for gentrification, as was the case of El Forat de la Vergonya in Barcelona, which met harsh repression too during the 2000s.

## Defacing spatial texture

Defacement can be directed against the texture, the materiality, of public space as it is perceived and made meaningful by people who inhabit it. Skateboarding is one familiar example of how a group of people can temporarily transform public space by defacing the material core that supports its habitual uses and perceptions. If we follow Borden's understanding of skateboarding as a 'performative critique of architecture' (Borden 2001), the city is for skateboarders reduced to a degree zero of meaning, only to re-emerge as the locus of a new awareness of meaningful differences. Among the important differences are those between soft and hard surface materials or between high and low objects – obstacles (benches, stairs, pavements, fences, etc.).

As the skateboarder defaces the street (and in many countries this is described as a criminal act) he or she makes repressed memories, which are connected with the urban texture, erupt or indeed create new possible experiences. 'These are my streets. I know every crack of every sidewalk there is down there' (quoted in Borden 2001: 191).

The practice of skateboarding involves groups of people collectively organizing their defacing presence in the city. A kind of commoning-through-defacement unfolds in such peculiar reinterpretations and reappropriations of the streets. The area outside the Museum of Modern Art in Barcelona is a good example of such a process. Young people have transformed the area into a collectively used common space in which they exhibit their outstanding skills. The police have attempted many times to regain control of the place and to reconvert it into the public square initially designed for the museum's visitors.

Skateboarding was the means to establish a fleeting common space and to show how space-commoning may transform public space. Skateboarding-designed tracks and parks attempt to contain and control the defacement potential of this performative critique of the city. In these publicly used spaces, groups of skateboarders are left to enjoy their art without producing infectious images of space-commoning.

Children playing where they should not – as when climbing on monuments or statues – often bring forth a materiality of public space which is completely hidden from view, as well as perfomatively evaluating the user-friendliness of the materials used in its making. Defacing official memory sites, children re-activate them as surfaces, obstacles and shelters in a redeemed public space.

## Defacing spatial traces

Finally, defacement can be directed against a crucial character-istic of public space: its power to absorb and retain traces. Many urban gentrification programmes include acts of erasing traces of the gentrified area's past, as we have seen. A very obvious strategy of remaking the meaning and use of existing spaces is to control and select their connections with the past, especially those connections based on material remnants.

What graffiti does, however, is not to efface or carefully hide traces but, rather, it juxtaposes traces, adds traces, 'deflects' traces and critically manipulates traces, as well as simply marking by traces an ephemeral presence. In all those cases, graffiti defaces buildings, sites or objects. Those who practise this ephemeral, fugitive art are always on the move, writing their own city on top of the existing one. To some, their acts can sometimes appear blasphemous or offensive. Sennett, interpreting the fear of graf-fiti, imagines the graffiti maker's battle cry: 'We exist and we are everywhere … we write all over you' (Sennett 1993: 207).

These defacement gestures, however, do not demand a total eclipse of the object's or the building's former image. Rather, graffiti makers want a comparison between what used to be there (usu-ally derelict, unused, out of sight) and what temporarily is made present. The memory shocks they produce can lead to revealing comparisons between a past violently erased and a controlled present as, for example, in the ironic graffiti image made on the Israel Wall in Palestine by Banksy, who bitterly staged a freedom opening on its grey, massive, ruthlessly dominant side (Banksy 2005). Milder memory shocks may be caused by ephemeral ruptures in everyday life's homogeneous settings made by graffiti images that capture the city dweller's gaze through the windows of the underground train or bus. Graffiti climb on walls, penetrate metro stations, travel on transport cars and train wagons or deface large advertisement images. In every case, the graffito redirects attention to the traces left on the skin of the city by small and great acts in a literal 'iconoclash' (Latour and Weibel 2002).

By being exposed to harsh weather and to alterations and distortions caused by those who try either to erase it or 'write' on it, graffiti become themselves targets of defacement acts (Schacter 2008: 47–8). The urban palimpsest created in such acts hides and reveals different layers of meaning inscribed on the city's body. The very act of official erasure (in the name of the law or protection from 'aesthetic pollution'), exposes itself as a violent act of war against dissident images through its often limited success in effacing the graffiti traces. What remains exposes the internal dynamics of defacement: defaced (rather than completely effaced) images which are themselves products of defacing acts take part in the creation of an ever-changing visual landscape in which hiding and revealing always clash and coexist. 'Defacement tampers with the borders between signifier, signified, and referent' (Nandrea 1999: 112).

Elusive and fugitive as it is, graffiti art often attempts to reappropriate public space as a crucial social area through which messages and shared values are transmitted. Graffiti art in such cases gestures towards a possible commoning-through-representations that criticizes, ironically deconstructs or, almost sacrilegiously, attacks dominant images of the city. Iconic or written messages are the means through which graffiti reclaim the city. There is of course a considerable difference between the narcissistic tags which emphatically declare 'I was there' and the collective works of 'crews' which often transmit messages at war with the dominant representations of the city.

We can perhaps trace further possible routes for alternative defacement practices in acts that consciously combine art and activism. In these performances, defacement acquires the status of a paradigmatic gesture that explicitly aims at redefining new possible urban experiences in search of 'liberated' and 'liberating' public spaces: in search, that is, of reinvented common spaces. Defacement can give form to gestures of symbolic appropriation as well as to gestures of inventive inhabiting. It is one of the many ways that cities become 'stages for the ephemeral reconfiguration of meaning on the streets' (Robinson 2006: 84).

Traverso's bicycle might be one example of such an inventive use of defacement. Taking his stencil of a full-scale bicycle to many countries of the world, Traverso, an Argentinian artist and activist, paints the same bicycle image on the walls of buildings, on street corners or inside community centres. His almost haunted 'bicycle' stands there as if temporarily left by someone. This bicycle image was initially crafted to remind us of all those people who disappeared during Videla's dictatorship. Tortured and executed by Videla's junta, the disappeared people left no traces, virtually suspended between death and life. This was how one of Traverso's friends disappeared in those days, leaving behind his deserted bicycle on a street corner.

Traverso made the image of the bicycle a kind of 'invented trace' of his disappeared friend. Reproducing it on the surface of different buildings, the artist subtly introduces this invented trace in places where other traces dominate. This is what he did by painting his bicycle on the wall of one of the buildings of the Alexandras Prosfygika housing complex. Such a gesture becomes part of the defacing palimpsests of urban graffiti. Traverso, however, does something more than that. He uses this stencil image to reactivate layers of public memory dormant in key places of collective memory all over the world. 'Traverso insists that his *bicis* are counter-monuments,' says Katherine Hite and she quotes him: 'Monuments meant to remember people just end up killing them all over again' (Hite 2012: 90).

Many artist groups were encouraged to use this almost totemic stencil image to mark areas in which horrible collective reminiscences were either suppressed or still wait for justice and redemption (ibid.: 93). As in the image painted on the Alexandras Prosfygika, Traverso's bicycle potentially works as a catalyst for collective memory: a strange image hides and reveals at the same time, creating small memory shocks. We expect to see a bicycle leaning against a wall somewhere in the chosen places, but since it is obviously a painted bicycle, why did someone paint it there? We know that a person can leave his or her bicycle somewhere, but nobody seems to be returning for *this* haunted bicycle.

Traverso says about his bicycles: '[The *bicis* were] physically at the limits of the corporeal and the intangible, they were opening the sense of different stories and interrogations for everyone who saw them' (ibid.: 106). Out of the ambiguity created by a graffiti-like image that defaces and draws attention at

the same time to what it defaces, Traverso creates the potentiality of a political gesture. Defacement thus becomes a way of
calling forth common space as a contestable social artefact
moulded by memory. Traverso spreads a message meant to
encourage memory-commoning and to ignite practices of
space-commoning through the reintroduction of repressed or
violently erased common memories into the public realm. There
is no guarantee for such an interpretation and no way to ensure
that Traverso's bicycle will activate and recreate traces of alternative memory. We can imagine, however, that such gestures
can possibly teach us ways in which we learn how to appropriate
defacement's dialectics. And if defacement reveals by hiding and
directs our attention to what it veils, defacement can be used to
bring to view repressed dreams and forgotten alternatives.

There is an interesting relation of inverse symmetry between
Traverso's bicycles and Christo's Reichstag. Through his gesture
Christo has made prominent a crisis in the appreciation of contemporary images: it is the crisis of aura which is attributed to
unique singular works. Christo's work has an ambiguous kind
of aura, an aura which generates interpretive ambivalences and
inconsistencies. It is because of this that the wrapped Reichstag
may assault, irritate or activate, or even inspire collective memory when it unexpectedly replaces the monumental building's
established aura with a new aura that puts the old one's reception
into crisis.

For his part, Traverso through his invented traces puts into
crisis the trace value which can be attributed to an image. He
mobilizes the power traces have in order to prove that certain
events took place and to testify about the existence of certain
people at certain times in order to rescue from oblivion events

and people whose traces were effaced by the military junta. Disappeared people return to collective memory through the shock that defacement creates: absent signs are reinvented through Traverso's use of defacement's peculiar dialectics. Inserting his graffiti in the urban palimpsest, he revealingly challenges dominant defacement acts. His invented staged traces challenge the elimination of traces and thus attempt to show that effacement will always be partial and at the mercy of defacement potentialities so long as there are people willing to use those potentialities in their struggles against imposed collective amnesia. Walter Benjamin has suggested that the trace is on the aura's antipode: 'The trace is appearance of a nearness, however far removed the thing that left it behind may be' (Benjamin 1999: 447). In Christo's gesture, defacement establishes an aura in crisis, and therefore puts into crisis the very tactics of creating a distance between the object and the viewer. This kind of ambiguity potentially releases the object from its monumentality without making it familiar, though. Glimpses of space-commoning may emerge in spectral form as viewers experience a clash between a renewed monumentality that fails to impose itself and an equally failed familiarity with a mundane object (a package). Common space may be envisaged in this context as the space of possible collective demythologizing appropriation (in between a renewed public mythology and the trivial private experience of consumer habits).

In Traverso's gesture, the invented nearness of an invented trace is perhaps the necessary means to defy power's undisputed right to select traces and arrange them in dominant narratives about or dominant images of the past. His haunted bicycles emblematically establish the possibility of common space. This kind of space may be created and used in practices that introduce to existing public spaces elements of a past that carry memories of collective struggles.

Sharing Benjamin's view that the past is full of not-realized opportunities and possibilities (Benjamin 1992: 247), we can employ defacement to search in the past for alternative possible futures. Maybe this is the deeper motive of the Zapatistas in the faraway cities and villages of south Mexico: they too seek to transform public space to common space by reactivating memories which redeem the egalitarian aspect of indigenous traditions. In an act of collective self-defacement, Zapatistas hide their faces using ski masks (Taussig 1999: 261). 'We have hidden our faces so that you can see us,' they say. Defacement becomes an act of demanding to be seen – an act of demanding to be recognized as equal, as having rights, needs and dreams. Isn't this after all an alternative politics of memory, a kind of potential emancipation and proliferation of shared memories in search of a different future?

Chapter 8

# Thought-images and representations of the city as commons

Common space emerges as an always-precarious spatial condition which people shape through commoning. Common space, thus, may be envisaged and projected through acts of collective representation and described through images and words shared by those who actually practise it.

Pierre Bourdieu has convincingly referred to the 'struggle over representations, in the sense of mental images' (Bourdieu 1991: 221) in his research into the ways in which people construct and reproduce space-bound identities (be it national, regional or city-connected identities). Representations, then, are not simply projections or interpretations of existing realities but are directly connected to struggles that mould reality both in terms of material interventions and in terms of battles over the naming and meaning of inhabited spaces. It is not that people only learn to recognize the social meaning of the places they are 'assigned to' by the society they belong to. People also learn to inhabit through shared forms of representation and imagination non-existent spaces, not-yet-existing spaces, possible spaces. Struggles indicate that there is an important stake in representations: representations that prevail can mould habits, behaviours and acts in the process of contributing to the reproduction of specific forms of domination.

As Maurice Godelier explicitly formulates it, 'mental realities ... appear not as the effects of social relations in thought, but as one of the internal components of these relations and as a necessary condition of their formation (as well as of their reproduction)' (Godelier 2011: 251). Representations, thus, become important in establishing shared mental realities (such as, for example, those which describe human relations by giving different forms of meaning to descent) which contribute to the shaping of social relations.

Representations of common space, representations of shared space (as common property of a group, as available common resource, as emblematic of a shared collective identity, and so on), are forms of making common space 'happen'. Before it can even be recognized as such, common space becomes a stake in struggles over representation. Common spaces can be misrecognized, corrupted or even usurped in and through these struggles. It is important, then, to investigate the ways in which people may possibly develop the tools to recognize common spaces, to invent them and to dream of them. These spaces are not simply the result of actions that produce them or acts of interpretation that name them. Common spaces can be experienced as such because they emerge in the process of being collectively used, defined, conceived and communicated.

Do people engage in struggles over representations by fighting to support certain images against images supported by others? Is common space depicted as a different set of images opposed to the dominant ones that present shared space according to prevailing views? Actually, common space, like any form of counter-dominant sets of common life practices, could be absorbed in the organized spectacle which according to Debord's

(1995) well-known formulation reduces human realities to relations between stereotyped images, if it were to become one more repertory of images. All of us know, for example, how effectively the commoning tradition of certain societies is represented in exotic tourist packages that depict common spaces as fossils of a bygone epoch of innocence.

Common space enters the field of the struggle over representations with precarious promises for winning the imagination of those who dream of a more just society if common space is not simply depicted through (idealized or not) images but through thought-images. But thinking-through-images is not a whimsical hybrid of ideas and images found only in abstract contemplations on the 'essence' of thought. It has been explored through the writings of thinkers who have added something really important to the history-long debates on the connection of words to images, namely a focus on the mundane, unnoticed aspects of social life. Following such a path, this chapter will explore the possibility of developing out of a hybrid concept, the concept of thought-image, an efficient weapon for the struggle over the meaning of common space.

The term was used to describe a kind of concise literary text written by theorists linked to the so-called Frankfurt school, Benjamin, Kracauer and Bloch. As Richter (2007: 7) describes it, 'The *Denkbild* (thought-image) … is a brief aphoristic prose text … that both illuminates and explodes the conventional distinctions among literature, philosophy, journalistic intervention and cultural critique.' This gives to these texts a 'fragmentary, explosive, and decentering force' (ibid.: 8).

Adorno's comment on Benjamin's *One-Way Street* may be considered as a concise description of the power of the *Denkbilder*:

'They do not want to stop conceptual thought so much as to shock through their enigmatic form and thereby get thought moving' (Adorno in Richter 2007: 12).

A *Denkbild* text becomes enigmatic and thus thought-provoking not because the images it uses are the product of an ingenious use of figurative language. Adorno compares these images to 'scribbled picture puzzles' (ibid.) and Richter evokes the peculiarity of hieroglyphics to explain the reading of the world that these texts suggest (Richter 2007: 19). Both writers try to capture the inventive construction of images through words which do not aim at illustrating thoughts or suggesting interpretations through comparisons (as often metaphors do). Those written images seem to suggest a different level of meaning in which thoughts cannot be separated from the images that attempt to represent them. Thoughts are not only expressed but are actually developed through such images.

In his own idiosyncratic writing and thinking, which is sometimes misunderstood as only poetic, Benjamin explored the potentiality of *Denkbilder* to activate a different kind of critical thinking: thinking in and through revelatory images. According to Weigel (1996: 53), Benjamin's 'thinking-in-images constitutes his specific and characteristic way of theorizing, of philosophizing and of writing'. Thus, the specificity of Benjamin's theory lies in this form of thinking which examines the ways in which 'the idea of reality is formed and the images of history are handed down'. So, 'images are not the object, but rather the matrix and medium of his theoretical work' (ibid.: x).

Benjamin's critical theoretical project was directed against the dominant mythology of capitalist modernity which he understood to have been developed through the phantasmagoria

of progress. Images were the most crucial element of this phantasmagoria and it was through images that this mythology
managed to infest people's imagination and thought (Benjamin
1983; 1999: 7–9). However, to reveal the mythological content
of prevailing images was not naïvely considered by Benjamin
to be the task of an explaining and elucidating reason. A more
delicate strategy was needed, and this strategy was first formulated in his work through the concept (and writing practice)
of thought-images. One has to use against myth myth's own
weapons in order to subvert or deactivate its power. And this
means that one has to treat images differently. What he described
as 'allegory', considered as the 'antidote to myth' (Benjamin
1980: I, 677; 1999: 268), is an inventive interpretative practice
of thinking through images that collects instances of mundane
or even trivial facets of modern life and uses them to trigger
a reflexive redemption of modernity's emancipating promises.
Such instances are taken to be emblematic representations of
crucial antinomies, important contradictions and revealing
ambiguities of urban modernity.

   Critical thought, then, would have to move in and around images to decipher and construct at the same time their enigmatic
meaning. Demythologizing strategies would simply attack those
images or attempt to analyse a supposedly fixed mythological
content. In Benjamin's critical project, however, such images neither pre-exist the thought that examines them nor can they be
taken to consist of mythological barriers to a hidden truth. These
images can become explosively revealing if critical thought
penetrates them without destroying them and learns from their
power to hide and reveal at the same time. This is why this strategy creates forms of sudden and precarious illumination. Images

intervene in thoughts, and images may divert as well as clarify the thought that develops in and through them.

This kind of thinking, often focused on allegedly insignificant facets of quotidian city life, was described as 'micrological' (Richter 2007: 5). Kracauer was equally considered to be involved in a reflexive 'phenomenology of the surface' and a 'revaluation of quotidian superficiality' (Levin 1995: 20). Both writers seem to try to unearth in the less heroic images of urban modern phantasmagoria the very logic of a society they criticize and the means to think beyond it. Their critical strategies offer us a way to explore the double role of mental images in social life: they may condense essential messages of dominant ideologies but they may also become vehicles of thoughts which defy, resist or overturn such ideologies.

Thinking-in-images can be something more than an idiosyncratic philosophical strategy. It can, rather, describe a more general attitude which might acquire an anthropological horizon, as it characterizes the way people treat their experiences and perceptions during their everyday praxis. People think through the things they perceive by using images of the world around them as means to generalize, to compare and even to form abstract concepts (Stavrides 2014b).

Thinking-in-images, as the *Denkbild* thinkers revealingly show to us, can be fixed on seemingly trivial images that do not possess the glorious status of emblematic icons. Those images can indeed be selected by everyday thinkers in search of means to understand their obligations or their aspirations. In this, those images can be almost 'irreducibly singular', to use a characterization Richter employs for written *Denkbilder* (Richter 2007: 9). But this singularity, this inventively crafted uniqueness, is just the vehicle of a process of comparability: people share thought-images when they attempt to communicate and collaborate, by using what they gather through their experiences. Experiences as well as employed images can be unique, but thinking through images gives to individual experiences a social meaning, by aligning them to a common horizon. In Rancière's terminology, this horizon is hegemonically created as the 'distribution of the sensible' (Rancière 2010: 36).

Sharing thought-images may be the nearest possible practice to thinking-in-common, if by this we don't, of course mean thinking in the same way or thinking about the same things, but thinking through shared experiences and shared questions. Thought-images are a powerful means to establish a translatability of thoughts and experiences between people who share (or develop) common worlds. If, as was already claimed in Chapter 2, commoning contributes to the creation and reproduction of a community's common world, thought-commoning (or thinking in common) is a specific form of crafting this common world.

City space, or inhabited space in general, is perhaps the richest source of images to which city-dwellers may refer and which people may construct as well as recognize in common. In inhabiting practices, people learn to perceive spatial relations and arrangements as indicative of social relations. Spatial relations may be condensed and emblematized in images which represent those social relations. Space, thus, is not only the necessary setting for social life and social practices but also the means through which to learn social roles and behaviours (Bourdieu 2000: 134; 1977: 89–91), as well as the means to reflect upon such learning. Spatial relations fixed into recognizable images become the means of comparing individual experiences and establishing a common ground in which and because of which such experiences are made meaningful in the context of a common world.

We know that many ancient civilizations have explicitly used the image of the settlement or the city to convey important messages to those who inhabited those spatial arrangements of common life (Stavrides 2014b). A whole range of different planning and ritual practices stem from this general principle. What is interesting, however, in the context of investigating thought-commoning, is the fact that dominant classes (or religious and political elites) seem to have always presupposed that people possess the ability to receive those messages and decipher them. Ranging from practices that invest on the city's layout cosmological meanings which only the chosen few could completely understand and interpret (for example in the Egyptian necropolises) to practices of imposing a recognizable-by-all pattern (for example the grid) in the arrangement of space which also conveys certain socially important messages, the process of interpreting a city as the image of a society is crucially important in shaping people's views about the very society they participate in.

An interesting and highly indicative example can be found in the construction of New Delhi. This city was created near the historic Indian city of Delhi to the plans of Edward Lutyens commissioned by King George V of Great Britain himself. The new city was to be arranged in a form that would convey as well as impose the social hierarchy on which British colonial power based as well as legitimized itself. As Jyoti observes, the city layout imitated the spatial organization and imagery of a specific ritual outdoor ceremony of Mughal India called *durbar* in which 'relative placement of people and objects was used to symbolize their relationship to the ruler. Proximity indicated status' (Jyoti

1992: 87). Mughal durbars were temporary spatial arrangements which provided to people and ruling elites a clear image of their society organized in the form of successive hierarchical levels of authority. Replacing the local ruler or the India's emperor with the Viceregal ruler (representative of the British crown), New Delhi was meant to legitimize the new hierarchy of British colonial rule by being shaped as a durbar built on stone and bricks. Indigenous visitors as well as indigenous princes and various colonial officials (of British or Indian origin, depending on their role) were meant to understand New Delhi as the image of a new society. This image was purposely created by a dominant colonial power which attempted to legitimize itself by borrowing emblematic spatial images from India's past in which local people were accustomed to recognize naturalized arrangements of power and equivalent social roles. India's people were used to thinking about their society as a coherent and obvious whole through the durbar images. Colonial planning tried to direct through Delhi's spatial layout and imagery the thoughts of the colonized in their effort to understand (and thus accept) the new society. In this case, then, authorities were aiming at implicitly constructing thought-images that would colonize people's ability to think about their society.

Critical thinking and critical writing can possibly provide us with the means to reverse this process by giving to thought-images the power to reveal a society's hidden or 'naturalized' hierarchy. In this case, *Denkbilder* help us to think critically about a specific society or even contemplate the possibility of a different society.

We can take as an example of such forms of critical thinking Kracauer's essay on hotel lobbies written in the early thirties

when this type of place was relatively new and perhaps more easily questionable. What Kracauer does in this essay is to observe
people perform through their acts and even through their mere
presence in such spaces an emblematic alienated individuality.
Temporarily detached from everyday life, people in the lobby
were 'sitting around idly' and were being 'overcome by a disinter-
ested satisfaction in the contemplation of a world creating itself,
whose purposiveness is left without being associated with any
representation of a purpose' (Kracauer 1995: 177). In the hotel
lobby, then, 'people find themselves *vis-à-vis de rien*' (ibid.: 176),
as nothing actually happens or has meaning beyond this simulation of participating in a shared space.

Kracauer attempts to think through the images of a hotel
lobby, taking them as *tableaux vivants* of a pseudo-community
comprised of alienated individuals. His critical understanding
of the characteristics of 1930s capitalist Weimar society was not
based on a descriptive appraisal of this society's reproductive
mechanisms but on a *micrological* reading of this society's spaces
and mundane practices. This interpretative–critical attitude ex-
cavates in images the very logic of a modern society. And it is
because this logic is not only expressed in those instances but
is actually co-shaped by them that the critical thinker may use
them not to enhance their power to embed this logic into the
very users of such spaces but to reveal its workings. Thinking
through the images of the hotel lobby, Kracauer does not simply illustrate his ideas about his society but is able to perform
'a minute decoding of the surface phenomena of modernity as
complex historical ciphers' (Levin 1995: 6).

Micrological thinking-through-images has certain simi-
larities with the very process through which everyday actors-

thinkers construct their own thought-images either in obedient readings of their society or in dissident ones. People seem to employ for their thoughts on their society images which are most readily available or can be most easily constructed out of their everyday experiences.

That is why perhaps it is not enough to criticize contemporary or modern societies by fighting against forms of legitimization based on exceptional monumental or heroic representations of the society's structure. Micrological dissident thinking can participate in struggles against the capillary diffusion of legitimized domination.

*Dissensus*, to return to Rancière's terminology, needs to develop in and through thinking-in-images if it aims not at moulding opinions and discourses that deviate from dominant ones but, importantly, at 'restaging the scene of the common' by upsetting the dominant distribution of the sensible. Sensible is what can be thought and perceived in a historically determined social context. Thought-images may unify the field of the 'sensible' by extending and diffusing its legitimacy but they may as well challenge it: 'every situation can be cracked open from the inside, recognized in a different regime of perception and signification' (Rancière 2009b: 49).

Rancière's emphasis on the understanding of a society's self-reproduction and self-explanation through a sustained distribution of the sensible, clearly, departs from views that attribute to dominant ideologies a leading (or even exclusive) role in the process of social reproduction. When he speaks about 'configurations of sense' which create specific forms of 'commonsense', he evidently includes in those configurations not only ideas and meanings but also perceptions, orientations and movements (Rancière 2009a: 120). Commonsense, thus, is not merely ideology but the result of an overall control on what can be said and perceived, on what can be understood as perceivable and thinkable. Against the domination of *consensus* that creates and sustains commonsense, *dissensus* and disagreement are not formed in the field of ideas and opinions only but directly challenge dominant configurations of sense. If such configurations classify experiences, practices, and subjects of action and thinking, dissensus 'declassifies', undoes 'the supposed naturalness of orders and replace[s] it with the controversial figures of division' (Rancière 1995: 32–3). This is why critical and dissident practices shaped solely by ideological criticism and faith in rational demythologization may lose their power to challenge domination if they do not attack the very structure of the sensible comprising simultaneously ideas and perceptions. Thinking-in-and-through-images may possibly contribute to these multi-levelled processes of challenging the distribution of the sensible because it connects ideas with images and builds upon their established as well upon their possible synergies.

The very metaphor used by Rancière for defining the core of politics as a polemic over the common is significant in understanding how dissident struggles challenge the dominant distribution of the sensible. In a formulation we have already encountered, Rancière argues that 'politics … restages the scene of the common' (Rancière 2009a: 121). Politics is presented as a set of practices that not only puts dominant representations into crisis but also constructs new constellations of perceived images, actors and plots. Restaging is a process that rearranges images in order to evoke different meanings and different roles. Restaging the common means rethinking the common as a structure of shared thoughts and experiences. This is why restaging the common can be shaped in and through thought-images which explore and extend the field of the possible.

Thinking-in-common as exercised through the circulation of thought-images may activate or even multiply what Casarino calls 'surplus common' (Casarino and Negri 2008). In his search for 'a common wealth that is not appropriated by capital' (ibid.: 20), he draws from Hardt and Negri's remark that 'revolt arises … [not on the basis of deprivation but] on the basis of wealth, that is, a surplus of intelligence, experience, knowledges and desire' (Hardt and Negri 2005: 212). Thus, he suggests that surplus is 'immanence as such' (Casarino and Negri 2008: 33) because it can escape value as well as any form of ontological predisposition. People may experience 'surplus common' because they may simply desire to create in common, to create the common.

It is not really possible to define a kind of common that may always escape capitalist capture. It is, however, possible to interpret Casarino's intricate argument as a suggestion to struggle for commoning practices that are always open to potentialities as such due to the fact that they establish relations beyond any value calculations. Commoning is not a means to an end but an always-in-the-making end produced by people who desire to be in common, who love sharing and share love. Isn't this a different way of formulating one of the core suggestions of this book, namely that commoning can remain as commoning only if it keeps on expanding to include newcomers? Thought-images may contribute to this potentiality of commoning (and sustain commoning as potentiality) because they can offer the means to mentally transcend existing realities of common worlds and thus envisage new possible forms of commoning and the common.

Surplus common may in this perspective be understood as the movement that is comprised both of commoning practices of creation–production and of practices of thinking-in-common about the common and beyond the already-existing common. Commoning may escape capitalist capture by being in a constant movement that sustains and expands it.

How does thinking-in-and-through-images possibly contribute to the creation of common spaces? Godelier, we may recall, has showed both theoretically and through comparative anthropological analysis that mental realities are internal components of social relations (Godelier 2011: 151). Representations, thus, contribute to the shared reality of a society and do not merely reflect it (distorting it, hiding it, etc.). What if, then, thought-images that hint towards possible spaces may acquire an important role in shaping different social relations? The possibility of forming such thoughts exists because of the very process of social reproduction which in no society is just a system of automatisms. John Holloway, among many contemporary political theorists, insists that capitalism is a process that has to ensure its power to go on every day (Holloway 2002). It needs to ensure its power to prevail not only in the society's relations with nature but in people's minds. Godelier affirms and generalizes this view by insisting that, although each society crafts limits to what can be thought and done inside it, obligations and restrictions exist because the forbidden or condemned practices are not unthinkable. An incest taboo, for example, has meaning only if incest is thinkable in a specific society (Godelier 2011: 173). Rancière, for his part, understands the very core of politics to be the actions that challenge the established distribution of the sensible (Rancière 2009a: 121) which is at the basis of any society's reproduction. All these thinkers, then, follow converging paths in analysing the struggle over representations as a struggle that may possibly generate ideas that go against and beyond the society in which this struggle takes place.

Comparing shared representations in different societies focused on the social meaning and value of what is considered as common may be very helpful in this research context. Godelier again offers us a convenient example. Referring to 'property rules regarding material and immaterial realities' in Siane society (in New Guinea), he shows that they are of two kinds. 'In the first, a man has rights over an object in the same way as a father (*merafo*) had rights over his children' (Godelier 2011: 79). This kind of property rights makes the man a mere mediator between the ancestors and the future descendants. In the same way that children are a part of the community which the father is entitled to look after, so people should look after common land, ritual knowledge, et cetera. The area of the common, one could say, projecting the discussion on commons to such anthropological data, is paralleled to the linkages created through common descent. On the other hand, 'a man or a woman has rights over an object if it is like his or her shadow (*amfonka*)' (ibid.). These goods are personally appropriated and are alienable (ibid.) and include clothes, planted trees, tools, et cetera.

Both children and a man's shadow are undoubtedly observable realities in this specific society. More than that, they can be present in every member's mind as mental images which connect the particularity of individual experience (my shadow tonight, these specific children) with a generalizable, almost emblematic quasi-image (shadow, children). From these images and through them, members of this society are meant to learn what can be shared or not and under what conditions. But this knowledge is not based on explicitly stated rules (land belongs to community) but on a social education shaped through thinking-in-images. Images in this case mediate between different levels of shared social experience and build upon a commonly acquired knowledge. One can certainly argue that these images only help to constitute convenient analogies in order to make people understand what they must appropriate and use collectively and what they may appropriate individually. One can even go so far as to say that such societies use these forms of expressing social rules because they belong to a stage of evolution in which social learning is not yet shaped through abstract and explicit regulations (luckily Lévi-Strauss has convincingly dismissed in his *Savage Thought* this evolutionist West-oriented fallacy). It seems, however, that in Siane society learning about what is common is directly connected to the construction of the common world and to the material and immaterial aspects which constitute its structure. What appears as a mere analogical form of socially important knowledge is also a form of shaping thinking-in-common. What Siane people learn to recognize as common property is based on what they learn to think about their relations to descendants and to their own self. Just imagine the intricate connotations involved in visualizing individual property as one's shadow! Just to trace one of them: the shadow belongs to a self but it is generated by a shared external force (for example the sun or some kind of light). In an analogous way, the planted tree (a shadow type of property) owes its existence both to an individual's labour and to common land. One has to get immersed in the common world of Siane society even to attempt to grasp the complexity of the ways in which these image-thoughts are connected to all the other image-thoughts employed in the construction of this shared world.

Let's try now to take the Siane property status thought-images as thought-images that may challenge the ideas we have about public or shared goods and spaces. Visualizing shared land through images that depict generational relations may probably indicate a different way of experiencing the sharing of space. Not only common use (which individuals can evaluate in a 'selfish' calculus) but also different forms of affective relations may bind people to common space. People may be guided to think that they create common space and care for it in the way they look after their children. Obviously this potential thinking about common space through images that challenge prevalent values departs from a legal reasoning that may even reach the conclusion that common or shared property is unthinkable or a contradiction in terms (Blomley 2008: 321–2).

One can also go as far as to see in Siane thought-images, when employed critically to challenge dominant views in our society, the possibility of seeing child raising as an integral part of commoning practices. Thought-images have this potentially inspiring power. They can trigger thoughts through images and develop possible images through thoughts as these develop. We can learn a lot from thought-images either when these are extracted from a different sociocultural context or when they are purposely created by critical writer-theorists. It seems that their possible contribution to envisaging common space is not their illustrative power (that can present to mind something non-existent) but their power to offer glimpses of shared spaces shaped through shared values.

By being strange hybrids of thoughts and images those pre-figurations differ greatly from the images, of commoned worlds offered by utopian thinking (either produced by utopian political and moral theorists or by literature writers). Depicted utopias of a communally organized urban environment tend to enclose a possible common world in images that lack the power to capture the transformative potentialities of history. If commoning is a process and common space is an always-precarious stake, attempting to prefigure common spaces would be more fruitful and less self-enclosing if shared thought-images were inventively created and exchanged. Expanding commoning will need all the power that such proliferating images may carry if it is to become a creative force in the transformation of contemporary cities.

# Chapter 9

# Representations of space and representations of emancipation

Creating images of freedom and emancipation has always been a crucial way in which people shaped their common hopes and aspirations for a better future. Exploited and disempowered people have used these images at least to escape temporarily from their everyday miseries. And critical writers and activists have used such images in attempts to inspire enslaved people to react to their oppression.

It is not the possible history of liberation-oriented images that this chapter will try to trace. What it will attempt to sketch, though, is a possible rethinking of the politics implicitly or explicitly connected to the creation of such images. Are the representations of a liberated future we construct indicative of the values and the promises we project to this future? And are there hidden in the shape and qualities of the imagined spaces of liberation the very limits and potentialities of a different future? Do these imagined spaces, furthermore, permit people to transcend dominant mythologies that capture and enclose individual and collectively expressed imagination in this effort to grasp a 'beyond'? And do imagined spaces of liberation necessarily or possibly coincide with attempts to prefigure common spaces as spaces distinct from public as well as private spaces?

Perhaps one of the dominant modern images of emancipated communities presents them as barricaded in a liberated stronghold, always ready to defend themselves. This image, embedded in the collective imaginary of the oppressed, tends to survey the geography of emancipation through a map clearly depicting free areas defined by a recognizable perimeter. Either as islands surrounded by a hostile sea or as continents facing other hostile continents, these areas appear as spatially definable and traceable. Utopias described through extensive plans of ideal cities are only the most consistent versions of such an imaginary geography of emancipation. There is, however, nothing inherently emancipating in a well-defined area declared as free.

Modern utopias, starting from those of the so-called utopian socialists, were conceived as harmonious communities inhabiting well-ordered cities with regulated mechanisms of production and distribution of goods. Fourier's *phalanstères* were utopian cities conceived as extended massive building complexes meant to house strictly specified (in terms of social characteristics and levels of income) ideal communities. It is not by chance that Fourier's images of these buildings have a striking similarity to the Versailles palace complex. In a city-building complex of monumental proportions a clear and recognizable geometry would characterize the overall layout, putting each and everyone in his and her place. A complex and self-sustainable world would include people from different classes but in numbers explicitly defined in order to guarantee and sustain a sought-for social harmony. This community, depicted in and through space, would then become the prototype of a liberated, harmonious and peaceful society.

Fourier's ideas were not only expressed through a manifesto for a future society (Beecher 1986). They took shape in explicit images through which this society was exhibited in its details.

The most important characteristic of these images, however, is that the future communities were meant to be identified with the specific imagined utopian city which would not expand or be developed through its history but would be built and maintained in its ideal dimensions as a city outside history.

It is not by chance that one of Fourier's followers, Victor Considerant, developed this idea of a city beyond history as well as beyond the specificities of any existing urban or geographical context by suggesting that it can be identified with a large steamship in the middle of the ocean (Frampton 1981: 22) – a free-floating community liberated from the restrictions of space and time.

'There is an entire series of utopias or projects for governing territory that developed on the premise that the state is like a large city' (Foucault 2001: 351). This idea is implicit in the reasoning of the so-called utopian socialists. They don't want simply to describe possible ideal communities but they try to solve the problem of governing them by recognizing the power that spatial arrangements have to regulate people's lives and social relations. Those social reform visionaries, then, depicted a future ideal society through images of a future ideal city. Although, however, they appeared to think about such future societies by developing these images, they were not able to control the semantic potential of the images employed. The Versailles-like building images of Fourier were already contaminated with connotations identifying them with a hierarchical spatial arrangement suitable for a hierarchical 'community', the palace. Outside this community was a completely different world. No matter how egalitarian or, at least, harmonious the relations we could suppose might be organized in and through Phalanstère, its outside would be absolutely defined as outside.

Godin's *Familistère* was a similar model city which was supposed to house a self-contained harmonious community. An enthusiastic American follower of Godin praised this social experiment as 'a social system based upon liberty and sympathetic human love' (Hayden 1982: 97). Considering Godin's Familistère, Foucault remarks that there is no architecture of freedom, as there are no liberating machines (Foucault 2001: 356). A familistère could become a well-intended, however terrifyingly effective, panopticon. Conceiving emancipation as being contained in specific spaces and attempting to imagine emancipating mechanisms through spatially embedded regulations eventually reduces emancipation to a localizable essence. True, emancipation has to do with a radical transformation of the existing social worlds. To locate it, however, in the image of a totally absent site (absent spatially as well as temporally) means to accept a kind of spatializing ethics: what is outside the evil existent is by definition unpolluted, purely 'other'.

Projecting the problem of the organization of an ideal society onto the problem of efficiently arranging different spaces in an ideal city implicitly presupposes that a city or a settlement may reflect the society which inhabits it. If an ideal city, then, is envisaged as a planned, unalterable urban territory with clear boundaries and specified areas for urban 'functions', then the society for which this city is to be built will equally be envisaged as 'eternal', clearly separated from its outside and functioning as a machine that never falters. To think of such a liberated, harmonious, emancipated, autonomous, et cetera society as a self-sufficient and self-perpetuating whole directly affects any struggle for emancipation that uses (or is inspired from) such ideal city images. Exactly as commoning is bound to be transformed to practices

of enclosure if it is limited by the strict boundaries of a closed society, emancipation can be transformed to its opposite when it is
forced to (or chooses to) be enclosed within the boundaries of
any symbolically or literally barricaded enclave.

Nineteenth-century 'socialist' utopias were envisaging new
kinds of rationally planned and controlled community spaces.
Spaces for common use were explicitly identified with the community of the inhabitants. In Godin's Familistère ('social palace')
in Guise, floor galleries and a huge inner court with a glass roof
created for the building's inhabitants bounded spaces which could
be defined as enclosed common spaces. In the self-contained
utopian cities of utopian socialists, common space was the means
of expressing a community's closed identity rather than a shared
place to be shaped through practices of commoning.

Utopian attempts to describe and depict the future society
as accurately as possible were based on the belief that the mal-
adies of exploitation and lack of freedom will be eliminated by
an efficient, centralized and rational form of organization of
both society and the space it inhabits. To this vision implicitly
pertains a view about state (or equivalent) authorities as produc-
ers and guarantors of what all people need to use and enjoy. By
not opening the possibility for future imagined communities to
devise their own ways of defining, producing, using and symbolizing the spaces (as well as the goods) to be enjoyed by all,
utopian thinkers were limited to a reformulation of the problem
of the public realm and failed to open roads towards a reinvention of the realm of the common.

The imaginary representation of human emancipation
and freedom in the form of an ideal city owes a lot to the criticism launched against the existing industrial cities. Romantic

criticism deplored these cities for their anti-human qualities and the alienating effects that machine rationality had imposed on urban life (Löwy and Sayre 2001, Larmore 1996). Modernists, on the other hand, as we have seen, criticized urban chaos and asked for rational planning of cities divided into functional zones. Both criticisms, although seemingly quite different (or even conflicting), converged in certain utopian models for a future urban society, as the 'garden city' movement (Howard 1902, Giedion 1982: 782–5) indicates.

A different kind of representation of freedom and emancipation, which was less critical of the vices of the industrial city and more enthusiastic about some of its manifestations, emerged mostly in the nineteenth and twentieth centuries. This kind of representation identifies freedom with unobstructed mobility and sees the modern city as the locus of unprecedented and ever-expanding movement flows. Nineteenth-century boulevards, considered as spatial arrangements which cracked opened the labyrinthine city neighbourhoods and 'freed' vehicle and pedestrian movement, offered the emblematic images of this new mobility culture. Twentieth-century highways added a new dimension to this representation of freedom: cars would become both the means and the symbols of mobility-as-freedom. According to Urry, 'a civil society of automobility, or the right to roam where and when one wants, involves the transformation of public space into public roads' (Urry 2000: 193; 2004 and 2007).

Images which eulogize continuous and unobstructed movement as freedom and emancipation tend to focus on individuality rather than on collective or shared experiences and practices. The imaginary representation of an enclave of freedom in the form of an ideal city presupposes an ideal community as a possibility. Culminating in the imagery of the free car-rider (not easily distinguished from the motorbike 'easy rider' hero in this perspective), representations of freedom-as-mobility focus on individual trajectories and 'adventures'.

In a possible genealogy of contemporary mobility myths, the Romantic praise for walking has a prominent role. 'The peripatetic poetry of Wordsworth and Coleridge' has indeed 'turned walking into an experience of virtue' (Cresswell 2011: 166). The lone walker, discovering nature in long walks outside the alienating metropolis, was the predecessor of the heroic *flâneur* who plunged himself into the metropolitan crowd 'as into a reservoir of electric energy' (Benjamin 1983: 132) to discover the city as an exciting world. Both types of walkers had the aura of brave individuals who dared to go against the current and free themselves from the constraints of everyday urban routines. Both were lonely observers of life (the life of nature or humans) who emphatically expressed a detached form of individuality: public space was for them a place for discoveries and adventure but not a space for collaboration or collective appropriation. Romantic strollers avoided the crowd and modern *flâneurs* were fascinated to observe it and even mix with it only, however, to corroborate their unique individuality as aesthetes. For both walkers the practice of purposely wandering randomly was an expression of the freedom to discover, the freedom to create oneself the freedom to imagine beyond mundane life and beyond the metropolitan crowd's habits.

It is highly questionable if Benjamin wanted to present *flânerie* as a potentially collective practice in the way Situationists attempted to do many years after in the practices of *derivé* and psychogeography. Benjamin, however, did not simply admire the *flâneur's* power to redeem the liberating promises of the modern city through his hypersensitive sight. *Flânerie* was for Benjamin a paradigmatic reflexive practice which sought to make chance and contingency the tools for an illuminating archaeology of urban modernity. We might say, then, that this idiosyncratic thinker was trying to construct through a self-conscious programmatic *flânerie* a knowledge to be used collectively in the reclaiming of modernity's emancipating potential.

Bauman explores a more recent culture of mobility connected to the important changes developed in modern societies. What he terms 'liquid modernity' is a period during which 'it is the most elusive, those free to move without notice, who rule' (Bauman 2000: 120). In this view an interesting distinction that divides the field of representations of freedom-as-mobility becomes important. According to Bauman, two figures dominate the images of continuous movement: the 'tourist' and the 'vagabond' (1998). The tourist is the true imagined hero of liquid modernity because he travels when he chooses to; travelling is the tourist's freedom. The vagabond is the one who is forced by circumstances to be always on the move. His freedom is more like a nightmare, although movement offers him at least the possibility of escaping specific burdens. Vagabonds may be considered to be those refugees who are forced to flee from an area of disaster or war, immigrants in pursuit of a more decent life and all the precarious workers who are always in search of work in different cities or countries.

May images connected to those two contrasting figures be used to convey potential prefigurations of common spaces? We know very well that mass tourism is a predominant model of contemporary travel. Only very few may or even want to travel alone (either as idiosyncratic aesthetes or as jet-flying managers and academics). Mass tourism usually crafts recognizable and familiar contexts of consumption in which individual consumers will be encouraged to buy individual experience trophies. 'Consumers are first and foremost gatherers of *sensations*; they are collectors of *things* only in a secondary and derivative sense' (Bauman 1998: 83).

Programmed participation in pseudo-events, which allegedly happen spontaneously in the visited places, develops a sought-for atmosphere of communion in tourist groups. Obviously one would not talk of common spaces in this case but perhaps of spaces staged as common or even of spaces deliberately presented as nostalgic substitutes for a lost community feeling. Organized mass tourism sometimes creates temporary quasi-utopias of commoning: boat cruises, for example, are often organized in this spirit by temporarily converting the boat into a floating ideal city of social harmony.

Vagabonds are individuals looking for hope and some kind of security. Immigrants and refugees more often than not seek forms of collaboration and mutual help in their journeys to potential freedom, potential well-being or, at least, survival. Images of these dark and inverse figures of tourists often present them as homeless, not belonging to a society ('*sans papier*') and victims of a fate that they were forced to share. Any kind of collective action on their part is thus either interpreted as the pure result of helplessness and common essential needs or (in racist xenophobic imageries) as a form of mafia-like mutual support. However, Bauman's vagabonds, who always constitute a destabilizing threat to the 'utopia of the society of tourists' (Bauman 1998: 97), create their own networks of commoning and their own communities even during the time when they travel and lack any permanent shelter.

Although often secluded in their metropolitan enclaves, they largely contribute to a reinvention of the common space because official public space either is not secure for them or explicitly excludes them. Self-enclosed community spaces can indeed be corrupted common spaces created out of fear or solidarity inside ethnically defined groups of metropolitan pariahs. But they can become nodes in an underground network of collectively used spaces that tacitly reinvents or reactivates public space. A barbecue organized by Philippino families in a small park on Sunday, a group of card or domino players from Russia that brings new life to a small neighbourhood square, Albanian mothers collectively watching their children playing in an almost abandoned public playground and an informal market of Nigerians in front of an underground station: these images of Bauman's vagabonds in today's Athens prove that common space can be created in and through official public space even by people on the move, even by uprooted or chased people and even by people who desperately look for a place to create a life no matter how 'often the site … is pulled from under their feet' (Bauman 1998: 87).

Drawing images from contemporary city life, a different representation of space focuses on multiplicity and diversity as means to describe a spatiality of emancipation. Strong roots support this view. 'Critiques of everyday life' (Gardiner 2000) and everydayness, already put forward during the 1960s, have provided us with a new way to deal with the social experience of space. If everyday life is not only the locus of social reproduction but also contains practices of self-differentiation or personal and collective resistance, molecular spatialities of otherness can be found scattered in the city. As De Certeau has put it, 'a migrational, or metaphorical, city slips into the clear text of the planned and readable city' (De Certeau 1984: 93). Spaces of otherness proliferate in the city because of diversifying or deviating practices. Spatialities of otherness thus become inherently time-bound. According to this view, space is reduced neither to a container of otherness (idealized in utopian cities) nor to a contestable and distributable good. Space is actually conceptualized as a formative element of human social interaction. Space thus becomes expressive through use, or, rather, because use ('style of use' as De Certeau specifies) defines users. Discontinuous and inherently differentiated space gives ground to differing social identities allowed thus to perform and express themselves.

In De Certeau's understanding of this proliferation of differences and 'delinquencies' departing from the social order (ibid.: 130), 'space occurs as the effect produced by the operations that orient it, situate it, temporalize it, and make it function in a polyvalent unity of conflictual programs or contractual proximities' (ibid.: 117). Contrary to space, place represents order: spatial and social order alike. Place is the learned language that a society's members use in the different contexts of their interaction: space is a spoken or 'practiced place' (ibid.). It is in and through space that people develop their differentiated trajectories. Exactly as the spoken word may depart from the canonical meaning of dictionaries, so space may become a reinvented place, a reappropriated place. Unfortunately, there is no place for common space in such representations of emancipation. An emphasis on molecular everyday differentiation, which is depicted as hidden behind a prevailing homogeneity and anonymity, tends to search for liberation in the latent trajectories of individuals.

Molecular differentiation and dispersed particularity do not seem, however, to escape the traps of normalizing identification. The social inculcation of diverse and finely nuanced human interaction patterns is a very important part of social reproduction. Inhabited space, in societies that lack 'the symbolic-product-conserving techniques associated with literacy', is, according to Bourdieu, the principal locus of this inculcation of dispositions (Bourdieu 1977: 89). Inhabited space seems to have resumed this role in post-industrial societies too, not because people have become less dependent on formalized education but because city life has become the educational system par excellence. A wide variety of embodied reactions are learned through using metropolitan space. Identifying oneself means being able to deal expressively with the risks and opportunities of city life. Where someone is allowed to be and how he or she conforms to spatial instructions of use is indicative of his or her social identity. Space identifies and is identified through use.

A contemporary liberating effort may indeed seek 'not to emancipate an oppressed identity but [rather] to emancipate an oppressed non-identity' (Holloway 2002: 156). If social reproduction is enforcing identity formation, an emancipating struggle might be better directed against those mechanisms that reduce humans to circumscribed and fixed identities. Spaces of emancipation should then differ from identity-imposing and identity-reproducing spaces. Space as identity (and identity as space) presupposes a clearly demarcated domain. Space as the locus of non-identity (identity, that is, which is multifarious and open) has to be, on the contrary, a loosely determined space, a space of transition.

We know from social anthropology that many societies are well aware of the ambiguous potentialities of these spaces.

Anthropologists have provided us with many examples of spaces that characterize and house periods of ritualized transition from one social position or condition to another. Ritual acts aim, above all, to ensure that an intermediary experience of non-identity (Turner 1977: 103, 169), necessary for the passage from one social identity to another, will not threaten social reproduction. Through the mediation of purification rites or guardian gods, societies supervise spaces of transition, because those spaces symbolically mark the possibility of deviation or transgression.

However, liminality, this experience of temporarily occupying an in-between territory as well as an in-between non-identity, can provide us with a glimpse of a spatiality of emancipation. Creating in-between spaces might mean creating spaces of encounter between identities instead of spaces characteristic of specific identities. When Simmel was elaborating on the character of door and bridge as characteristic human artefacts, he was pointing out that 'the human being is the connecting creature who must always separate and cannot connect without separating' (Simmel 1997: 69). This act of recognizing a division only to overcome it without, however, aiming to eliminate it, might become emblematic of an attitude that gives to differing identities the ground to negotiate and realize their interdependence. Emancipation may thus be conceived not as the establishing of a new collective identity but rather as the establishing of the means to negotiate between emergent identities. Difference thus is not connected to privilege but to potentiality.

In-between spaces are spaces to be crossed. Their existence is dependent upon their being crossed, actually or virtually. It is not, however, crossings as guarded passages to well-defined areas that should interest us. It is more about crossroads, thresholds connecting separated potential destinations. The spatiality of the threshold can represent the limit of a spatiotemporal experience that becomes the operating principle of a network of places. Thresholds, by replacing checkpoints that control access through interdictions or everyday 'rites of passage', provide the ground for a possible solidarity between different people allowed to regain control over their lives.

Those spaces essentially differ from the non-places Augé describes (Augé 1995). No matter how temporary or general, the identities imposed in non-places are effective in reducing human life to the rules of contemporary society. 'Transit identities' are nonetheless identities. Intermediary spaces can be the locus of an emancipating culture only when people assume the risk of accepting otherness as a formative element of their identities. Shared worlds and common spaces are thus envisaged and performed as meeting grounds rather than as identifying areas of belonging.

Social experiences of this kind have been actualized in various social and historical settings. Carnivalesque transgressions flooding the streets of a city have sometimes resulted in carnival riots: social acts of appropriating the city as a network of passages belonging to nobody and everybody. During the short-lived Paris Commune or the days of Chile's Unidad Popular we had acts of establishing public space as a space of encounters between emancipated otherness. Communards or Chilean *pobladores*, like Argentinian *piqueteros* or anti-globalization demonstrators, actually produced threshold spaces and not only strongholds to be defended. Zapatistas, in their long march for dignity, were also creating intermediary spaces of liberation, spaces temporally inhabited by those invisible and suppressed others.

As we have seen so far in this book, threshold spatiality can shape common spaces so long as those spaces participate in

networks of expanding commoning. Imagined spaces of liberation or emancipation are not necessarily linked, as this chapter
attempts to demonstrate, with the prospect of space-commoning.
Liberation can even be trapped in representations that either
enclose in advance a future society of commoners or focus on
individuality or identity and thus depart from the prospect of commoning. Imagining spaces of transition, spaces-as-thresholds,
may, conversely, contribute to the prefiguring of possible practices of space-commoning. It seems that common space may be
captured in representations of a society beyond capitalism and
domination that stem from a threshold-like imagination. In
between the present and the future, in between absolute outside
and a recognizable inside, representations of common space are
representations of liminal experiences and liminal practices.
Common space is liminal, and the representations that attempt
to prefigure it are bound to be equally liminal.

Prefigurative politics is a form of understanding political
action that highlights a consistency between means and ends.
The future society and corresponding values should be reflected
in the practices and ethics of the movements that fight for such
a society, according to this view, which acquired an important
momentum during the sixties (Breines 1989) as well as recently
in discussions about the Occupy movements (Smucker 2014). In
Boggs's classic definition, prefigurative means 'the embodiment,
within the ongoing political practice of a movement, of those
forms of social relations, decision making, culture, and human
experience that are the ultimate goal' (Boggs 1977).

Do the self-organized settlements of Latin American
homeless movements prefigure a different kind of communal
bond or do they actualize it? Does not the parallel existence of

antagonistic community models – hegemonic and counter-hegemonic – make some less real or less functioning than the others? Is the production of common spaces part of prefigurative polities or the actualization of new relations in space and through space? Probably the answer is both: even if collective actions have prefigurative aims and aspirations they sometimes contribute actively to real changes in the life of those involved and even provoke changes in the society itself. One should not forget that a network of self-managed homeless settlements or of occupied factories already creates, actualizes, a parallel network of social and economic relations. Common space may thus be both an example that shows the potentialities of commoning and a concretization of those potentialities in a specific time and place. As we will see in the extensive discussion of the occupied Navarinou Park case that follows, prefiguration and actualization of the liberating potentialities of space-commoning emerge in different ways depending on the representations shared between those who use and mould the park as a common space.

## An occupied threshold common space

Let us try, then, to explore the way representations of common space may interact with practices of space-commoning by examining a concrete example. In the case of the occupied Navarinou Park in Athens, which has already been briefly mentioned, close observation of the acts and shared representations of those who have created it may possibly show that the idea and the experience of threshold crossing correspond to the project of expanding commoning. Navarinou Park may thus become an example of liminal space performed and represented as liminal, in search of space-commoning forms that gesture towards an emancipated society.

Perhaps the most important manifestation of the enduring power of the spirit of the December 2008 youth uprising in Athens was the creation of the occupied Navarinou Park. It was a case of collective action that was characterized by both a decisive distantiation from state-supported policies (and relevant demands asking for the state's intervention) and a genuinely creative spirit. Those two important characteristics, as we will see, make the Navarinou Park initiative an important experiment in collective autonomy. It was early in March 2009 that a handful of activists issued an open invitation to people to squat a car park in the Exarchia neighbourhood of Athens. The idea was to transform this outdoor space into a small park open to all. The plot belongs to the Technical Chamber of Greece (TEE) which bought it in 1972.

In 1990, the TEE offered the land to the Athens Council in order to turn it into a square and provided it would be reimbursed by increasing its building coefficient allowance in one of its other properties in Maroussi. Due to several delays and changes in urban development law, this exchange never took place and this piece of land remained for years leased as an open-air parking space. Once the leasehold for the parking expired in 2008, the TEE brought up again the issue of re-developing the land, and this attracted the interest of Exarcheia residents. The Exarcheia Residents' Initiative, which had already been working on the matter for a year and a half, informed the neighbourhood, took action and requested the immediate conversion into an area of high vegetation. On the 7th March 2009, along with the collective 'Us, Here and Now and for All of Us', it organized an event where all residents and enthusiastic supporters united to squat on the space and demand the obvious, that the parking turns into a park! They broke the asphalt with drills and cutters, they brought trucks carrying soil, planted flowers and trees and in the end they celebrated it.[14]

If commoning is a set of relations and practices which not only produces goods to be shared under certain conditions but also a common world which contains shared values, habits and opinions, then commoning emerged in Navarinou Park as a multi-levelled and sometimes contradictory process of decisions, acts and initiatives. A common world open to newcomers is a world that is constantly reshaped by those who create it and at the same time a world that reshapes them.

Were there no limits to this openness? Obviously this initiative excluded or, rather, wanted to exclude practices of racism, profit making and collaboration with the state. Of course, equality and solidarity were declared to be non-negotiable shared values. But when it comes to specific problems connected to a predominantly hostile context of capitalist relations, then declared values do not suffice. To give an example: how does the Navarinou Park assembly treat or want to treat those who are victims of capitalism's specific horrors, as, for example, are the drug addicts? We are all crippled, torn apart by the contradictions and antagonisms that pervade us as individuals (Holloway 2002: 144–5). How can we collectively deal with this? Can drug addicts be 'convinced' to 'respect' the rules of common use of the occupied park? Are they to be thrown out (and how? by whom?) because with them come the micro-dealers (or they themselves act as micro-dealers) and then unfolds the obscure network of relations with the police? Or, in a seemingly simpler case: who is going to convince those who fantasize an area of freedom as a place in which they can do what they want in spite of the needs of others that they must clean the place they use at night and not destroy the collectively created gardens and benches or be noisy at the times of day when the neighbourhood people are trying to rest, et cetera?

When equality becomes a stake to be negotiated between those who create and use the park, then equality becomes a principle that needs to take distinct forms in the context of concrete or potential human relations. People involved in the Navarinou Park experience soon discovered that they had constantly to invent forms of mutual awareness and mutual recognition. Commoning pushed everybody to reinvent himself or herself as well as new relationships with the 'others'.

For some, the project of liberation or emancipation may be described as a process that creates completely independent sociospatial entities which become capable of reproducing themselves with no recourse to their hostile social and political surroundings. 'Autonomous areas', thus, are meant to create their own rules of self-regulation and people inhabit them by following those rules. For some of the creators and users of Navarinou Park, this kind of autonomous status was and is imagined to be the venture's defining target. For them, this space epitomizes the very exceptional character of the Exarchia neighbourhood in which Navarinou Park is located, which is an area fantasized as a free alternative stronghold by lots of anarchist militants. The state itself along with the dominant media often project views and images which negatively reaffirm this myth by presenting Exarchia as an anomic place where clashes with the police and drug dealing prevail. It is not by chance, of course, that these views are projected especially in periods during which violent police raids are planned and executed. As if to strengthen this myth of Exarchia's constant threat, police units in riot gear 'guard' the main entrances of an imaginary perimeter of the area.

This kind of imagined or demonized 'autonomy' was never really what characterized Exarchia. Although undoubtedly lots of events and initiatives of anti-system orientation have taken place in the area (the famous November 1973 anti-dictatorship occupation of the National Technical University of Athens buildings included), Exarchia is far from being a liberated enclave. An alternative youth culture prevails in the centre of the neighbourhood but it is heavily commodified. And certainly drug dealing is not an anti-system activity (and there is proof that the police selectively tolerate such activities, which undermines, this alternative or dissident culture).

It is perhaps possible that the state wanted and still wants to sustain this myth because it can intervene in the area when it chooses to crush paradigmatically and emblematically any dissident behaviour by giving, at the same time, the impression that these behaviours only exist in the Exarchia enclave. What the December youth uprising did was to shift the media and police focus from Exarchia to various other neighbourhoods, public buildings and public spaces in Athens and other major cities (Stavrides 2010a). The state could not present the December uprising as one more Exarchia-centred incident of 'rioting hooliganism'.

Navarinou Park was obviously not created at the edge of Exarchia by chance. As a member of the neighbourhood group remarked, '[T]he park might have also succeeded elsewhere but it probably would not have lasted anywhere else. Being in Exarchia assures the constant presence of people in the park, day and night, which in a way is its best protection' (An Architektur

2010: 3). However, the power of this collective initiative lies in its openness towards the rest of the city. From the very beginning, the established participative procedures (an assembly, working groups) had to deal with a dilemma that sometimes evolved into a fierce disagreement. Is the occupied park a place of the movement, part of the anti-capitalist movement's network of squatted places and open only to those who belong to the movement, or is the park an open common space that has to provide to different people the opportunity to enjoy and create what capitalist urbanism has deprived them of (green areas, urban gardening, free access to alternative events, open and imaginative playground areas, etc.)?

Especially during periods of direct confrontation with aggressive state policies and relevant police measures, the first view often took the form of an organized use of the park as a stronghold as well as a – mostly fantasized – 'base of operations' against the police squads stationed nearby. The second view attempted to broaden the horizon of the park's use and managed to convince lots of neighbours to consider the place as a green area for everyday use (often bringing along their children).

We could discern in the struggle between those two viewpoints, which still has its difficult moments, an implicit dispute about the meaning of autonomy and self-management. The first viewpoint understands autonomy as a form of separation that guarantees and ensures the consistency of the venture and its avant-garde role. According to this view the park is a liberated enclave or a 'free space', as some name it. The second viewpoint understands autonomy as a radical break with the state mechanisms, which, however, does not create barriers that separate 'enlightened activists' and 'exemplary acts' from the rest of society. This view remained radical and inventive without losing contact with the neighbourhood. On the contrary, the first viewpoint made it at times extremely difficult for less engaged or everyday people to be in the park.

The park was from the start and because of the very material conditions of its production (with no actual dividing barriers one could possibly defend) an open space. It had an osmotic relation with its surroundings and passers-by could easily describe it as a public space. However, the park was and is something different: it is common space. It was the very people involved in the park's creation, life and maintenance who produced rules of 'good use' and organized practices of care and protection (of both the space and its users). It was those people who searched and still search for appropriate rules of expanding commoning.

In Navarinou Park, people could have created distinct working groups in which participation would be based on each one's knowledge and abilities. This, however, would latently reproduce a role taxonomy based on the 'innocent obviousness' of existing differences. What makes Navarinou Park an experiment in self-management and expanding commoning is that any form of work and cooperation is implicitly or explicitly an act of inclusive self-governance. Collecting the rubbish can become a test in such a context as can be a discussion in the park's assembly regarding direct democracy. In both cases, subjects of action and practices themselves become comparable and relevant: what is at stake is to invent forms of collaboration based not on homogenization but on multiplicity (Hardt and Negri 2005: 348–9). The rules established by the assembly formed institutions of expanding commoning as did the rules that established a rotation of duties (as, for example, in the collection of rubbish). Such institutions try to be flexible because newcomers need to be included in them without being integrated into a pre-existing taxonomy of roles.

Navarinou Park's open assembly explicitly tried to establish equality in terms of decision making. Everyone had the right to participate. Furthermore, decision making was not based on voting but on consensus reached through extended and sometimes exhaustive debate. As happens in many similar cases, to establish equality of opinions is a difficult process. It depends on who is willing to participate, what is the stake of the decision, how decisions are linked to specific tasks, and who chooses to take the burden. And of course an important issue is how one forms one's opinion and what kind of access to knowledge, education, experience and bodily abilities one has. Frequently, advantages in all those fields latently legitimize certain opinions as superior to others. How does one treat, for example, the opinion of somebody who rarely participates in the everyday hard work of the park's maintenance? And do those who participate more frequently than others have the right to decide against the opinions of others?

The main argument of those who accept forms of concentration of power in groups or individuals involved in a movement's initiative is efficiency. Quick or coherent decisions, they say, need to be taken by representatives, who, of course, should be elected democratically. The park's experience has shown that an obstinate insistence on direct democracy can also create coherent decisions (decisions that do not change the targets or the framework all the time) and an efficient distribution of tasks collectively agreed upon.

Navarinou Park is not an island in the urban archipelago of Athens. It is not even an alternative island in a sea of urban uniformity imposed by the dominant values and practices, as some militant activists tend to fantasize. Navarinou Park is a kind of *liminal* space which invites *liminal* practices by people who experience the creation of potentially *liminal* identities. No sanitary zone surrounds the park, although police raids and drug dealing sometimes threaten its threshold status. The park does not belong to a certain collectivity, community or authority but it is daily produced as an in-between space. It is a space in between surrounding public spaces, in between housing blocks, a space between a neighbourhood with a rich history of youth struggles and an adjacent upper-middle-class neighbourhood with expensive cafés (Kolonaki) and between university buildings and an extensive book and software market. The park is also a peculiar threshold between a dense urban fabric and a natural landscape. It belongs to a network of central streets (one of them with rather heavy traffic) but it also appears as an unexpected oasis with trees, bushes, vegetable gardens and flowers. This unexpected juxtaposition of urban and natural environment adds to the park's liminal status. Not entirely a secluded urban garden but not a city square either, the park is actually a park-square, an urbanized natural threshold. That is why it can contain so many different activities and why it can comprise so many different overlapping spaces. Even though each of the park's areas is defined by specific self-constructed urban furniture (benches, playground constructions, outdoor theatre seats, etc.), all of them blend into each other, as do their users. Different cultural or political events may often coexist with everyday uses (children play while a discussion takes place at the park's outdoor theatre, and so on).

Maybe the park experience urges us to abandon a view of common space that fantasizes uncontaminated enclaves of emancipation (Stavrides 2009: 53: Negri 2009: 50). It seems that the dominant experiences of urban enclosures and the dominant imaginary of recognizable identity enclaves colonize the thought and action of those who attempt to go beyond capitalist hegemony. Threshold experience and threshold images offer a counterexample to the dominant enclave city. Rather than perpetuating an image of the capitalist city as an archipelago of enclave islands, we need to create spaces that inventively threaten urban order by upsetting dominant taxonomies of spaces and life types. Those spaces-as-thresholds acquire a dubious, precarious perhaps but also virus-like existence. Their power lies in their openness, in their ability to overspill their boundaries and in their gestures towards those who are not included yet.

## Commoning the state?

Collectively recognized representations of a desired common future are shaped in and by specific cultural contexts. Imagined cities and heavenly utopias reflect shared cultural values and, even when they are used to challenge some of those values, they are created with culture-infused images. This is why perhaps the opening of the discussions and aspirations for commoning to non-Western views on community, society and 'common good' potentially creates new ways of problematizing the political meaning of practices, ideas and representations related to commons.

Referring to the experience of the 'Oaxaca commune', Esteva connects this collective reappropriation of the city to forms of understanding, representing and performing community which have deep roots in Mexican indigenous cultures. Using the notion of *communalidad*, 'coined by two indigenous intellectuals',

Esteva shows that it describes more than a 'juxtaposition of commons and polity'. *Communalidad* is also 'a mental space, a horizon of intelligibility: how you see and experience the world as a We' (Esteva 2012:). This We permeates language, communal work, fiestas and the common symbolic ties to communal territory. In such a context then, the politics of taking back the city and taking back society are linked. *Communalidad* was alive in the experiment of self-governance that took place in Oaxaca during the days of the Oaxaca uprising. In a way, *communalidad*, as a horizon of shared intelligibility, shaped the political imaginary of those who participated. Common space did not simply 'happen' as the uprising unfolded, but also became a reinvented communal territory that actively shaped the uprising. What distinguishes Oaxaca's insurgent *communalidad* from traditional indigenous *communalidad*, however, is the fact that in the occupied city the 'we' was in-the-making. And, furthermore, this 'we' was threatening to overspill the boundaries of the city and send a message to the rest of the country that a different form of social organization is possible and effective in dealing with the small and big problems of living together. As an Oaxaca activist expressed it: 'we realized that we can do without them' (meaning the government and the institutions of the state and market).

Another important Latin American indigenous term that may be employed in ways that substantially differ from Western ideas of the common good is *buen vivir*. The term is often used to indicate a whole array of indigenous notions, as in the Aymara (Bolivia) *sumaq qamana*, the Quechua (Peru, Ecuador, Bolivia, Chile, Colombia and Argentina) *sumak kawsay*, the Peruvian Amazonian groups' *ametsa asaiki*, the Guarani (Paraguay, Uruguay, Argentina, Brazil and Bolivia) *nandereko*, et cetera.

What all these terms share is the 'idea that well-being is only possible within a community' (Gudynas 2011: 441). 'The concept does not split mankind from nature' (Prada 2013: 145). Mother Earth is considered alive and sacred and any relationship with Nature, which is always 'mediated by the community' (ibid.), is based on respect and 'a communion and dialogue' (ibid.)

*Buen vivir*, then, understands the creation of community shared worlds as a process that is based on exchanges between people and nature which are not exploitative or aggressive but dialogic and expanding through dialogue. The fact that Nature may be considered as an alive interlocutor not only is important in the context of indigenous spiritual beliefs but also has direct results in the ways these people understand commons goods, 'resources' (a word already infused by a economocentric logic) and those practices that in a different vocabulary are called commoning.

By learning from nature's diversity and respecting the wide range of differences between different people, indigenous *buen vivir* is both a plural idea and a world-view focused on plurality. An important principle of *buen vivir* is complementarity, 'the underlying premise of the interdependence between different human beings' (ibid. 146). Risking translations that possibly violate the inherent logic of the term, *buen vivir* is both an ethics of commoning and a set of community-based practices that aim at guaranteeing a certain form of collective well-being.

*Buen vivir* has been actively employed as a guiding principle of movement actions and aspirations in many countries in Latin America. Indigenous movements explicitly have mobilized representations and values connected to *buen vivir* in order to criticize existing colonial and capitalist relations. They have also employed *buen vivir* mentality in the ways they shaped both their forms of organization as well as their methods of constructing social relations that go beyond dominant arrangements of power. Aymara political struggles in Bolivia and indigenous struggles in Ecuador as well as the Zapatista-inspired struggles in Mexico share critical reappropriations of *buen vivir* cosmovision.

In all these cases, *buen vivir* has been a pluralistic and culture-specific way of understanding common good, a stake and a means to approach forms of social organization that attempt to go beyond Western imaginations of welfare and well-being. This has led to the recasting of future aspirations of progress, both the dominant and the counterhegemonic ones: instead of considering the future as the culmination of a process of continuous betterment, *buen vivir* urges for efforts to reinstall a lost equilibrium. According to such an approach, capitalism has destroyed both the dialogic relation of community to nature and the communal bonds of complementarity. 'Development' is the sacred name given by the capitalist cult of progress to a set of practices that plunder both the earth and human energies supposedly in the process of ensuring a betterment of humankind's well-being. Opposed to such a view, which understands growth not as an organic metaphor but as a Faustian mobilization of even greater means to extract value from the exploitation of men and nature alike, is a view that reconsiders the horizon of the common: Capitalist appropriation of natural resources and human energies (affects, cognitive power and acquired skills included) is a set of violent acts of enclosing what should be shared, profiting from what potentially belongs to all and destroying whatever may become the means to achieve a different balance between society and nature. A *Buen vivir* mentality explicitly challenges the development imaginary and puts into crisis ideas and values that have trapped the anti-capitalist imaginary by limiting it to aspirations which cannot go beyond the modernist obsession with eternal progress. It even challenges the idea of revolution as the event that will separate history to a 'before' and an 'after' completely different from each other, the idea of revolution as the quintessence of sudden genesis of the 'new'. Another indigenous term is more relevant here: *pachakutik* (Becker 2011), which 'is the beginning of a new/old cycle, the end of something and the beginning of something else, not like the tabula rasa but more akin to the restoration of What has been lost/forgotten' (Zibechi 2012: 184).

It is clear that in terms of the polities of commoning, *buen vivir, communalidad* and *pachakutik* introduce a view of the commons – of what is to be shared – that connects the definition of a shared world to values that challenge the capitalist logic (capitalist models of social organization included). What has been an interesting and debatable development in the political uses of these indigenous terms is their use in the new constitutions of two Latin American states, Ecuador (approved in 2008) and Bolivia (approved in 2009). Does this mark a shift in the political meaning of those forms in the context of reconceptualizing the 'common good' of a society and the practices of commoning connected to the definition and creation of common good?

Ecuador's constitution bears the marks of the anti-neoliberalism movements that overthrew the IMF's governments and changed the country's political and economic orientations. In this constitution, *buen vivir* 'is described as a set of rights, which include those referr[ing] to health, shelter, education, food, environment and so on' (Gudynas 2011: 443). Interestingly, 'along with the "Rights of Buen Vivir" and under the same title, "Rights", is a chapter on "Rights of Nature"' (Systemic Alternatives 2011: 10). To interpret the *buen vivir* cosmovision as a set of rights to be protected and guaranteed by the state is already a way of limiting the term's power to redefine what is to be considered good for society and what is to be considered as common good and well-being.

The state is not challenged as a form of social organization and as an arrangement of power but is declared to become the most important promoter of a kind of redistributive 'development'. As the Buen Vivir National Plan for 2013–16 declares, *buen vivir* is not a new development paradigm. However, the plan explicitly focuses on economic growth by directing public investment to '"sowing the oil" (reinvesting oil revenues) and harvesting a productive framework with which to built a "knowledge society"' (ibid.: 12 and Ecuador, Republica de 2009).

Bolivia's constitution incorporates *buen vivir* logic mainly as a set of ethical principles that are guaranteed by the state. Those principles are connected to the construction of a 'plurinational state' that sustains and supports a plural society. According to Prada, 'this involves devolving the administration of local activities in accordance with local customs' (Prada 2013: 150).Whether this will lead to 'the deconstruction of colonial state structures and the incorporation and recognition of the community principles in state administration' (ibid.) remains to be seen. There is a common element, however, in the reconceptualization of common good and society's well-being in both constitutions. The state, no matter how much transformed, in order to be in the service of society has a leading role in social and economic planning and a leading role in directing the change of the corresponding societies to non-capitalist or post-capitalist ones (Brand 2013, Prada 2013, Walsh 2010). The very logic of the state, which has historically shaped itself as a form of social organization in which asymmetries of power support technologies of governing and rulers are explicitly different (and separated) from those ruled, is not challenged.

Faced with this new imaginary of a benign interventionist state, which differs, of course, in certain important aspects from the established neoliberal state, movements inspired by commoning principles and forms of organization have to rethink and, perhaps, redirect their actions. Can *buen vivir*-related values and cosmovisions contribute to a rethinking of a future society beyond capitalism and domination? Could this be expressed in new state-like forms of social organization, or should we search for patterns of action and models of organization that go beyond the state as a social and political form?

Answers to these questions are actually being suggested and challenged by movements of our time. Directly connected to the very specific forms of social organization and cooperation that aspire to create open worlds of commoning, those answers shape and are being shaped by the politics of commoning expressed in movement practices and struggles. What has been considered as the historical opportunity for promoting alternative economic and social policies by the so-called left or progressive governments in Latin America (or, more recently, in Europe) may very well be a new arena for Ranciere's 'polemic over the common'. Will societies in movement produce and sustain areas of freedom that will create possibilities for the development of active, expanding networks of commoning? Will dispersed initiatives and movement struggles take advantage of institutional opportunities created by state-directed reforms (reforms that may be influenced by *buen vivir*-like visions of the common or inspired by Western approaches to human emancipation)? History unfolds today in ways that challenge existing models of radical change. What seems to be more important, however, is that people in movement towards a post-capitalist future have to invent forms of organization and cooperation that match the very aims of their implicit or explicit mobilizations. The Zapatistas' Subcomandante Marcos once said that we need to fight capitalism in ways that don't look like capitalism. We need to go beyond capitalism through expanding networks of commoning, by employing and inventing liminal institutions of commoning and by accepting communities as plural and open worlds. We need to go beyond the historically specific form of social organization that we call the state, beyond the historically specific form of social reproduction that we call development and beyond the historically specific prioritization of the economy that has become necessary in and through capitalism's predominance. A world beyond capitalism is already being constructed, experienced and represented in the practices and networks of contemporary expanding commoning. And, if common space is not only an objective of commoning but also one of its most important shaping factors, let us carefully observe the emergence of common spaces in today's metropolises. In these spaces the seeds of a different future are being planted and taken care of.

# Conclusion: reinventing the city through commoning

Throughout this book, I have attempted to explore the characteristics of common space without forgetting that common space is not an accomplished state of things, a concrete materiality, but a process. What makes this endeavour even more complicated and probably incomplete is the fact that this process is not like any other process of construction. The metaphor of construction directs our thought to a process connected to specific subjects of action who use specific tools. However, in space-commoning there are no tools and no subjects of action that are not transformed by the very process in which they get involved. Common space emerges through practices of commoning, and it is a product of certain forms of commoning but, at the same time, common space shapes commoning practices as well as the subjects of commoning.

We need to abandon the idea that space is a concrete product which can be 'used', bought and sold, and represented in the concrete form of a container which pre-exists its usage. The dominating ideology of the market supports and corroborates the idea that space can be exhaustively defined in terms of its qualities and accurately measured as a quantity: the law of value and the practices of profit making demand that space becomes one more merchandise which can be evaluated and owned.

Nevertheless, space is a lot more than that. Space is an active form of social relations, a constituent aspect of social relations and a set of relations itself. Space matters because it is not an inert container of social life but an integral part of its manifestations and its events. Space gives form to encounters because it is a structured system of relations. That is why, at the same time, it is possible to project expressively values and ideas through spatial comparisons. It matters a lot how far away and how near people are, how they can interpret their distances and how they can handle and symbolize various levels and forms of proximity. And it is equally important that people place things high or low, in the same way as they 'place' ideals and aspirations and that they judge acts and individuals by employing spatial metaphors. Space as a system of relations between positions is the most pervasive means to express social relations as well as to make them 'happen'.

Common space is relational and relative. It is not only a medium and a shaping factor of social relations, as every kind of space is, but also an always-in-the-making set of relations which ceases to be a motor force of commoning when enclosed in a bounded system of position relations. For common space to remain as common there needs to be a mechanism that continuously processes the contribution of those who are invited to use common space. In other words, common space cannot be fixed in the form of a product (no matter how collectively it was produced) because it keeps on producing those who produce it. The production and uses of common space cannot be separated.

Throughout the book, however, we have encountered practices which attempt to specifically locate common space and representation acts which try to envision common space as a describable material entity explicitly demarcated by spatial limits. We have encountered communities which identify the boundaries of their common space with their own boundaries, delimiting, thus, complete and secluded common worlds. Common space might in such a prospect be considered as a bounded shared world.

If we accept that common space is a type of space that simply has a different ownership status than public and private space, we miss the potentiality inherent in the process of space-commoning. More than an ownership status, space-as-commons is a set of social relations which potentially challenges the very foundations of ownership. Common spaces, enclosed within communities or groups, may easily be converted to enclaves of privilege or misery – enclaves of collective privileges or enclaves of collective misery. In order for common space to be radically different from public and private space it needs to overspill the boundaries of any spatial taxonomy, whether this taxonomy is based on legal criteria (ownership, accessibility, etc.), political criteria (forms of authority which control space) or economic criteria (value attributed to space by a certain historically embedded system of market relations). Common space can possibly best be described when it is contrastingly compared to private and public, but common space is essentially incommensurable with public and private. Common space remains common when it keeps on destroying the boundaries between public and private not by absorbing one into the other (as in the privatization of public or the enforced erosion of private realms, as in statist ideologies and practices), but by transforming their historically shaped antithesis into a myriad of new syntheses. We have observed how common spaces offer opportunities for reshaping personal identities and aspirations, but a lot needs to be done in theory and research in order to study systematically how new forms of understanding the self emerge in practices of urban commoning. We have enough indications, however, to say that common spaces challenge situated identities as well as the fixity of boundaries of any pre-existing community from which individuals draw their own self-images.

Common space, then, cannot be reduced to a place, although acts of commoning unfold in specific places and times, indeed take place. Common space needs to radiate in order to exist as a potential force and result of commoning. Common space needs to include newcomers, and this objective reconfigures it incessantly as a network of contested, reinterpreted and re-evaluated spatial relations. However, common space is not sheer spatial formlessness and contingency. It 'happens' in specific sociohistorical contexts and it expresses the intricacies of its emergence in and through commoning practices which have to struggle against dominant practices of enclosure. The political importance of pursuing today's experiences as well as representations of common space lies in the possibility of combining this pursuit with the struggle for an emancipated society. Can the processes through which common spaces emerge in the life of the metropolis as well as in the dreams of its inhabitants contribute to such a prospect?

This book, a modest contribution to discussions that are crucially important for the everyday needs and aspirations of many people (well beyond the circle of well-intentioned academics and activists), suggests that common space may 'happen' in, against and beyond capitalism (to borrow J. Holloway's expression). This means that common space should not be reduced either to an idealized beyond or to a realistic opportunity for the betterment of social life. We have practices that produce common spaces in today's capitalism and struggle to keep them alive against the forces of the market and the capitalist state. We have practices that become oriented towards the creation of common spaces as a form of the collective survival strategies of the vulnerable and the dispossessed. And we need to learn from these struggles. We need to learn from the everyday practices of immigrants and street vendors which sometimes produce precarious and short-lived common space cells in official public spaces. Their efforts, albeit often connected to survival networks, may direct our attention to the differences of public and common and may even teach us that space-commoning may be shaped and invented through quite different forms of group solidarity.

We need also to learn from struggles to establish common spaces as a form of prefiguration of different social relations. Protest camps, Occupy movements and demand-focused struggles experiment with forms of space-commoning or discover, as they unfold, the importance space has for shaping egalitarian relations between those who struggle.

So far, these are the cases in which common space emerges in and against capitalism. In all of these manifestations of space-commoning, common space destabilizes the dominant urban order. If, as we have seen, this kind of order is based on the process of normalization which is established through the three different modalities of dominating power (sovereignty, discipline and security), then common space becomes a rupture in that order. We know that capitalism may amend ruptures and even absorb the energies which caused them by converting them to propelling fuel for its reproduction. Common space can be and has been enclosed either by being integrated into the logic and regulations of the enclave city (as in the case of gated community 'common' spaces or in the case of controlled ghetto 'common' spaces) or by being converted to a marketable entity in the way all other products of commoning are being 'captured' too. In both cases common space is deprived of what can keep it as a live challenge to dominant spatial and social taxonomies: its power to expand and to exceed the boundaries of any group of privileged or disadvantaged commoners.

Capitalism may also try to enclose common space within the boundaries of an alternative economy. Commoning, however, acquires the dynamics of an anti-capitalist force when it defies the very logic of economy. Commoning is thus a set of practices and relations that hints towards a different kind of social values and priorities. Enclosing commoning within the market is potentially killing commoning. This, of course, does not mean that all the everyday experiments in alternative and shared economy are pointless. Quite the contrary: commoning has to really exist in space and time in order to be able to threaten the existing rules and norms of capitalism.

We know that alternative economy projects and initiatives may very well offer solutions to current neoliberal policies by 'compensating the cuts in social services' through essentially unpaid labour (Caffentzis and Federici 2014). Also, some kinds of commons, although outside the market, as in the case of community-owned and collectively used land, may actually be the means through which established forms of domination are prolonged. This happens, for example, in a strictly patriarchal society in which only men decide how common land is to be used (De Angelis 2012a: 12).

Can there be politically effective and theoretically consistent ways in which to identify commoning practices that are immune to capitalist enclosure or co-optation? Probably not. But there is one important precondition that keeps open the possibility for real existing commoning practices to transcend the limits of real existing capitalism. Commoning needs to try to become always more rather than less in order to remain a live challenge to the existing social order.

David Harvey believes that 'Enclosure is a temporary political means to pursue a common political end' (Harvey 2012: 79). This, in a nutshell, is the logic of efficiency which is so pervasive in classic anti-capitalist organized political movements. In other words this means that anti-capitalist struggle may accept the use of capitalist 'tools' (actually, values) for as much as it is needed in order to win an anti-capitalist movement's victory. This view is rightly criticized as an instrumentalist approach to the problem of organization. As many contemporary movements have indicated through their acts and words, means should try to look like the ends if the aim is to move towards human emancipation. To cite Zapatista Marcos once more, 'We should find ways to fight capitalism that don't look like capitalism.'

Commoning practices that aspire to struggle against capitalism can only defend themselves through commoning. What the Occupy movements (the occupied Syntagma Square experience included) explicitly show is that against the enclosure and containment fabricated by the dominant media, the police and governments, movements always seek to expand the created common spaces (either actually or virtually through social media). Commoners may need to barricade themselves in certain cases to be able to confront market or police aggression, but at the same time they should incessantly try to include newcomers in a struggle to exceed any sanitary perimeter that is bound to trap them.

In and against capitalism: we need also to discover the potentialities of common space in its power to shape a world beyond capitalism. In this prospect we can think, we can judge and we can compare. And we can think-through-images without abandoning ourselves to the seductive promise of images that they are able to capture and to represent the future in advance. As we have seen, thinking-in-images is, potentially, thinking-in-common, sharing dreams for the future without these dreams replacing the process of inventively creating the future. Real existing commoning practices offer the images and the means to shape the forms of commoning that may surpass capitalism. But in order to draw from these practices not only examples but also criteria, we must realize that common space is not an end product of commoning but, indivisibly, a means and a shaping factor of commoning.

In order for practices that produce common space, and are being shaped in the process of producing it, to be able to exceed the limits of capitalism, they must be practices of expanding commoning. 'Extending the realm of the non-commodified field of reproduction' (De Angelis 2012a: 19) is as important as extending the realm of the non-commodified field of production. For Zibechi, the creation of alternative spaces includes the constructing of 'non capitalist social relations within them' (Zibechi 2012: 40).

This process cannot be simply an additive process. What is often theorized as the problem of 'jumping scales' (Harvey 2012: 151), the problem, that is, of distinguishing between means appropriate for different levels of human communities to engage in commoning beyond capitalism, can be formulated as the problem of qualitative leaps in expanding commoning.

Experiences already referred to or analysed in this book that have to do with commoning at the scale of the city show that the urban milieu can be traversed by networks of commoning which reconfigure public space and social life. This was the case for the Oaxaca commune in Mexico (Esteva 2010, 2012), the El Alto struggle for the defence of water-as-commons (Zibechi 2010, Lazar 2010) and the network of neighbourhood assemblies during the *Argentinazo* in Buenos Aires (Sitrin 2006) as well as the lesson of the Paris Commune (to name just one important historical example). The corresponding cities' life was strongly influenced by the metastatic processes through which common spaces spread all over the urban fabric, transforming the very characteristics of urban spatiality. One can even argue that those changes were not only temporary or short-lived but left their marks on the cities. The legacy of those periods of extensive urban commoning is part of the commoning dynamism which survives in these cities even though state suppression against rebellious commoners has in most cases been harsh and extensive too.

Zapatista municipalities, although mostly organized in rural areas and comprising small-scale towns and villages, hint at a different level or scale of expanding commoning. As we have seen, in these sociopolitical experiments not only extensive circuits of commoning were and are being tested but also important political artifices of power sharing, such as the establishing of extensive rotation in duties and governing posts and the institutional framework of participation in collective self-governance.

To be obliged to govern by obeying the community that temporarily assigns this duty to different chosen members ('*mandar
obedeciendo*', as the Zapatistas say), is the most accurately defined real existing political practice of power sharing. At the level
of larger communities or societies or even networks of societies,
one can only think of forms of inter-community negotiations
based on the very preconditions that prevent commoning from
turning into its opposite.

An equally important social experiment that employs expanding circuits of commoning is unfolding today in Kurdistan
(TATORT Kurdistan 2012). An extensive network of communities
which have organized themselves according to the principles of
'Democratic Confederalism' (Öcalan 2011) has emerged in Syrian
state territory (Graeber 2014). Abdullah Öcalan, the imprisoned
leader of the PKK who has been influenced by Murray Bookchin's
work on communalism (Bookchin 2007), retheorized the project of Kurdish liberation by introducing a new perspective on
this struggle for emancipation and self-determination. For him,
'Democratic Confederalism is a non-state social paradigm ... Its
decision-making processes lie with the communities' (Öcalan
2011: 33).

According to the 'Social Contract' of the Autonomous Region
of Rojava in Syria (consisting of the three cantons of Afrin, Jazira
and Kobane), a document that is meant to be a kind of Constitution, 'all cantons in the Autonomous Regions are founded upon
the principle of local self-government' (Rojava 2014: Article 8).
'The Autonomous Regions form an integral part of Syria. It is a
model for a future decentralized system of federal governance in
Syria' (Article 12). According to the same charter, which explicitly describes the different levels of autonomous self-governance,

'natural resources, located both above and below ground, are the public wealth of society' (Article 39). Also, in a somewhat awkward phrasing, 'all buildings and land in the Autonomous Regions are owned by the Transitional Administration are public property. The use and distribution shall be determined by law' (Article 40).

Rojava's social experiment is a set of institutions and practices that attempts to establish a form of social organization that goes beyond the nation-state and a form of economy that attempts to go beyond capitalist predominance. Commoning of resources, together with community- and cooperative-based practices of production create a close interdependence between a political model of self-governance and an economic model of autonomy.

Judging from the active struggle in Rojava (Western Kurdistan) to create a society based on democratic confederalism, one could think that the problem of 'jumping scales' is always specific in terms of history and territory: the very dense and complex history of the area – which is inhabited by people with different cultures, traditions and religions – and the conditions of war between different states and armed guerrilla forces create a context in which the establishment of a different society meets unprecedented problems and opportunities. What makes the Rojava experiences comparable to those of the Zapatistas is that in both regions the form of self-governance chosen is inherently oriented towards expansive equalitarian inclusion: new cities, villages and regions (or cantons) may choose to enter this open political system based on a non-negotiable equality between cultures and religions so long as they respect the basic individual and collective rights. Expanding commoning is, thus, the underlying principle both of the creation of common worlds open to newcomers and of the sharing of resources, goods and services between people who equally participate in defining and protecting what is to be considered as common. This is perhaps why, both in Chiapas and Rojava, the level of people's improvisation and participatory inventiveness is so high (Biehl 2014). People have to invent through practices of cooperation the means to construct a society beyond capitalism and domination.

'Equality' is a somewhat abstract objective, whether it describes relations between individuals or between groups or communities. To consider, however, equality both as a precondition and as a permanent goal of human emancipation may have a performative influence. Although in terms of logic to say that something is both a precondition and a possible result of a certain set of practices is a paradox, in terms of political action it can signify the power a goal has to influence the means to pursue it. We have to start from considering people equal to be able to collectively devise struggles, forms of organization and institutions of negotiation inside the movements in the process of establishing and sustaining equality. It matters little if we call this process 'real democracy', 'radical libertarianism' or even 'true communism' (if we choose to reclaim terms misused or distorted beyond recognition throughout recent history). Expanding commoning through the sharing of power will be in any case the core as well as the centre of gravity of this process.

Commoning may possibly defy capitalist enclosure not through establishing or aspiring to establish heroic enclaves of otherness (no matter how egalitarian or self-managed they might be) but through always expanding commoning practices that include newcomers. This creates unprecedented problems in the very process of establishing the rules of commoning.

Any specific community of commoners always has to devise rules for commoning practices to be regulated within its social and spatial boundaries. However, a community of commoners which is focused on expanding commoning has to be open to its own transformation if those invited to participate in sharing are considered as equally responsible for creating and observing the commoning rules. Expanding commoning, considered as opened commoning, poses the problem of open commoning institutions. We have seen that those institutions may be forms of social predictability in which comparability and translatability of actions are established as necessary conditions through which common ground is created in open negotiations over the common. And it has been argued in this book that comparability and translatability may function as forces that ensure egalitarian negotiations in the shaping of commoning rules so long as the ultimate goal and precondition of sharing is kept alive: the sharing of power. Here lies the necessary link between commoning and the beyond-capitalism realm of an emancipated society.

The sharing of power creates both different rules for commoning and different processes of subjectivation of commoners. The discussions on the meaning of democracy, on the uses and effects of horizontality and on the values of solidarity and equality, discussions which became vital for social movements and the anti-capitalist political movements alike, are directly connected to the important issue of power sharing.

Horizontality and radical or direct democracy have been tested on various occasions in recent movement history. We also have examples of societies which in the past used mechanisms to limit or ban the accumulation of power. Far from sustaining a quasi-religious utopia of essentially good people living together in eternal harmony, the idea of horizontality accepts that power is a constitutive element of human relations. We cannot avoid power since even contingent circumstances may always give advantages to some individuals over the others (a lucky or physically gifted hunter in a hunter society, for example). An emancipated society must devise the means to prevent those advantages from being used as opportunities for domination. We know at least, after Foucault, that the molecular structure of power (the possibility of one person imposing his or her will over another) will always exist in various historically dependent forms. But domination is not a necessary result of power: social artifices of equality (and horizontality is certainly a prominent one) may be (and have been) invented to struggle against domination.

Commoning, and urban commoning in particular, considered as a process that 'secretes' common space, may become a force to shape a society beyond capitalism so long as it is based on forms of collaboration and solidarity that decentre and disperse power. Collaboration in solidarity asks individuals not simply to work together on equal terms and to share equally the products of commoning but also to be formed as subjects of sharing. Subjects of sharing are subjects who accept their incompleteness, subjects who accept that they can be transformed through sharing and subjects who recognize in sharing the power of opening to potential worlds, the power of encountering ever-new expanding horizons of commoning. For such subjects-commoners, sharing is already a form of experiencing subjectivation as an open collective process. Collective subjects, thus, are being formed and transformed without everybody being reduced to fit to perpetuated role taxonomies. If commoning has the power to hint at a world not only beyond capital but also beyond domination, then it must have the power to destroy the antithesis between the individual and the collective. Expanding commoning through institutions that prevent any accumulation of power is possibly the only social context that supports creative individuals in their non-hierarchical collaboration. Creative individuality may only thrive in and through commoning so long as commoning never ossifies in the enclosed reality or fantasy of a homogenized common world.

# Notes

1  The Brigadas Populares member was interviewed by the author in November 2010.

2  The observations that follow are based on a visit to the João Candido settlement in September 2009 and discussions with inhabitants and MTST activists.

3  A discussion with USINA members in September 2009 has been very helpful in clarifying their involvement in urban movements.

4  Research programme (funded by NTUA, 2009–2011): *Transformations of the public–private space relations in the social housing complexes built in Greek cities*. Research team: S. Stavrides (chief researcher), M. Kopanari, P. Koutrolikou, F. Vatavali, C. Marathou and V. Guizeli.

5  'Fear does not revolutionize experience, it only renders it un-certain and precarious … At the base of fear lies the experience of being fully and irremediably exposed to the world' (Carolis 1996: 43–4).

6  For an extended appraisal of the Athens December uprising see Stavrides 2010a, Memos 2010, Sotiris 2009 and Mentinis 2009.

7  'The critical matter is that while most messages were very similar, the sender for each receiver was someone known, someone that had the receiver's address in his/her cell phone's address book. Thus, the network of diffusion was at the same time increasing at an exponential rate but without losing the proximity of the source, according to the well known "small worlds" phenomenon' (Castells et al. 2007: 201). See also Cué 2004.

8  'Common space', according to Hénaff and Strong, 'admits

no criteria; it is open to all in the same way. It is not owned or controlled … all can go there to extract from it what is there' (Hénaff and Strong 2001: 4). This is more or less an understanding of common space as pre-existing its social uses (including its potential enclosure), whereas, as we have seen so far, common space is primarily and necessarily a social artefact created through practices of space-commoning.

9  Available at www.democra ciarealya.es/manifiesto-comun/ manifesto-english/

10  Available at http://aganak tismenoihrakleio.blogspot.com/ (Heraklion Assembly blog). Patras city Aganaktismenoi have uploaded their Assembly decisions and discussions http:// patras-democracy.blogspot.com/ (for the referred fragment see patras-democracy.blogspot .com/search/label/%CE%A3% CF%85% CE%BD%CE%AD% CE% BB%CE%B5%CF% 85% CF%83%CE%B7). Syntagma square occupation assembly resolutions, including the one mentioned, are available at http:// real-democracy.gr/content/poioi -eimaste-1

11  Clearly distinguished from the 'people' and the 'masses', the multitude is an 'active social subject' which 'although it remains multiple and internally different is able to act in common and thus rule itself' (Hardt and Negri 2004: 100).

12  Agamben's theorizations gesture towards a 'community without subjects' in which humans are to succeed 'in making of the proper being-thus not an identity and an individual property but a singularity without identity, a common and absolutely exposed singularity' (Agamben 1993: 65).

13  Hardt and Negri prefer the term 'singularity' instead of the term 'identity'. For them, singularity is defined by and oriented towards multiplicity and is 'always engaged in a process of becoming different' (2009: 338–9). They also share with Agamben an understanding of 'co-belonging' which departs from the dominant understanding of community as identity (see also Stavrides 2010b: 125).

14  From the Navarinou Park web page http://parkingparko .espivblogs.net/englishfrench/ about-the-park/

# Bibliography

Abul-Magd, Z. (2012) 'Occupying Tahrir Square: The Myths and the Realities of the Egyptian Revolution', *South Atlantic Quarterly* 111/3 (Summer): 565–72.

Agamben, G. (1993) *The Coming Community*, Minneapolis: University of Minnesota Press.

Agamben, G. (1998) *Homo Sacer: Sovereign Power and Bare Life*, Stanford University Press.

Agamben, G. (2000) 'Form of Life', in his *Means Without End*, Minneapolis: University of Minnesota Press.

Agamben, G. (2001) 'Genova e il Nuovo Ordine Mondiale', *Il Manifesto*, 25 July.

Agamben, G. (2005) *State of Exception*, University of Chicago Press.

Albet i Mas, A. and Garcia Ramon, M. D. (2005) 'Urban Planning and Social Integration in Barcelona: From Public Management to Deregulated City', in Seminars of the Aegean, *Rethinking Radical Spatial Approaches*, Athens and Thessaloniki: NTUA and AUTh: 231–43.

Alexander, J. C. (2011) *Performative Revolution in Egypt: An Essay in Cultural Power*, New York: Bloomsbury Academic.

An Architektur, (2010) 'On the Commons: Insert on the Navarinou Park', *An Architektur*, 23.

Anderson, E. (2000) *Code of the Street: Decency, Violence and the Moral Life of the Inner City*, New York: W. W. Norton and Company.

Atkinson, D. (1998) 'Totalitarism and the Street in Fascist Rome', in N. R. Fyfe (ed.), *Images of the Street: Planning, Identity and Control in Public Space*, London: Routledge.

Atkinson, R. and S. Blandy (2005) 'Introduction: International Perspectives on the New Enclavism and the Rise of Gated Communities', *Housing Studies* 20/2: 177–86.

Augé, M. (1995) *Non-Places: Introduction to an Anthropology of Supermodernity*, London: Verso.

Augé, M. (2004) *Oblivion*, Minneapolis: University of Minnesota Press.

Aureli, P. V. (2011) *The Possibility of an Absolute Architecture*, Cambridge, MA: MIT Press.

Banksy (2005) *Wall and Piece*, London: Century.

Baudrillard, J. (1983) *Simulations*, New York: Semiotext(e).

Bauman, Z. (1998) *Globalization: The Human Consequences*, Cambridge: Polity Press.

Bauman, Z. (2000) *Liquid Modernity*, Cambridge: Polity Press.

Becker, M. (2011) *Pachakutik: Indigenous Movements and Electoral Politics in Ecuador*, Lanham, MD: Rowman & Littlefield.

Beecher, J. (1986) *Charles Fourier: The Visionary and His World*, Berkeley: University of California Press.

Bektaş, A. (2013) '"I've Gone to Resist, I'll be Right Back": Against the Dictatorship of Development', in anon. *This Is Only the Beginning: On the Gezi Park Resistance*. At www.indybay.org/uploads/2014/03/03/this_is_only_the_beginning.pdf (accessed 14 October 2014).

Benjamin, W. (1980) 'Zentralpark', in his *Gesammelte Schriften*, Frankfurt: Suhrkamp.

Benjamin, W. (1983) *Charles Baudelaire: A Lyric Poet in the Era of High Capitalism*, London: Verso.

Benjamin, W. (1985) 'Naples', in his *One Way Street and Other Writings*, London: Verso.

Benjamin, W. (1990) *The Origin of German Tragic Drama*, London: Verso.

Benjamin, W. (1992) 'Theses on the Philosophy of History', in his *Illuminations*, London: Fontana Press.

Benjamin, W. (1999) *The Arcades Project*, Cambridge, MA: Belknap Press.

Berman, M. (1983) *All That Is Solid Melts into Air*, London: Verso.

Bhabha, H. (2004) *The Location of Culture*, Abingdon and New York: Routledge.

Biehl, J. (2014) 'Impressions of Rojava: a Report from the Revolution'. At http://roarmag.org/2014/12/janet-biehl-report-rojava/ (accessed on 25 March 2015).

Blau, E. (1999) *The Architecture of Red Vienna 1919–1934*, Cambridge, MA: MIT Press.

Blomley, N. (2008) 'Enclosure, Common Right and the Property of the Poor', *Social and Legal Studies* 17/3: 311–31.

Boggs, C. (1977) 'Marxism, Prefigurative Communism and the Problem of Workers' Control', *Radical America*, Winter 1977–8. At https://libcom.org/library/marxism-prefigurative-communism-problem-workers-control-carl-boggs (accessed 9 March 2015).

Bollier, D. and S. Helfrich (eds.) (2012) *The Wealth of the Commons. A World beyond Market and State*, Amherst, MA: Levellers Press.

Bookchin, M. (2007) *Social Ecology and Communalism*, Oakland: AK Press.

Borden, I. (2001) 'Another Pavement, Another Beach: Skateboarding and the Performative Critique of Architecture', in Iain Borden, Joe Kerr and Jane Rendell (eds.), *The Unknown City*, Cambridge, MA: MIT Press.

Bourdieu, P. (1977) *Outline of a Theory of Practice*, Cambridge University Press.

Bourdieu, P. (1991) *Language and Symbolic Power*, Cambridge: Polity Press.

Bourdieu, P. (2000) *Pascalian Meditations*, Cambridge: Polity Press.

Boyer, M. C. (1994) *The City of Collective Memory*, Cambridge, MA: MIT Press.

Brand, U. (2013) 'The Role of the State and Public Policies in Processes of Transformation', in Rosa Luxemburg Stiftung/Transnational Institute (eds.), *Beyond Development: Alternative Visions from Latin America*, Quito: Fundación Rosa Luxemburg.

Breines, W. (1989) *Community and Organization in the New Left, 1962–1968: The Great Refusal*, New Brunswick: Rutgers University Press.

Brown, A. (ed.) (2006) *Contested Space: Street Trading, Public Space, and Livelihoods in Developing Cities*, Bourton-on-Dunsmore: Practical Action.

Brown, A., M. Lyons and I. Dankoco (2010) 'Street Traders and the Emerging Spaces for Urban Voice and Citizenship in African Cities', *Urban Studies* 47/3: 666–83.

Busquets, J. (2005) *Barcelona: The Urban Evolution of a Compact City*, Rovereto: Nicolodi/ Harvard University Graduate School of Design.

Caffentzis, G. and S. Federici (2014) 'Commons against and beyond Capitalism', *Community Development Journal* 49/ S1: i92–i105.

Caldeira, T. (2000) *City of Walls: Crime, Segregation and Citizenship in São Paulo*, Berkeley: University of California Press.

Carolis, M. De (1996) 'Toward a Phenomenology of Opportunism', in P. Virno and M. Hardt (eds.), *Radical Thought in Italy: A Potential Politics*, Minneapolis: University of Minnesota Press.

Casarino, C. and A. Negri (2008) *In Praise of the Common: A Conversation on Philosophy and Politics*, Minneapolis: University of Minnesota Press.

Castells, M. (1977) *The Urban Question*, London: Arnold.

Castells, M. (1983) *The City and the Grassroots*, London: Arnold.

Castells, M. (2010) *The Rise of the Network Society*, Malden, MA: Wiley Blackwell.

Castells, M. and G. Cardoso (eds.) (2005) *The Network Society: From Knowledge to Policy*, Washington, DC: Johns Hopkins Center for Transatlantic Relations.

Castells, M., M. Fernández-Ardèvol, J. Linchuan Qiu and A. Sey (2007) *Mobile Communication and Society: A Global Perspective*, Cambridge, MA: MIT Press.

Chomsky, N. (2012) *Occupy*, London: Penguin Books.

Conrads, U. (1971) *Programs and Manifestos on 20th-Century Architecture*, Cambridge, MA: MIT Press.

Coy, P. (ed.) (2001) *Political Opportunities, Social Movements and Democratization*, Oxford: Elsevier Science.

Cresswell, T. (2011) 'Towards a Politics of Mobility', in N. Edjabe and E. Pieterse (eds.), *African Cities Reader: Mobilities and Fixtures*, Vlaeberg: Chimurenga and the African Centre for Cities.

Cué, C. (2004) *Pásalo! Los cuatro días de marzo que cambiaron un país*, Barcelona: Península.

Davis, M. (1992) *City of Quartz: Excavating the Future in Los Angeles*, London: Vintage.

De Angelis, M. (2004) 'Separating the Doing and the Deed: Capital and the Continuous Character of Enclosures', *Historical Materialism* 12: 57–87.

De Angelis, M. (2007) *The Beginning of History: Value Struggles and Global Capital*, London: Pluto.

De Angelis, M. (2012a) 'Crises, Movements and Commons', *Borderlands* 11. At www .borderlands.net.au/vol11no2 _2012/deangelis_crises.htm (accessed 20 September 2014).

De Angelis, M. (2012b) 'Crises, Capital and Co-optation: Does Capital Need a Commons Fix?' in D. Bollier and S. Helfrich (eds.), *The Wealth of the Commons: A World beyond Market and State*, Amherst, MA: Levellers Press.

De Angelis, M. and S. Stavrides. (2010) 'Beyond Markets or States: Commoning as Collective Practice (a public interview)', *An Architektur* 23 (also at www.e-flux.com/ journal/view/150).

De Certeau, M. (1984) *The Practice of Everyday Life*, Minneapolis: University of Minnesota Press.

Deleuze, G. (1988) *Foucault*, Minneapolis: University of Minnesota Press.

De Peuter, G. and N. Dyer-Witheford (2010) 'Commons and Cooperatives', *Affinities* 4/1: 30–56.

Detienne, M. and J. P. Vernant (1991) *Cunning Intelligence in Greek Culture and Society*, University of Chicago Press.

Donald, J. (1999) *Imagining the Modern City*, London: Athlone Press.

Dyer-Witheford, N. (2006) 'The Circulation of the Common'. At www.fims.uwo.ca/people/ faculty/dyerwitheford /Commons2006.pdf (accessed 7 March 2015).

Ecuador, Republica de (2009) *Plan Nacional para el Buen Vivir 2009-2013: Construyendo un Estado Plurinacional e Intercultural*, Quito: Secretaria Nacional de Planificacion y Desarrollo.

Edensor, T. (2000) 'Moving Through the City', in D. Bell and A. Haddour (eds.), *City Visions*, Harlow: Pearson Education.

Esteva, G. (2010) 'The Oaxaca Commune and Mexico's Coming Insurrection', *Antipode* 42/4: 978-93.

Esteva, G. (2012) 'Hope from the Margins', in D. Bollier and S. Helfrich (eds.), *The Wealth of the Commons: A World beyond Market and State*, Amherst, MA: Levellers Press. At http://wealthofthecommons.org/essay/hope-margins.

Esteva, G. (2014) 'Commoning in the New Society', *Community Development Journal* 49/S1: i144–i159.

Federici, S. (2004) *Caliban and the Witch: Women, the Body, and Primitive Accumulation*, Brooklyn NY: Autonomedia.

Feigenbaum, A., F. Frenzel and P. McCurdy (2013) *Protest Camps*, London: Zed Books.

Féral, J. (2002) 'Theatricality: The Specificity of Theatrical Language', *SubStance* 31/2-3: 94–108.

Ferrell, J. (2002) *Tearing Down the Streets: Adventures in Urban Anarchy*, New York: Palgrave Macmillan.

Foucault, M. (1993) 'Of Other Spaces: Utopias and Heterotopias', in J. Ockman (ed.), *Architecture–Culture 1943–1968: A Document Anthology*, New York: Rizzoli.

Foucault, M. (1995) *Discipline and Punish: The Birth of the Prison*, New York: Vintage Books.

Foucault, M. (2001) 'Space, Knowledge and Power'. in J. Faubion (ed.), *The Essential Works of Foucault, 1954–1984*, Vol. III, *Power*, New York: New Press.

Foucault, M. (2009) *Security, Territory, Population: Lectures at the College de France, 1977–1978*, Basingstoke: Palgrave Macmillan.

Frampton, K. (1981) *Modern Architecture: A Critical History*, Oxford University Press.

Franck, C. and Q. Stevens (eds.) (2007) *Loose Space: Possibility and Diversity in Urban Life*, London: Routledge.

Frisby, D. (2003) 'Straight or Crooked Streets? The Contested Rational Spirit of the Modern Metropolis', in I. B. Whyte (ed.), *Modernism and the Spirit of the City*, New York: Routledge.

Galatoula, T. (2013) 'The Indignants of Athens as a Multitude of Singularities', *Stirling International Journal of Postgraduate Research* 1/2. At www.stryvling.stir.ac.uk/index.php/inspire/issue/current (accessed 13 October 2014).

Gardiner, M. (2000) *Critiques of Everyday Life*, London: Routledge.

Giedion S. (1982) *Space, Time and Architecture*, Cambridge, MA: Harvard University Press.

Giugni, M., D. McAdam and C. Tilly (eds.) (1999) *How Social Movements Matter*, Minneapolis: University of Minnesota Press.

Godelier, M. (1999) *The Enigma of the Gift*, Cambridge: Polity Press.

Godelier, M. (2011) *The Mental and the Material*, London: Verso.

Graeber, D. (2014) 'Why is the world ignoring the revolutionary Kurds in Syria? *Guardian*, 8 October.

Graham, S. and S. Marvin (2001) *Splintering Urbanism: Networked Infrastructures, Technological Mobilities and the Urban Condition*, London: Routledge.

Gudynas, E. (2011) 'Buen Vivir: Today's Tomorrow', *Development* 54/4: 441–7.

Halbwachs, M. (1992) *On Collective Memory*, University of Chicago Press.

Hamel, P., Lustiger-Thaler H. and M. Mayer (eds.) (2000) *Urban Movements in a Globalising World*, London: Routledge.

Hamilton-Baillie, B. (2008a) 'Shared Space: Reconciling People, Places and Traffic', *Built Environment* 34/2: 161–81.

Hamilton-Baillie, B. (2008b) 'Towards Shared Space', *Urban Design International* 13/2: 130–8.

Hamilton-Baillie, B. and P. Jones (2005) 'Improving Traffic Behaviour and Safety through Urban Design', *Proceedings of ICE Civil Engineering* 158: 39–47.

Hanssen, B. (1998) 'Christo's Wrapped Reichstag:

Globalized Art in a National Context', *The Germanic Review* 73/4: 350–67.

Hardt, M. (2010) 'The Common in Communism', *Rethinking Marxism* 22/3: 346–56.

Hardt, M. and A. Negri (2005) *Multitude: War and Democracy in the Age of Empire*, London: Hamish Hamilton.

Hardt, M. and A. Negri (2009) *Commonwealth*, Cambridge, MA: Harvard University Press.

Harvey, D. (1996) *Justice, Nature and the Geography of Difference*, Oxford: Blackwell.

Harvey, D. (2012) *Rebel Cities: From the Right to the City to the Urban Revolution*, London: Verso.

Harvey, D., M. Hardt and A. Negri (2009) 'Commonwealth: An Exchange', *Artforum* 48/3: 210–21.

Hayden, D. (1982) *The Grand Domestic Revolution*, Cambridge, MA: MIT Press.

Hénaff, M. and T. B. Strong (2001) *Public Space and Democracy*, Minneapolis: University of Minnesota Press.

Hetherington, K. (1997) *The Badlands of Modernity: Het-erotopia and Social Ordering*, London: Routledge.

Hirschon, R. (1998) *Heirs of the Greek Catastrophe: The Social Life of Asia Minor Refugees in Piraeus*, New York: Bergahn Books.

Hite, K. (2012) *Politics and the Art of Commemoration: Memorials to Struggle in Latin America and Spain*, New York: Routledge.

Holloway, J. (2002) *Change the World Without Taking Power*, London: Pluto Press.

Holloway, J. (2010) *Crack Capitalism*, London: Pluto Press.

Holston, J. (2008) *Insurgent Citizenship: Disjunctions of Democracy and Modernity in Brazil*, Princeton University Press.

Hou, J. (ed.) (2010) *Insurgent Public Space*, London: Routledge.

Howard, E. (1902) *Garden Cities of To-Morrow*. At www.archive.org/details/gardencitiesoftoOOhowa (accessed 19 October 2014).

Hughes, N. (2011) '"Young People Took to the Streets and All of a Sudden All of the Political Parties Got Old."

The 15M Movement in Spain', *Social Movement Studies* 10/4: 407–13.

Huyssen, A. (2003) *Urban Past:. Urban Palimpsests and the Politics of Memory*, Stanford University Press.

Jeffrey, A., C. McFarlane, and A. Vasudevan (2012) 'Rethinking Enclosure: Space, Subjectivity and the Commons', *Antipode* 44/4: 1,247–67.

Jensen, O. B. (2013) *Staging Mobilities*, Aalborg University Press.

Jimenez, C. (2008) 'From the Lettered City to the Sellers' City: Vendor Politics and Public Space in Urban Mexico, 1880–1926', in G. Prakash and K. M. Kruse (eds.), *The Spaces of the Modern City: Imaginaries, Politics, and Everyday Life*, Princeton University Press, 214–46.

Joyce, P. (2002) 'Maps, Blood and the City' in P. Joyce (ed.), *The Social in Question: New Bearings in History and the Social Sciences*, London: Routledge.

Joyce, P. (2003) *The Rule of Freedom: Liberalism and the Modern City*, London: Verso.

Jyoti, H. (1992) 'City as Durbar: Theater and Power in Imperial Delhi', in N. Alsayyad (ed.), *Forms of Dominance*, Aldershot: Avebury Ashgate.

Kaejane, G. (2011) 'Seven Key Words on the Madrid-Sol Experience, 15M'. At http:// fromtheplazas.wordpress .com/translations/seven-key -words/ (accessed 14 October 214).

Kamel, N. (2012) 'Tahrir Square: The Production of Insurgent Space and Eighteen Days of Utopia', *Progressive Planning* 191: 36–9.

Khan-Magowedov, S. O. (1978) *Pioneers of Soviet Architecture: The Search for New Solutions in the 1920s and 1930s*, London: Thames and Hudson.

Koepnick, L. (2002) 'Aura Reconsidered: Benjamin and Contemporary Visual Culture', in G. Richter (ed.), *Benjamin's Ghosts: Interventions in Contemporary Literary and Cultural Theory*, Stanford University Press.

Koolhaas, R. (1994) *Delirious New York: A Retroactive Manifesto for Manhattan*, New York: Monacelli Press.

Kopp, A. (1970) *Town and Revolution. Soviet Architecture and*

*City Planning 1917–1935*, New York: George Braziller.

Kracauer, S. (1995) *The Mass Ornament*, Cambridge, MA: Harvard University Press.

Larmore, C. (1996) *The Romantic Legacy*, New York: Columbia University Press.

Latour, B. and P. Weibel (eds.) (2002) *Iconoclash: Beyond the Image Wars in Science, Religion, and Art*, Cambridge, MA: MIT Press.

Lazar, S. (2010) *El Alto, Rebel City: Self and Citizenship in Andean Bolivia*, Durham, NC: Duke University Press.

Le Corbusier (1970) *Towards a New Architecture*, London: Architectural Press.

Le Corbusier (1987) *The City of To-morrow and Its Planning*, New York: Dover Publications.

Lefebvre, H. (1991) *The Production of Space*, Oxford: Blackwell.

Lefebvre, H. (1996) *Writings on Cities*, Oxford: Blackwell.

Lefebvre, H. (2004) *Rhythmanalysis: Space, Time and Everyday Life*, London: Continuum.

Lemke, T. (2011) *Biopolitics: An Advanced Introduction*, New York University Press.

Levin, T. (1995) 'Introduction', in S. Kracauer, *The Mass Ornament*, Cambridge, MA: Harvard University Press.

Linebaugh, P. (2008) *The Magna Carta Manifesto*, Berkeley: University of California Press.

Linebaugh, P. and M. Radiker (2000) *The Many-headed Hydra: Sailors, Slaves, Commoners, and the Hidden History of the Revolutionary Atlantic*, Boston, MA: Beacon Press.

Loukaitou-Sideris, A. and R. Ehrenfeucht (2009) *Sidewalks: Conflict and Negotiation Over Public Space*, Cambridge, MA: MIT Press.

Löwy, M. and R. Sayre (2001) *Romanticism against the Tide of Modernity*, Durham, NC: Duke University Press.

Marcuse, P. (1995) 'Not Chaos, but Walls: Postmodernism and the Partitioned City', in S. Watson and K. Gibson (eds.), *Postmodern Cities and Spaces*, Oxford: Blackwell.

Marcuse, P. and R. Van Kempen (eds.) (2002) *Of States and Cities: The Partitioning of Urban Space*, Oxford University Press.

Massey, D. (2005) *For Space*, London: Sage.

Mauss, M. (1967) *The Gift: Forms and Functions of Exchange in Archaic Societies*, New York: W. W. Norton.

Memos, C. (2010) 'Neoliberalism, Identification Process and the Dialectics of Crisis', *International Journal of Urban and Regional Research* 34/1: 210–16.

Mentinis, M. (2009) 'Peace, Legality, Democracy', *Radical Philosophy* 154: 67–8.

Methorst, R., J. Gerlach, D. Boenke and J. Leven (2007) 'Shared Space: Safe or Dangerous? A Contribution to Objectification of a Popular Design Philosophy', *WALK 21 Conference*. At www.walk21 .com/papers/Methorst%20 Shared%20Space.pdf (accessed 25 September 2014).

Midnight Notes Collective (1990) 'The New Enclosures', *Midnight Notes* 10.

Miller Lane, B. (1985) *Architecture and Politics in Germany 1918–1945*, Cambridge, MA: Harvard University Press.

Miraftab, F. (2004) 'Invented and Invited Spaces of Participation: Neoliberal Citizenship and Feminists' Expanded Notion of Politics', *Wagadu: Journal of Transnational Women's and Gender Studies* 1 (June). At www.rro-jasdatabank.info/neolibstate/ miraftab.pdf (accessed 20 October 2014).

Miraftab, F. and S. Wills (2005) 'Insurgency and Spaces of Active Citizenship. The Story of Western Cape Anti-eviction Campaign in South Africa', *Journal of Planning Education and Research* 25/2: 200–17.

Mittermaier, A. (2014) 'Bread Freedom, Social Justice: The Egyptian Uprising and a Sufi Khidma', *Cultural Anthropology* 29/1: 54–79.

Moody, S. and S. Melia (2013) 'Shared Space: Research, Policy and Problems', *Proceedings of the Institution of Civil Engineers – Transport* at http:// eprints.uwe.ac.uk/17937/8/ tran1200047h.pdf (accessed 25 September 2014).

Morgenthau, H. (1930) *An International Drama*, London: Jarrolds.

Motta, S. (2009) 'New Ways of Making and Living Politics: The Movimiento de Trabajadores Desocupados de Solano and the "Movement of Movements"', *Bulletin of Latin American Research* 28/1: 83–101.

Mumford, E. (2000) *The CIAM Discourse on Urbanism, 1928–1960*, Cambridge, MA: MIT Press.

Müştereklerimiz (2013) 'Today We Are All Someone New'. At www.opendemocracy.net/m%C3%BC%C5%9Ftereklerimiz/today-we-are-all-someone-new (accessed 10 June 2014).

Nandrea, L. (1999) '"Graffiti Taught Me Everything I Know about Space": Urban Fronts and Borders', *Antipode* 31/1: 110–16.

Negri, A. (2009) 'On Rem Koolhaas', *Radical Philosophy* 154: 48–50.

Notes From Nowhere (2003) *We Are Everywhere: The Irresistible Rise of Global Anticapitalism*, London: Verso.

Öcalan, A. (2011) *Democratic Confederalism*, London: Transmedia.

Ostrom, E. (1990) *Governing the Commons: The Evolution of Institutions for Collective Action*, Cambridge University Press.

Ostrom, E., R. Gardner and J. Walker (1994) *Rules, Games and Common-Pool Resources*, Ann Arbor: University of Michigan Press

Papavasileiou, E. (2003) 'A Personal Account and an Appeal', *Avgi* (Greek newspaper), 2 November.

Peterson, N. (1993) 'Demand Sharing: Reciprocity and the Pressure for Generosity among Foragers', *American Anthropologist* 95/4: 860–74.

Pickvance, C. G. (1995) 'Where Have Urban Movements Gone?' in C. Hadjimichalis and D. Sadler (eds.), *Europe at the Margins: New Mosaics of Inequality*, London: John Wiley and Sons.

Pickvance, C. G. (2003) 'From Urban Social Movements to Urban Movements: A Review and Introduction to a Symposium on Urban Movements', *International Journal of Urban and Regional Research* 27/1: 102–9.

Postvirtual (2013) 'Historical Atlas of Gezi Park'. At http://postvirtual.wordpress.com

/2013/06/27/historical
-atlas-of-gezi-park/ (accessed
14 October 2014).

Prada Alcoreza, R. (2013) 'Buen
Vivir as a Model for State and
Economy', in Rosa Luxem-
burg Stiftung/Transnational
Institute (eds.), *Beyond De-
velopment: Alternative Visions
from Latin America*, Quito:
Fundación Rosa Luxemburg.

Rancière, J. (1995) *On the Shores
of Politics*, London: Verso.

Rancière, J. (2006) *The Politics of
Aesthetics*, London: Continuum.

Rancière, J. (2009a) 'A Few
Remarks on the Method of J.
Rancière', *Parallax* 15/3: 114–23.

Rancière, J. (2009b) *The Emancipated Spectator*, London:
Verso.

Rancière, J. (2010) *Dissensus: On
Politics and Aesthetics,* London: Continuum.

Richter, G. (2007) *Thought-
Images. Frankfurt School Writ-
ers' Reflections from Damaged
Life*, Stanford University Press.

Robinson, J. (2006) *Ordinary
Cities: Between Modernity
and Development*, London:
Routledge.

Roggero, G. (2010) 'Five Theses
on the Common', *Rethinking
Marxism* 22/3: 357–73.

Rojava (2014) Charter of the Social Contract. At http://
peaceinkurdistancampaign
.com/resources/rojava/
charter-of-the-social
-contract/ (accessed 7 March
2015).

Schacter, R. (2008) 'An Eth-
nography of Iconoclash:
An Investigation into the
Production, Consumption
and Destruction of Street-art
in London', *Journal of Material
Culture* 13/35: 35–61.

Schmitt, C. (2005) *Political
Theology: Four Chapters on the
Concept of Sovereignty,* Uni-
versity of Chicago Press.

Smucker, J. M. (2014) 'Can
Prefigurative Politics Replace
Political Strategy?' *Berkeley
Journal of Sociology* 58: 74–82.

Sennett, R. (1993) *The Conscience
of the Eye*, London: Faber and
Faber.

Sennett, R. (1994) *Flesh and
Stone: The Body and the City in
Western Civilization*, London:
Faber and Faber.

Sennett, R. (1995) 'Theory',
*Harvard University Graduate*

*School of Design News (GSD)* Summer issue: 54–6.

Sennett, R. (2009) *The Craftsman*, New York: Penguin Books.

Simmel, G. (1997) 'Bridge and Door', in N. Leach (ed.), *Rethinking Architecture*, London: Routledge.

Simone, A. (2008) 'The Last Shall Be the First: African Urbanities and the Larger Urban World', in A. Huyssen (ed.), *Other Cities, Other Worlds: Urban Imaginaries in a Globalizing Age*, Durham, NC: Duke University Press.

Sitrin, M. (ed.) (2006) *Horizontalism: Voices of Popular Power in Argentina*, Oakland: AK Press.

Sitrin, M. (2012) 'Pulling the Emergency Brake', *Tidal: Occupy Theory, Occupy Strategy* 2: 6–8.

Smith, N. (1996) *New Urban Frontier: Gentrification and the Revanchist City*, London: Routledge.

Smith, N. and P. Williams (eds.) (1986) *Gentrification of the City*, Boston, MA: Allen and Unwin.

Soja, Ed. W. (2000) *Postmetropolis: Critical Studies of Cities and Regions*, Malden MA: Blackwell.

Solà-Morales Rubió, Ignasi de (1995) 'Terrain Vague', in C. Davidson (ed.), *Anyplace*, Cambridge, MA: MIT Press.

Solnit, R. (2009) *A Paradise Built in Hell: The Extraordinary Communities That Arise in Disaster*, New York: Penguin.

Sorkin, M. (ed.) (1992) *Variations on a Theme Park*, New York: Hill and Wang.

Sotiris, P. (2009) 'Rebellion of Greek Youth', *Radical Philosophy* 154: 65–6.

Souza, M. L. de (2006) 'Together with the State, despite the State, against the State: Social Movements as "Critical Urban Planning" Agents', *City* 10/3: 327–42.

Stavrides, S. (2002a) *From the City-Screen to the City-Stage* (in Greek), Athens: Ellinika Grammata.

Stavrides S. (2002b) 'Inhabitation and Otherness: Refugees and Immigrants in the City', in T. Koubis, T. Moutsopoulos and R. Scoffier (eds.), *Athens 2002 Absolute Realism*, Eighth International Exhibition of Architecture, Venice Biennale,

Athens: Hellenic Ministry of Culture – Association of Greek Architects.

Stavrides, S. (2009) 'Espacialidades de Emancipacion y "la Ciudad de Umbrales"', in J. Holloway, F. Matamoros and S. Tischler (eds.), *Pensar a Contrapelo: Movimientos Sociales y Reflexion Critica*, Buenos Aires: Herramienta.

Stavrides, S. (2010a) 'The December 2008 Youth Uprising in Athens: Spatial Justice in an Emergent "City Of Thresholds"', *Spatial Justice* 2. At www.jssj.org/article/la-revolte-de-la-jeunesse-athenienne-de-decembre-2008-la-justice-spatiale-dans-une-ville-des-carrefours-emergente/ (accessed 23 October 2014).

Stavrides, S. (2010b) *Towards the City of Thresholds*, Trento: Professionaldreamers.

Stavrides, S. (2012) 'Squares in Movement', *South Atlantic Quarterly* 111/3 (Summer): 585–96.

Stavrides, S. (2013) 'Contested Urban Rhythms: From the Industrial City to the Post Industrial Urban Archipelago',

in R. J. Smith and K. Hetherington (eds.), *Urban Rhythms: Mobilities, Space and Interaction in the Contemporary City*, London: Wiley-Blackwell.

Stavrides, S. (2014a) 'Open Space Appropriations and the Potentialities of a "City of Thresholds"', in M. Mariani and P. Barron (eds.), *Terrain Vague: Interstices at the Edge of Pale*, New York: Routledge.

Stavrides, S. (2014b) 'What Does a Settlement's Layout Show about the Society that Inhabits it? On the Importance of Thinking-Through-Images', in S. Souvatzi and A. Hadji (eds.), *Space and Time in Mediterranean Prehistory*, New York: Routledge.

Surin, K. (2001) 'The Sovereign Individual and Michael Taussig's Politics of Defacement', *Nepantla* 2/1: 205–20.

Svoronos, N. (1972) *Histoire de la Grèce Moderne*, Paris: Presses Universitaires de France.

Swyngedouw, E. (2009) 'Civil Society, Governmentality and the Contradictions of Governance-beyond-the-State: The Janus-face of Social Innovation', in D. MacCallum,

F. Moulaert, J. Hillier and S. Vicari Haddock (eds.), *Social Innovation and Territorial Development*, Surrey: Ashgate.

Swyngedouw, E. (2011) 'The Zero-Ground of Politics: Musings on the Post-Political City', in T. Kaminer, M. Rombles-Duran and H. Sohn (eds.), *Urban Asymmetries. Studies and Projects on Neoliberal Urbanization*, Rotterdam: 010 Publishers.

Systemic Alternatives (2011) *Vivir Bien: Notes for the Debate*. At https://systemicalternatives.files.wordpress.com/2014/07/buen-vivir-english-30-jul-2014.pdf (accessed 7 March 2015).

Tafuri, M (1990) *The Sphere and the Labyrinth: Avant-gardes and Architecture from Piranesi to the 1970s*, Cambridge, MA: MIT Press.

TATORT Kurdistan (2012) *Demokratische Autonomie in Nordkurdistan*, Hamburg : Mesopotamien Verlag (also at http://demokratischeautonomie.blogsport.eu/files/2012/10/da-webversion.pdf accessed 7 March 2015).

Taussig, M. (1999) *Defacement: Public Secrecy and the Labor of the Negative*, Stanford University Press.

Thomas, M. J. (1978) 'City Planning in Soviet Russia (1917–1932)', *Geoforum* 9: 269–77.

Tilly, C. and L. Wood (2012) *Social Movements 1768–2012*, London: Paradigm.

Tsougrani, B. (2000) 'When Memory Shoots Oblivion', *Rizospastis* (Greek newspaper), 11 June.

Turner, V. (1974) *Dramas, Fields and Metaphors*, Ithaca, NY: Cornell University Press.

Turner, V. (1977) *The Ritual Process*, Ithaca, NY: Cornell University Press.

Turner, V. (1982) *From Ritual to Theatre: The Human Seriousness of Play*, New York: PAJ.

Tzanavara, H. (2000) 'They Tear Down History', *Kyriakatiki* (Greek newspaper), 25 March.

Urban, F. (2012) *Tower and Slab: Histories of Global Mass Housing*, New York: Routledge.

Urry, J. (2000) *Sociology beyond Societies: Mobilities for the Twenty-first Century*, London: Routledge.

Urry, J. (2004) 'The "System" of Automobility', *Theory, Culture and Society* 21/4–5: 25–39.

Urry, J. (2007) *Mobilities*, Cambridge: Polity Press.

USINA (2006) 'Self-administered Vertical Habitation for Densely Populated Urban Conditions – Copromo, União da Juta e Paulo Freire Projects. Brazil', in BSHF *Report, December 2006*. At http://courses .arch.ntua.gr/fsr/134924/ BSHF_Final_Usina_Brasil.pdf (accessed 25 September 2014).

Vahl, H. G and J. Giskes (1990*) Traffic Calming through Integrated Urban Planning*, Paris: Amarcande.

Van Gennep, A. (1960) *The Rites of Passage*, London: Routledge and Kegan Paul.

Virno, P. (1996) 'Virtuosity and Revolution: The Political Theory of Exodus', in P. Virno and M. Hardt (eds.), *Radical Thought in Italy: A Potential Politics*, Minneapolis: University of Minnesota Press.

Virno, P. (2004) *A Grammar of the Multitude*, Los Angeles: Semiotext(e).

Vlachos G., G. Yannitsaris and E. Hadjicostas, (1978) 'Housing the Asia Minor Refugees in Athens and Piraeus between 1920 and 1940', *Architecture in Greece* 12: 117–24.

Vrychea A. (2003) 'A Spurious Remodelling', *Avgi* (Greek newspaper), 15 June.

Walsh, K. (2010) 'Development as Buen Vivir: Institutional Arrangements and (De)colonial Entanglements', *Development* 53/1: 15–21.

Wa-Mungai, M. (2009) 'Innovating "Alternative" Identities', in K. Njogu and J. Middleton (eds.), *Media and Identity in Africa*, Edinburgh University Press.

Wa-Mungai, M. (2010) 'Hidden $ Centz: Rolling the Wheels of Nairobi Matatu', in H. Charton-Bigot and D. Rodriguez-Torres (eds.), *Nairobi Today: The Paradox of a Fragmented City*, Dar es Salam: Mkuki na Nyota.

Weigel, S. (1996) *Body- and Image-Space. Re-reading Walter Benjamin*, London: Routledge.

Zednicek, W. (2009) *Architektur des Roten Wien*, Vienna: Verlag Walter Zednicek.

Zibechi, R. (2007) *Autonomías y emancipaciones: América Latina en movimiento*, Lima: Programa Democracia y Transformación Global and Fondo Editorial de la Facultad de Ciencias Sociales, Unidad de Post Grado, UNMSM.

Zibechi, R. (2010) *Dispersing Power: Social Movements as Anti-State Forces*, Oakland: AK Press.

Zibechi, R. (2012) *Territories of Resistance: A Cartography of Latin American Social Movements*, Oakland: AK Press.

Zukin, S. (1995) *The Cultures of Cities*, Cambridge: Blackwell Publishers.

# Index